FODOR'S TRAVEL PUBLICATIONS

are compiled, researched, and edited by an international team of travel writers, field correspondents, and editors. The series, which now almost covers the globe, was founded by Eugene Fodor in 1936.

OFFICES
New York & London

Fodor's Tokyo:
Editor: Gail Chasan
Area Editors: Jean Pearce, Peter Popham, Hollistar Ferretti, Helen Brower
Maps and City Plans: Pictograph, C.W. Bacon

FODOR'S

TOKYO
1988

FODOR'S TRAVEL PUBLICATIONS, INC.
New York & London

ISBN 0-679-01572-8
ISBN 0-340-41872-9 (Hodder & Stoughton)

CONTENTS

FOREWORD

Fodor's *Tokyo* consists of material adapted from our larger *Japan*. As in the larger book, the team of resident journalists has put together information on the widest range of establishments and activities in Tokyo, and, within that range, presents you with selections that will be safe, worthwhile, and of good value. The descriptions we provide are just enough to enable you to make your own informed choices from among our selection.

While every care has been taken to ensure the accuracy of the information contained in this guide, the publishers cannot accept responsibility for any errors which may appear.

All prices quoted in this guide are based on those available to us at the time of writing. In a world of rapid change, however, the possibility of inaccurate or out-of-date information can never be totally eliminated. We trust, therefore, that you will take prices quoted as indicators only, and will double-check to be sure of the latest figures.

Similarly, be sure to check all opening times of museums and galleries. We have found that such times are liable to change without notice, and you could easily make a trip only to find a locked door.

When a hotel closes or a restaurant produces a disappointing meal, let us know, and we will investigate the establishment and the complaint. We are always ready to revise our entries for the following year's edition should the facts warrant it.

Send your letters to the editors of Fodor's Travel Publications, 201 E. 50th Street, New York, NY 10022. European readers may prefer to write to Fodor's Travel Guides, 9-10 Market Place, London W1N 7AG, England.

FACTS AT YOUR FINGERTIPS

 CLIMATE. The tourist season in Japan is generally thought to begin in March, to carry on in strength through November, and to taper off by the following February. That is, although spring and autumn are top favorite seasons, Japan is a year-round tourist country.

Climate. Japan has four clear-cut seasons of equal length, each one with its own character and customs, and each with much to commend it. Generally, spring is described as being warm, summer as hot, autumn as cool, and winter as cold.

Spring peaks in Tokyo with the opening of the cherry blossoms near the beginning of April. Summer in the capital is sticky and hot, so this is the season for seeking out beach and mountain resorts. Autumn is spasmodically tempestuous when typhoons approach the city. Winter is usually dry and bright; even in Tokyo, famous for its smogs, the sky is pellucid.

Average temperatures in the city range from 4.1°C in January to 25.2°C in July, with a year-round median of 15°C. Rainfall averages 125 millimeters per month, while the average humidity is 69 percent.

 PACKING. Your first consideration will be the season, and in this regard Japan makes it easy for you. The four seasons are models of their kind, so dress accordingly. Winter clothes for December to February; spring clothes, including rainwear and folding umbrellas, for March to May; summer clothes, including swimsuits and some light rainwear, and umbrellas that double as parasols, for June to August; and autumn clothes and rainwear for September to November.

 TOURIST INFORMATION. There is a plethora of informative leaflets and pamphlets put out by the *Japan National Tourist Organization*. Your nearest Japanese Embassy or Consulate or office of Japan Air Lines is also well equipped to answer general questions. For specific advice, stay with JNTO. Main offices are at the following addresses:

Kotani Bldg., 1–6–6 Yurakucho, Chiyoda-ku; Narita Airport, Airport Terminal Bldg., Narita, Chiba Pref.;
Kyoto Tower Bldg., Higashi-Shiokojicho, Shirogyo-ku;
630 Fifth Avenue, New York, NY 10111;
333 North Michigan Avenue, Chicago, IL 60601;
1519 Main Street, Dallas, TX 75201;
360 Post Street, San Francisco, CA 94108;
624 South Grand Avenue, Los Angeles, CA 90017;
165 University Avenue, Toronto M5H 3B8, Ontario, Canada;
167 Regent Street, London W.1, England;
115 Pitt Street, Sydney, N.S.W., Australia;
Suite 3606, 2 Exchange Sq., 8 Connaught Pl., Central, Hong Kong;

1

56 Suriwong Road, Bangkok, Thailand.

Travelers' Aid. The *Japan Association of Travel Agents,* headquarters at Zen-Nittso Kasumigaseki Bldg., 3–3–3 Kasumigaseki, Chiyoda-ku, Tokyo 100 (592–1271), aims at the development of the tourist industry in Japan. It will deal with any tourist's complaints concerning services handled by JATA members. JATA has branch offices in Nagoya, Osaka, Fukuoka, Sapporo, Sendai, Okayama, and Naha.

Guides will be provided by a travel agent, or if you prefer, you may telephone the *Japan Guide Association Headquarters,* Shin Kokusai Bldg. (213–2706). The association is closely related to JTB, the nation's semi-official Japan Travel Bureau.

TIPS FOR BRITISH VISITORS. Passports. You will need a valid U.K. passport, but not a visa (as long as your passport is not endorsed "Holder is subject to control under the Commonwealth Immigration Act" and your stay is less than six months). You may also be required to prove you have sufficient funds for your stay, and a valid onward or return ticket with all necessary documentation. Currency and customs allowances are the same as for U.S. citizens.

Information. The best British source of Japanese travel information is the *Japan National Tourist Organization,* 167 Regent St., London W1R 7FD (tel. 01–734 9638).

Insurance. We heartily recommend that you take out travel insurance before embarking. If you book your ticket using a credit card, you may find that the insurance for the actual trip is included. If not, try *Europ Assistance,* 252 High St., Croydon CR0 1NF (tel. 01–680 1234). They have a wide selection of coverages and are a long-established and experienced insurance firm.

Tour Operators. Among the many long-haul operators who have tours to Japan are the following:

Albany Travel (Manchester) Ltd., 190 Deansgate, Manchester M3 3WD (tel. 061–833 0202).

Asia-Pacific Holidays, 103 Waterloo Rd., London SE1 8UL (tel. 01–928 5511).

Bales Tours Ltd., Bales House, Barrington Rd., Dorking, Surrey RH4 3EJ (tel. Dorking (0306) 885991).

Far East Travel Centre, 3 Lower John St., London W1A 4XE (tel. 01–734 7050).

Kuoni Travel Ltd., Kuoni House, Dorking, Surrey RH5 4AZ (tel. Dorking (0306) 885044).

Meon Villa Holidays, 32 High St., Petersfield, Hants. GU32 3JE (tel. 0730 4011).

Oriental Magic Holidays, Prudential House, Topping St., Blackpool, Lancs. FY1 3TU (tel. 0253 23951).

Air Fares. As Japan is such a long-haul destination, far and away the best bets for reasonable fares are package tours. The current (late '87) regular fares London/Tokyo are—First Class, £3,942 round-trip; Club Class, £1,882 round-trip; Economy APEX, £863 round-trip, basic period, £900 peak periods. The APEX fare needs one month prior booking, and a minimum stay in Japan of 14 days, maximum of three months. *JAL* address in Britain is Hanover Court, 5 Hanover Sq., London W1R 0DR (tel. 01–408 1000).

WHAT IT WILL COST. Japan has a long-standing reputation for being expensive. In the past this has been fiercely contested by the Japan National Tourist Organization, but the leap in value of the yen against the dollar and other major currencies during the past 18 months has put the matter beyond dispute. In a survey compiled of living costs in the world's major cities by Business International, the Geneva-based consultancy, Tokyo led the pack by several points, with second city Osaka offering the only real competition. This survey reflected the living costs of expatriate executives and thus included the astronomical rents for which Tokyo has become notorious, so travelers can avoid some of these expenses. And those determined to see the city on a shoestring will still find it possible.

Usually it is advantageous to be a couple, for whom a double or twin room costs from ¥20,000 – ¥25,000 per night. Tax and service charges are additional. Usually no discounts for long stays are offered. JNTO also pointed out in its survey that because Tokyo is a safe city, its hotels are well patronized by local people and so are not exclusive, and therefore excessively costly, places.

A super deluxe Japanese inn is not cheaper, and in fact can be more expensive. However, as you go down the price scale you will find that it is still possible, even in Tokyo, to find clean, unadorned rooms in simple hotels and inns for as little as ¥5,000 per head per night. If you don't mind bunks or dormitory accommodations, you can pay even less.

HOW TO GET THERE. Japan is reachable by air and by sea. Tokyo's international airport is at Narita, which is actually in the neighboring prefecture of Chiba and at least an hour's journey by road from the Tokyo City Air Terminal. The former international airport at Haneda now mostly caters to domestic flights, with the exception of certain flights from Taiwan, and of carriers bringing VIPs.

The city's seaport is Yokohama, a half-hour journey by train to the south.

BY AIR

Flight time from Honolulu to Tokyo is nine hours, from Los Angeles to Tokyo is 11½ hours. The duration of the recently introduced nonstop flight from London to Tokyo is 11 hours 35 minutes. The Polar flight is about 18 hours, with a stop at Anchorage, Alaska.

First-class, executive-class and economy-class cabins are available on many major carriers. If you are an independent traveler paying full fare (not in a group or using any kind of discount ticket), you may change your carrier for different sectors of your trip. Some trans-Pacific airlines have arrangements with steamship companies to fly passengers across, join a cruise ship for part of the itinerary (among the islands of Indonesia perhaps, or into Korea or Mainland China), then return by plane.

Group rates for package and charter tours remain the most economical. It is always worth enquiring into "excursion," "APEX," and any other special fares. Even typical economy fares between Los Angeles and Tokyo, for example, can vary by several hundred dollars depending on how long in advance the reservation is made (and paid for), how long a stay is involved, whether any land arrangements are tied in, how many stopovers are included, and other factors.

Some charter tour packagers simply block-book seats on major airlines at reduced prices. Some major airlines offer special charter-like prices in order to boost travel on certain routes during certain periods. Regardless of formal status, all flights must meet the same U.S. federal government standards of aircraft maintenance and safety, crew qualifications, and reliability.

Given the distance and cost involved in any trip to Japan, many travelers try to maximize the time and money spent by taking in other locales in the area. Korea is only a short, separate trip away from Japan. A popular sweep through Southeast Asia would include Taiwan, Hong Kong, Bangkok, and Singapore. Between Bangkok and Singapore, a stop may be made at Kuala Lumpur, capital of Malaysia.

If you are so ambitious as to decide upon a visit to the South Seas, from Japan you may fly to Manila, Bali, then go on to Sydney, Australia, and Auckland, New Zealand. As well as all the hinterland of these countries opening up for you, you are also placing yourself well for advancing into the islands of Micronesia and Melanesia.

Luggage. Regulations for air travelers from the United States base baggage allowances on size. Economy-class passengers may each take two pieces of baggage provided that the sum of their dimensions is not over 2m. 70cm., or 106 inches (neither piece being more than 1m. 58 cm., or 62 inches, combined height, width, and length). First-class allowance is two pieces up to 1m. 58 cm., or 62 inches, overall dimensions each, total 3m. 16 cm., or 124 inches. There is also a 32-kilogram (70-pound) limit for each piece of luggage. Penalties for regulation contravention are severe.

To and from Britain. If you're traveling to Japan on a scheduled airline ticket, you'll realize the return fare is equal to a round-the-world fare, as Tokyo is halfway around the globe from London. You may wish, therefore, to take advantage of a wide number of stopovers allowed on such a ticket. These, on the Southern route, represent nearly every major tourist destination in the northern hemisphere. You can pop in to the Middle East, India, Singapore, Bangkok, Hong Kong, Taiwan. From Tokyo, you can return the same way to stop at different cities, or continue around the world to Hawaii and North America, before crossing the Atlantic to home.

More than 30 airlines operate international services to Japan. Their counters are divided, at Narita Airport, into two wings. The airlines are listed below, with their code letters, under the building wings where they are located.

North Wing		*South Wing*	
Air-India	AI	Air France	AF
Aeroflot Soviet Airlines	SU	Air Lanka	UL
American Airlines	AA	Alitalia	AZ
Bangladesh Biman	BG	All Nippon Airways	NH
Civil Aviation Administration of China (CAAC)	CA	British Airways	BA
Continental Airlines	CO	British Caledonian	BC
Delta Airlines	DL	Canadian Pacific Air	CP
Egypt Air	MS	Cathay Pacific Air	CX
Garuda Indonesian Airways	GA	Iberia	IB
Iran Air	IR	Japan Asia Airways	EG
Iraqi Airways	IA	Korean Air	KE
Japan Air Lines	JAL	Lufthansa German Airlines	LH
KLM Royal Dutch Airlines	KL	Northwest Airlines	NW
Malaysian Airlines System	MH	SAS Scandinavian Airlines	SK
Pakistan International	PK	Singapore Airlines	SQ
Philippine Airlines	PR	Swiss Air	SR
Qantas Airways	QF	Thai Airways International	TG
Sabena Belgian Airlines	SN	Varig Brazil Airlines	RG

| United Airlines | UA |
| UTA French Airlines | UT |

BY SEA

An increasing number of passenger ships as well as freighters having limited accommodation for passengers are calling at ports in the Far East. Since schedules are extremely variable, it is advisable to make your inquiries and bookings well in advance.

Among the American travel agencies handling travel by sea are: *Air and Marine Travel Service,* 501 Madison Avenue, New York, NY 10022; *Cameo Travel Service,* 501 Fifth Ave., New York, NY 10017; *Cruises & Tour,* 250 W. 57th St., New York, NY 10019.

The following list gives some of the possibilities of travel by sea.

Pearl Cruises of Scandinavia, with an office under this name in San Francisco, regularly schedules cruises to China aboard this company's flagship, the one-class M/S *Pearl* of Scandinavia. The *Pearl,* 12,456 tons, cruises from Hong Kong to China, Korea, Kobe in Japan, and back to Hong Kong. Tours are sold in both the U.S. and Europe for twelve two-way cruises on the route annually.

Royal Viking Sea, of the Royal Viking Line, 1 Embarcadero Center, San Francisco, CA 94111, has a 100-day Grand Circle Pacific cruise that calls at major ports of the Far East and the Pacific.

The Cunard Line's *Queen Elizabeth II* calls at 29 ports from New York, on round-the-world cruises.

P. and O. Cruises have the *Canberra* which does a 100-night Pacific cruise.

Hapag-Lloyd's new cruise ship, M/V *Europa,* sails east from Genoa, taking 112 days to go around the world, calling at Kobe, Nagoya, and Yokohama in Japan.

The *Sea Princess,* 20,636 tons, takes 56 days to travel around the world. She calls at Kobe and Yokohama in Japan.

International Cruise Center in Mineola, NY is the general agent for all Soviet ships visiting the Orient. For information, call (516) 747–8880 or (212) 517–8346 locally, or (800) 221–3254 toll-free.

JAPANESE TRAVEL AGENCIES AND TOURS. (Addresses for the agencies and companies below are given at the end of this section.) The *Japan Travel Bureau* claims to be the oldest travel agency in the Far East. This bureau offers a variety of Tokyo tours. For details, look under "Tours" in the *Practical Information* section of this guide.

The following travel agencies and companies are equipped to handle all or some of your travel and related problems should you come to Japan on your own.

American Express International, Shuwa Kamiyacho Bldg., 4–3–13 Torano-mon, Minato-ku, Tokyo; *Air Voyages Co.,* 1–14–4, Jingumae, Shibuya-ku, Tokyo; *Executive Travel,* Orient New Akasaka Suite, 2–8–15 Akasaka, Minato-ku, Tokyo; *Fuji Tours International,* Ryuwa Bldg., 2–3–5, Yurakucho, Chiyo-da-ku, Tokyo; *Fujita Travel Service,* 6–2–10, Ginza Chuo-ku, Tokyo; *Hankyu Express International,* 3–3–9, Shimbashi, Minato-ku, Tokyo; *Hanshin Travel Service,* 2–6–20, Kyobashi, Chuo-ku, Tokyo; *Japan Gray Line,* Pelican Bldg., 3–3–3, Nishi-Shimbashi, Minato-ku, Tokyo; *Thomas Cook/Wagons-Lits,* No. 20 Mori Bldg., 2–7–4, Nishi Shimbashi, Minato-ku, Tokyo.

Japan Air Lines has an information service at 457–1121 in Tokyo; *Japan Travel Bureau,* Foreign Tourist Department, Nittetsu Nihonbashi Bldg., 1–13–

1, Nihonbashi, Chuo-ku, Tokyo; *Kinki Nippon Tourist,* Kintetsu Bldg., 19–2, Kanda-Matsunagacho, Chiyoda-ku, Tokyo; *Kuoni Travel,* Asahi Tokai Bldg., 2–6–1 Otemachi, Chiyoda-ku, Tokyo.

New Orient Express, Tanaka-Tamuracho Bldg., 2–12–15, Shimbashi, Minato-ku, Tokyo; *Nippon Express,* Nittu Bldg., 3–12–9, Sotokanda, Chiyoda-ku, Tokyo; *Nippon Travel Agency,* Shimojima Bldg., 1–2–17 Higashi-Shimbashi, Minato-ku, Tokyo; *Overseas Travel Service,* Shin-Yurakucho Bldg., 1–12–1, Yurakucho, Chiyoda-ku, Tokyo; *Shosenkoku,* 1–2–2 Uchisaiwai-cho, Chiyoda-ku; *SITA World Travel,* Hibiya Park Bldg., 1–8–1, Yurakucho, Chiyoda-ku, Tokyo; *Joe Grace's Travel Center,* 1404 Chateau Bunkyo, 1-15–19, Nishikata, Bunkyo-ku, Tokyo; *Unitours Nippon Ltd.,* 1–11–2, Nihonbashi, Kayaba-cho, Chuo-ku, Tokyo. *Yusen Air & Sea Service,* Sanshin Bldg., 1–4–1, Yurakucho, Chiyoda-ku, Tokyo.

 TRAVEL DOCUMENTS. Your first essential document is your passport, without which you cannot leave your own country. **U.S. residents** must apply in person to their nearest U.S. Passport Agency, or to their local county courthouse. In some areas, selected post offices are also equipped to handle passport applications. If you still have your latest passport issued within the last eight years, you may use this to apply by mail. Otherwise, take with you: (1) a birth certificate or certified copy thereof, or other proof of citizenship; (2) two identical photographs, 2 ins. square, full face, black and white or color, on non-glossy paper and taken within the past six months; (3) $42 for those 18 years of age and up, $27 for those under 18 ($35 if you apply by mail); (4) proof of identity, such as a driver's license, previous passport, any governmental ID card. Social Security and credit cards are *not* acceptable. U.S. passports are valid for ten years. If it gets lost or stolen, immediately notify either the nearest American Consul or the Passport Office, Dept of State, Washington, D.C. 20524.

If you are **not an American citizen,** but are leaving from the United States, you must have a Treasury Sailing Permit, Form 1040D, certifying that all federal taxes have been paid. Apply to your local IRS office for this. You will have to present various documents: (1) passport; (2) travel tickets; (3) tax returns filed for the last two years; (4) W-2 forms for the most recent full year; (5) most recent current payroll stubs or letter; (6) check to be sure this is all!

To return to the U.S., you need a re-entry permit. If abroad less than two years, your Alien Registration Card will get you in on return. Apply for the Re-entry Permit at least six weeks before departure in person at the nearest office of the Immigration and Naturalization Service, or by mail to the Immigration and Naturalization Service, Washington D.C. This entitles the noncitizen resident to stay abroad a total of two years. (Naturalized American citizens may now stay abroad an unlimited length of time, even in the country of their origin.)

Canadian citizens entering Japan must have a valid passport. In Canada, apply in person to regional passport office in your area. Or write to the Passport Office, Dept. of External Affairs, Ottawa, Ontario K1A 0G3. A $21 fee, two photographs, and certification of citizenship or a Provincial birth certificate are required. Canadian citizens living in the U.S. need special forms from their nearest Canadian consulate.

Visas. The nationals of Canada and several non-English speaking countries are exempted from visa requirements so long as they do not stay for longer than three months (six months in the case of Austria, Germany, Ireland, and the United Kingdom, among others), nor seek employment in Japan. Visas are also not required for transit passengers continuing their journey by the same or first connecting flight within 72 hours, nor for steamship passengers on overland tours of under 15 days between two ports.

Americans must obtain a visa from any Japanese consulate. Passport photographs and confirmed air or sea passage may be required; visas are either commercial or tourist. Tourist visas are granted for 90 days and are valid for 5 years. Business visas will often allow a longer stay, depending on the business at hand. Tokyo Immigration Offices are at 3–3–20, Konan, Minato-ku, and on the 6th floor, World Import Mart, Sunshine City, Ikebukuro.

Tourists must receive special permission to stay longer than 90 days and must register with their local ward offices within the 90 days of entry. They are then issued with their Registration Cards. This registration is mandatory. All non-Japanese must carry their passports with them at all times until receiving Alien Registration Cards, which must then always be carried. Alien Registration Cards have to be surrendered upon leaving Japan.

CUSTOMS UPON ENTERING. Japan is strict about firearms, pornography, and narcotics other than alcohol or tobacco. Anyone caught with drugs is liable to detention, deportation, and refusal of re-entry into Japan. Certain fresh fruits, vegetables, plants, and animals are also illegal.

Duty-free allowances for nonresidents are: 3 bottles of alcohol; 400 cigarettes, 100 cigars, or 500 grams of tobacco; two ounces of perfume; two watches or clocks, each worth less than ¥ 30,000; and goods other than the above with a total market value not above ¥ 100,000. If you have possessions following you, you must fill in on arrival a "declaration of unaccompanied goods."

HOW TO GET AROUND. Public transport in Tokyo is cheap, safe, frequent, comprehensive—and grievously overcrowded, as all the world knows. Surface and subway trains are readily mastered once you have obtained a map with roman letters. Buses, however, are tricky, because the destinations are only written in Japanese.

Pedestrians please note: When you are crossing a road in Japan, look to the right first and then to the left before stepping out into traffic. Keep-to-the-left is the rule for vehicles and for pedestrians, except where there is no sidewalk; then you walk on the right so that you face vehicular traffic.

Some terms in general use in addresses:

-ken	prefecture (state)
-shi	city
-ku	ward
-machi	district within a ward, or a town
-chome	a block or group of blocks within a ku or a machi
-ban	"number," meaning a house or building number

Some other common geographical terms:

-kawa or -gawa	river
-wan	bay
-bashi or -hashi	bridge
-ko	lake
-yama	mountain
sen	line (rail, bus, or subway)
eki	station
kita	north

minami	south
nishi	west
higashi	east

CURRENCY. Japanese currency floats without a fixed official exchange rate between the yen and the U.S. dollar or the pound sterling or other currencies. Foreign currencies can be converted at banks and hotels and some shops. You may reconvert from Japanese yen to your original currency.

Traveler's checks and credit cards are safe and simple ways to carry money. Personal checks are completely useless in Japan. Many establishments honor the credit cards of organizations such as American Express, Barclaycard, Diners Club, MasterCard, Visa, and Carte Blanche. Traveler's checks are sold by banks and agencies. Amongst those widely used are those of the Bank of America, Cook's, and American Express. Japan's Bank of Tokyo and Fuji Bank sell traveler's checks in yen at their offices in the United States.

Japanese money is issued in ¥10,000, ¥5,000, and ¥1,000 notes. There are silver ¥500, ¥100, and ¥50 yen coins. The ¥10 yen coin is copper in color, and the ¥5 bronze. ¥1 coins, that are practically without value, are aluminum.

It is a good idea upon arrival in Japan to acquire a good stock of 100 yen and 50 yen coins. You'll need these constantly for local transport fares and vending machines.

Note: All prices mentioned in this book are indicative of costs at press time. We suggest that you keep an eye open for fluctuations in exchange rates while planning your trip—and while on it. Press time, U.S. $1.00 = ¥145.

HOTELS AND INNS. Hotel reservations should be made well in advance to avoid any disappointment with a room which you have to take on short notice. A good rule is to have your travel agent request your hotel accommodation at least three months prior to arrival. It is possible to make quick bookings up to seven days before arrival at several of Japan's top hotels, through Japan Travel Bureau International in the U.S., New York, Los Angeles, San Francisco, Honolulu.

You can confidently expect to find service and accommodation superlative in the upper categories of hotels and inns, and accommodation good and clean in the lesser-priced establishments that don't offer service. Hotel construction continues apace in Japan, resulting in superb buildings with advanced facilities. Tokyo's best luxury hotels without doubt qualify for leading world class status in terms of service and elegance.

Business hotels, hostels, and cheaper inns usually include tax and service charges in their rates. Major hotels do not. The tax levied is 10 percent of your total bill, minus ¥1,500 per head per night, and service charges are 15 percent. Tax is not levied on bills under ¥4,000. If your dining bills are separate and paid after each meal, you are not liable for tax until you go over ¥2,500.

The descriptions below will give you some idea of the types of low-cost accommodation available in Tokyo.

Business Hotels. These are connected with the Japan Business Hotel Association and provide convenient and inexpensive accommodation for pleasure travelers as well as for business people. Service is not provided. Expect to pay ¥5,000 per person per night, and be pleased if you get a lower rate.

Minshuku. These are private homes that accept paying guests for overnight stays. Each visitor or group is accommodated in a private room, but all guests come together around the family dining table. Guests are expected to lay their bedding at night, to provide their own toilet gear and nightwear, and to tidy up in the morning. Minshuku charge about ¥5,000 per person per night with two meals. Reservations have to be made in advance, and that is not easy to do until you get to Japan. You could begin by communicating with the *Japan Minshuku Association* at 201, New Pearl Building, 2–10–8, Hyakunin-cho, Shinjuku-ku, Tokyo, and asking for a list of their 25,000 minshuku throughout Japan and the addresses of different reservation centers.

Inns. Those registered with the Japanese Group Inns are moderately priced —not high-class, but friendly, hospitable, and economical. You touch the Japanese way of living here, since the rooms are floored with straw tatami mats, and you sleep on quilts on the floors. You join in the Japanese bathing habit, too, scrubbing yourself clean and sluicing off the soap before entering the hot tub. Expect to pay at least ¥4,500, and to be charged extra for breakfast and dinner (which, for curiosity's sake alone, you are well advised not to skip).

Youth Hostels. Visitors who are not already members in their own countries pay ¥450 extra per night for a "Welcome Stamp." Six accumulated stamps are equivalent to one year's membership. The overnight charge including sheet rental is about ¥2,000. With two meals you pay about ¥1,000 more. The Japan YHA national office is at Hoken Kaikan, 1–2, Sadohara-cho, Ichigaya, Shinjuku-ku, Tokyo 162. Advance booking is indicated, and travelers should be checked in before 9:00 P.M. Stay in any one hostel is restricted to three consecutive nights.

LAUNDRY. Top-class hotels take care of your laundry and dry cleaning in 24 hours if it is urgent, in two to three days otherwise. Coin-operated laundries exist in residential districts. Often public bathhouses have a washing machine or two, where your laundry gets swished around while you're in the tub.

DINING OUT. Restaurants often have set lunches which are much cheaper, and quicker-served, than both à la carte dishes and dinners. Exquisite Japanese food is as costly as gourmet Western food, but everyday Japanese dishes, available everywhere, are inexpensive, low in fat content, and moderate in calories. Japanese green tea is usually included with ordinary Japanese fare. Cheap restaurants have show windows with attractive wax models of the dishes they offer, and prices are clearly marked. Scout around among the dining rooms of department stores, restaurants in big office buildings, and in underground shopping arcades.

TIPPING is not customary in Japan. The service charge that is added to hotel and restaurant bills takes the place of individual tipping. Taxi drivers are not tipped. Prices are set for porters. Some beauty parlors post notices asking patrons not to tip. Japanese people dislike being treated as if they were beggars, and tipping, to them, places them in this category.

On the other hand, little gifts are never wrong as tokens of appreciation for any special services willingly given. Never forget to say "thank you." Simple politeness goes a long way.

BUSINESS HOURS, HOLIDAYS, AND LOCAL TIME. Banks, business houses, and government offices are closed on Sundays each week. Banks are open from 9:00 A.M.–3:00 P.M. from Monday to Friday, and until noon on Saturdays. They are not open on the second and third Saturdays of the month, and on these days the post office, too, does not handle money or insurance business. Business houses and government offices are open from 9:00 A.M. –5:00 P.M. from Monday to Friday and until noon on Saturdays. Some business houses observe a five-day week. Department stores are open from 10:00 A.M. –6:00 P.M. and usually take a weekday holiday instead of Sunday. Food stalls in department stores stay open until 6:30 or 7:00 P.M. Local shops often stay open until 9:00 P.M. and do not take regular holidays.

Japan has twelve national holidays in a year. These are:

January. *New Year's Day,* January 1. In most cities and towns, the ladies put on their best kimonos and go out to their family shrines, or else the most fashionable temples, and pay their respects to their ancestors, and admire each other's attire. Children go out with their fathers to fly kites. National holiday. Most shops, stores and offices closed through January 3.

Adults' Day on the 15th, to honor youth who have reached voting age, which is 20 in Japan. National holiday, but no special observances, usually.

February. *National Foundation Day,* on the 11th. National holiday celebrating accession to the throne of the first emperor, Jimmu.

March. On the 3rd, *Girls' Day,* while not a holiday, is observed in most homes, the girls displaying sets of expensive dolls (never played with), and receiving congratulations from the relatives. You will see sets of these dolls in some public places on display.

Vernal Equinox Day, a national holiday to celebrate the coming of Spring. Visit to ancestral graves. Celebrated on the 20th or 21st.

April. *The Emperor's Birthday,* on the 29th, is a national holiday, and the beginning of "Golden Week." There being two more national holidays in the space of a week, business comes to a standstill at this time, and everyone tries to go touring around the country.

May. *Constitution Day* to commemorate promulgation of the country's new, peaceful, basic law, a postwar creation. National holiday held on the 3rd.

Children's Day, formerly called Boys' Day. From bamboo poles families hang cloth streamers in the shape of the carp, which symbolize strength. Also a national holiday.

September. *Respect for the Aged Day.* National holiday, on the 15th.

Autumnal Equinox Day, to celebrate the first day of autumn and to venerate one's ancestors. National holiday, held on the 23rd.

October. *Sports Day.* A new national holiday, on the 10th, commemorates the Tokyo Olympics of 1964.

November. *Culture Day,* on the 3rd, is a national holiday which is supposed to encourage the people to love peace, freedom and culture, but on which nothing much happens except that the people rest. Before the war, this day was celebrated as the Emperor Meiji's Birthday, and many older people today still visit Meiji Shrine in Tokyo to pay respect to the memory of the great man who brought Japan into the community of nations.

Labor Thanksgiving Day, also a national holiday held on the 23rd. Frequently combined with celebrations of a good harvest in the countryside but in itself merely a special day of rest. Before war's defeat brought about the disestablishment of the Shinto religion, this day was a national holiday of Thanksgiving only. Then as now, the emperor offers new rice wine (sake) fermented from this year's crop, to the gods.

Time in Japan is 10 hours ahead of Greenwich Mean Time, and 15 hours ahead of Eastern Daylight Savings Time.

THE JAPANESE CALENDAR. The Japanese year is often indicated by the reign of the emperor. This year is the 62d of the Showa (the formal name for Emperor Hirohito's reign).

TELEPHONES AND MAIL. Telephones. Along the streets you'll find blue and green public pay telephones in booths, and red pay telephones in front of some shops. A local call costs ¥10 for 3 minutes. Insert another ¥10 coin before the time is up to keep going. The larger red telephones are for long distance calls, and they accept up to ¥60 at a time. There is no time limit on domestic long-distance calls, but you must keep feeding in ¥10 coins at intervals of a few seconds. Yellow long-distance telephones take ¥100 coins at a time. Green telephones accept special telephone cards as well as coins. If you do not know the area code, dial 100 for long-distance service, and 104 for information, in Japanese.

Overseas calls: book your calls at your hotel through the operator. To make operator-assisted overseas calls from anywhere in Japan, dial 0051. Be prepared to wait for about 20 seconds before you hear the ringing tone. For station-to-station calls, rates are lower than personal calls. For a collect call, give the number and the operator will connect you if the party agrees to pay the charge. This service is available between Japan and U.S.A., Canada, Korea (Republic of), Hong Kong, Taiwan, Australia and most European countries. Charges to Europe are ¥2,250 on weekdays for 3 minutes, to the U.S.A. ¥1,890. Subscribers registered with KDD can make calls much cheaper through direct dialing, with a charge unit of six seconds. Check with your hotel.

Mail rates vary according to destination. These are:

	Asia, Australia	Canada, U.S.A.	Europe
Air mail letter			
up to 10 grams	¥130	¥150	¥170
for each extra 10 grams	¥70	¥110	¥110
Air mail post card	¥90	¥100	¥110
Aerogram	¥120	¥120	¥120

Ordinary **cablegrams** are ¥118 per word to the United States, and ¥192 per word to most of Europe. Seven words is the minimum. Letter telegrams, somewhat slower, are about half the ordinary rate. Minimum of 22 words.

ELECTRIC CURRENT. Hotels usually have outlets for 100 volts only. Eastern Japan including Tokyo is on a 50-cycle basis, western Japan including Kyoto and Osaka is on 60 cycles. The dividing line between eastern and western is roughly halfway between Tokyo and Nagoya, near the city of Shizuoka.

HINTS TO HANDICAPPED TRAVELERS. Language Service Volunteers of the Japanese Red Cross have published a book: *Accessible Tokyo.* A copy of this, from 1–1–3, Shiba Daimon, Minato-ku, Tokyo, will be of great assistance to a traveler on crutches or in a wheelchair.

MEDICAL TREATMENT. The *International Association for Medical Assistance to Travelers* is a worldwide association offering a list of approved English-speaking doctors, whose training meets British and American standards. Write to IAMAT, 417 Center St., Lewiston, NY 14092. In Japan

IAMAT has member hospitals or clinics in Tokyo, Yokohama, Osaka, Kyoto, Kobe, Hiroshima and Okinawa. The fixed fees are: office calls $20; house and hotel calls $30; weekends, holidays, nights $40. Other IAMAT offices are: in Canada at 123 Edward Street, Toronto, Ontario MGE 1B9; in Europe at Got-thardstrasse 17, 6300 Zug, Switzerland; in Australia at St. Vincent's Hospital, Victoria Parade, Melbourne 3065.

SECURITY. In this country of low crime rate, you still need to take reasonable precautions. Leave your valu-ables in hotel safe-keeping—there is no sense offering temptation. Lost property often finds a way back to the owner if it is clearly labeled with name and address; small items are often recoverable from where they were left (if you can remember where you put them down), from Lost Property offices of railways and taxi companies, or from local police boxes.

Emergency numbers, dialed without charge from public telephones, are: 110 for police; 119 for fire services and ambulances. Such calls have to be made in Japanese.

CUSTOMS DEPARTING. Americans who are out of the United States at least 48 hours and have claimed no exemption during the previous 30 days are now able to bring in $400 worth of purchases duty-free. For the next $1000 worth of goods beyond the first $400, inspectors will assess a flat 10 percent duty, rather than hitting you with different percentages for various types of goods. The value of each item is determined by the price actually paid (so keep your receipts). All items purchased must accompany the passenger on his return. Every member of the family is entitled to this exemption, regardless of age, and the allowance can be pooled.

Not more than 200 cigarettes, or one carton, may be included in your duty-free exemption, nor more than a quart of wine or liquor (none at all if your passport indicates you are from a "dry" state or are under 21 years old). Only one bottle of perfume that is trademarked in the U.S. may be brought in, plus a reasonable quantity of other brands.

Antiques are defined, for customs purposes, as articles manufactured over 100 years ago and are admitted duty-free. If there's any question of age, you may be asked to supply proof.

It is illegal to bring into the U.S. foreign meats, plants, fruit, soil, etc., without permission as they can spread destructive diseases. Write for the pamphlet, *Travelers' Tips,* Program Aid 1083 to: Treasury Department, Office of Regional Commissioner of Customs, Region II, Custom House, New York, NY 10048. In the last several years a large number of birds, animals and marine mammals have also come under protection as endangered species, and cannot be brought into the U.S.

British Customs. British subjects may import the following goods, duty-free: 200 cigarettes, or 100 cigarillos, or 50 cigars, or 250 grams tobacco; plus one liter of alcohol of more than 22 percent proof, or 2 liters of alcohol not more than 22 percent proof, or 2 liters of fortified or sparkling wine and 2 liters of still table wine; plus 50 grams of perfume and ¼ liter of toilet water; plus other goods to the value of £32.

Canada. Residents of Canada, after 7 days away, may, upon written declara-tion, claim an exemption of $300 per calendar year, which includes an allowance of 40 ounces of liquor, 50 cigars, 200 cigarettes, and 2 pounds of tobacco. For details ask for Canada Customs brochure, "I Declare."

Australia. Duty-free allowances include 200 cigarettes or 250 grams of cigars and tobacco, and one liter of liquor. Dutiable goods to the value of A$400 included in personal baggage are also duty free. Duty on additional items vary from item to item. New Zealand regulations are similar.

Everyone. If you have brought with you any foreign-made articles such as cameras, binoculars, expensive timepieces, it is wise to have receipts from the retailer showing that the items were bought in your home country. If you bought such articles on previous holidays abroad, and have already paid duty, carry with you those relevant receipts. Otherwise, on returning home, you may be charged duty again—and for British residents, VAT as well.

As you leave Japan, you must not carry anything with you that resembles a weapon, even if it is a pair of scissors. All baggage is searched to reduce hijacking risks.

"Using the airport" fee, collected at the check-in counters, is ¥2,000 per person.

EXPLORING TOKYO

by
JOHN TURRENT

John Turrent was on the editorial staff of The Japan Times *from 1978 until 1984, writing regularly for the daily newspaper,* The Student Times, *and* The Japan Times Weekly. *He is now working as a freelance writer and translator in Tokyo. Mr. Turrent is co-author and author, respectively, of the guidebook* Around Tokyo, *volumes 1 and 2.*

The first impression many people have of Tokyo is of a city teeming with people and traffic, a concrete jungle of modern office buildings stretching as far as the eye can see. The rush-hour crush for which the capital of Japan is notorious is a fact of life here. To experience it at first hand, head for Shinjuku Station in western central Tokyo between the hours of 8:00 and 9:00 in the morning and try changing trains there. Several railway lines pass through Shinjuku, including the green-colored Yamanote loop line, the Chuo line, which runs from Tokyo Station out to the western suburbs, and the private Keio and Odakyu lines, both of which start at Shinjuku. And as if that weren't enough, Marunouchi subway line trains also stop there.

The squeeze, accompanied by plenty of pushing and shoving and heaving, should be enough to convince you that Tokyo, with a population of over 11 million people, is indeed an overcrowded city. The

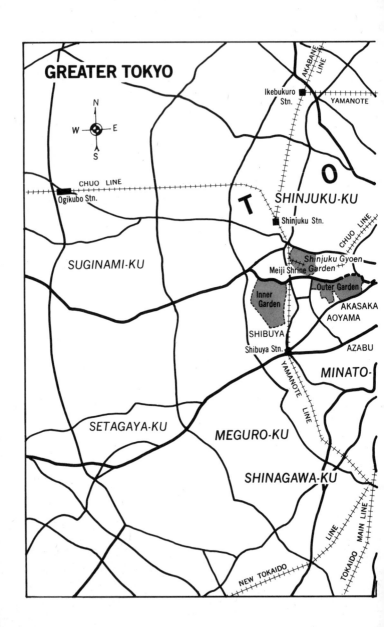

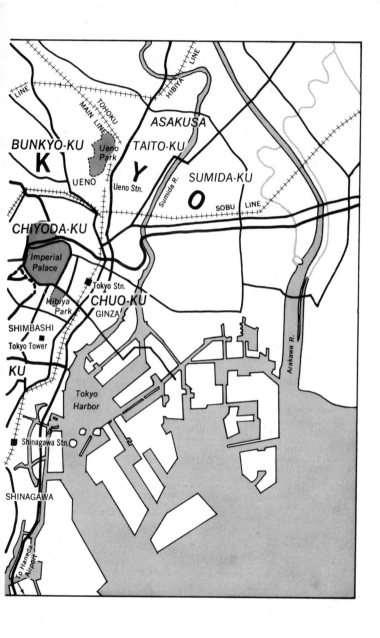

Shinjuku experience is repeated at various degrees at many other stations around the capital, especially the main Tokyo, Shinagawa, Shibuya, Ikebukuro, and Ueno stations on the Yamanote line, all starting points for other lines fanning out into the suburbs. While recovering your composure after being bundled off the train, spare a thought for the many citizens of the capital who have to suffer the rush hour every working day of the week.

Fortunately, first impressions do not have to be lasting ones. Having got over the worst aspect, it is a good idea to take a look at the city from a different angle by climbing to one of Tokyo's high spots, of which there are several possible choices. Your hotel might rise high enough to offer a panoramic view of the capital. If not, head for the nearest skyscraper with an observation floor.

The biggest cluster of skyscrapers in Tokyo is a 10-minute walk from the west exit of Shinjuku Station—within this grouping the Keio Plaza Hotel, Center Building, Nomura Building, and Sumitomo Building all have observation floors. Other possibilities are Kasumigaseki Building, near Toranomon Station on the Ginza subway line, the World Trade Center Building near Hamamatsucho Station on the Yamanote line, and Sunshine 60 (the largest of them all at 240 meters) near Ikebukuro Station on the Yamanote line. Last but not least, there is Tokyo Tower, which, when it was built in 1958, was the tallest independent steel tower in the world at 333 meters. It has two observation platforms, at 150 and 250 meters, and is located at Shiba Park, not far from the World Trade Center Building. As in the case of some of the skyscrapers, an entrance fee is required at Tokyo Tower.

From the observation platform of your choice, you will be able to enjoy spectacular views of the capital and its surroundings. On a clear day, especially after a good rainfall has cleared away all the smog, you should be able to see Mount Fuji to the south, and the hills and mountains of Chichibu to the west. To the southeast you can see Tokyo Bay, particularly fine views of which can be had from the World Trade Center Building and Tokyo Tower, which rise nearby. To the north, you might be able to make out the hills of Nikko in Tochigi Prefecture.

In this way, the mammoth city can be put into perspective. You can picture it as a small village by the sea, which is what it was when Ota Dokan built the first castle stronghold in the area in 1457. That first castle, which was located in today's Hibiya district, did not last long, but the town of Edo (as Tokyo was then known) began to develop and prosper in the 17th century, most notably under the guidance of the first Tokugawa shogun, Ieyasu.

Edo, which was modeled after Kyoto, was chosen by Ieyasu as his capital because of its situation near the sea, with mountains nearby. It is said that Edo had already developed into the largest city in the world by the mid-18th century, when it had a population of about 1 million. Edo became the capital of all of Japan in 1868 when the shogunate was overthrown and imperial rule restored throughout the nation. It was then that the city's name was changed to Tokyo, which means "eastern capital."

Tokyo continued to expand rapidly after 1868, when a period of Westernization brought in a new look in the form of red-brick, Western-style architecture. However, Tokyo has been reduced to rubble on two occasions in the 20th century: in 1923 by a huge earthquake and in 1945 by wartime air raids. This is the reason why Tokyo today appears to be such a thoroughly modernized city.

Except for part of the Tokyo Station building and the occasional structure hidden among glass and ferro-concrete, the red-brick architecture of the Meiji Period has largely disappeared now. Beneath the skyscrapers, though, there are still many traces of Tokyo's past to be seen, and it is these that make up the capital's attractions. The concrete jungle image is a true one if you limit yourself to central areas such as Marunouchi and Shinjuku, but Tokyo is actually a city with a wealth of history and culture, greenery, and even has islands to offer. Its high spots are certainly not limited to its skyscrapers.

Getting Around the City

Tokyo consists of 23 central wards, 26 cities, 6 towns, and 9 villages. Its farthest point, which cannot be seen even from the top of the tallest skyscraper, is the Ogasawara, or Bonin, island group, located in the ocean to the southeast and reached in about 30 hours by boat. The central point is the Imperial Palace, a favorite among tourists.

Despite the size and congestion involved, Tokyo is quite an easy city to get around in. Nearly all the famous spots are accessible by overground train or subway, or a combination of both. The central area is served by the Yamanote loop line, which runs from Tokyo Station in the east down south to Yurakucho, Hamamatsucho, and Shinagawa, then up the western side of the city's central area via Shibuya, Shinjuku, and Ikebukuro, then back to Tokyo station via Ueno in the northeast. There are a total of twenty-nine stations on the Yamanote line.

The other main line that you'll be using in the central Tokyo area is the Chuo line, which cuts across the city from east to west, starting at Tokyo Station and operating out into the western suburbs of the capital, passing through Ochanomizu, Yotsuya, and Shinjuku stations on the way. Trains on the Chuo line are painted orange, and those on the Yamanote line green.

Working round the city clockwise from Tokyo Station, the main areas of the city that tourists visit, either for sightseeing or shopping purposes, are Ginza (for its department stores and nightlife), the Roppongi and Akasaka entertainment districts in Minato Ward in the south, Shibuya, Shinjuku, and Ikebukuro in the west for shopping and entertainment, and Ueno and Asakusa in the northeast, for the popular Ueno Park and Asakusa Kannon Temple tourist sights.

Imperial Palace

The palace stands where Edo Castle used to be. After the Meiji Restoration in 1868 brought the Edo Period to an end, construction of a new palace for the emperor was begun on the site and completed in 1888. This Meiji Palace, as it was called, was reduced to ashes in the 1945 air raids, along with much of the rest of Tokyo, although the moats and stone bridges remained intact. A new palace was completed

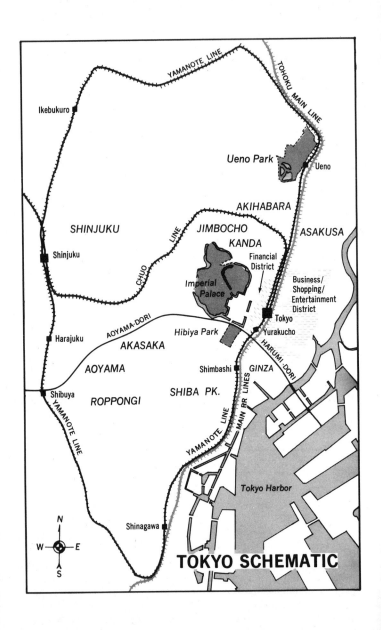

TOKYO SCHEMATIC

in 1968, and the path around the grounds has now become a popular jogging course. The public is allowed over the main Nijubashi bridge and into the private grounds on two occasions during the year, at New Year's and again on the Emperor's Birthday, April 29. The palace is located in Chiyoda Ward and is reached from the Sakuradamon, Nijubashimae, Otemachi, or Takebashi subway stations.

The Outer Garden and East Garden are open to the public. The former, which has a giant fountain as its symbol (illuminated at night), can be reached in 5 minutes from Nijubashimae Station on the Chiyoda subway line, while the latter (open only until 4:00 P.M. and closed on Mondays and Fridays) can be reached from Otemachi or Takebashi subway stations. Entrance is free.

DISTRICT BY DISTRICT

Shimbashi–Ginza–Nihonbashi

This is the business, shopping, and entertainment district on the southeast side of the Imperial Palace. Shimbashi Station is distinguished by the steam locomotive displayed outside its eastern exit. There are several hotels located in the vicinity of Shimbashi Station, including Shimbashi Daiichi Hotel, Ginza Daiichi Hotel, Nikko Hotel, and Ginza International Hotel. The Imperial Hotel can also be reached from Shimbashi Station.

The Shimbashi area is a small but popular place to go eating and drinking in the evenings. The many restaurants and bars located on the narrow side streets near the station usually are cheaper than those found in the Ginza area to the north, and the atmosphere of these places tends to be less restrained.

Between Shimbashi and Yurakucho stations are a number of department stores (Matsuzakaya, Hankyu, Mitsukoshi, Matsuya, and the recently opened Hankyu-Seibu) and other Ginza shops of long-standing fame: Wako, Mikimoto Pearls, Nishi-Ginza Electric Center, and the International Arcade, the latter housing several tax-free shops and quite rightly called one of Tokyo's best bargain centers. It is situated under the railway lines, a short walk from Yurakucho Station.

There's lots to see in this area and, with map in hand, you will be able to plan your own course. For example, a Ginza walking course might take you along Chuo Dori Avenue from Shimbashi Station, until you reach Matsuya Department Store. Turn left here, and you'll come out at Yurakucho Station. After stopping at the impressive Hankyu-Isetan department stores, the Sukiyabashi Shopping Center, Nishi Ginza Electric Center, and International Arcade, cross over to the other side of the railway lines to visit the Imperial Hotel with its arcade of top-class stores, and then on to Hibiya Park and, if time allows, the Imperial Palace as well.

The area around Tokyo Station is mainly taken up by office buildings. It is a busy business district by day, and almost a deserted ghost town at night. Two large bookstores are located near the station, Yaesu Book Center and Maruzen Book Store, which is on Chuo Dori Avenue; both stock English-language books. On the Yaesu exit side of the station, next to Daimaru Department Store, is the Kokusai Kanko

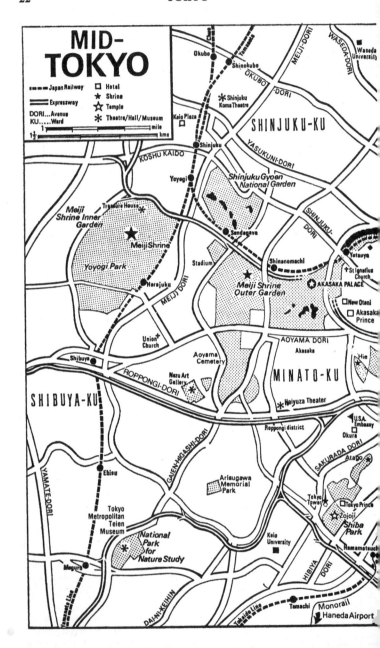

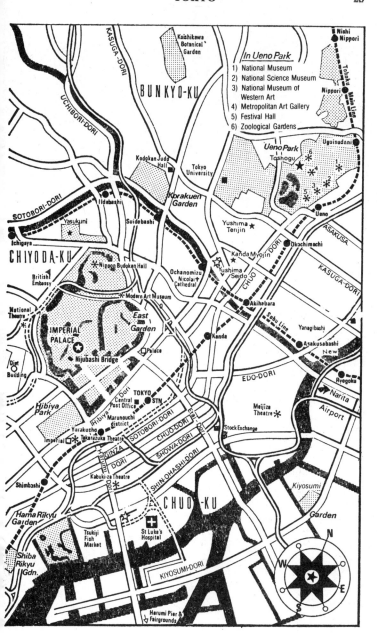

In Ueno Park
1) National Museum
2) National Science Museum
3) National Museum of Western Art
4) Metropolitan Art Gallery
5) Festival Hall
6) Zoological Gardens

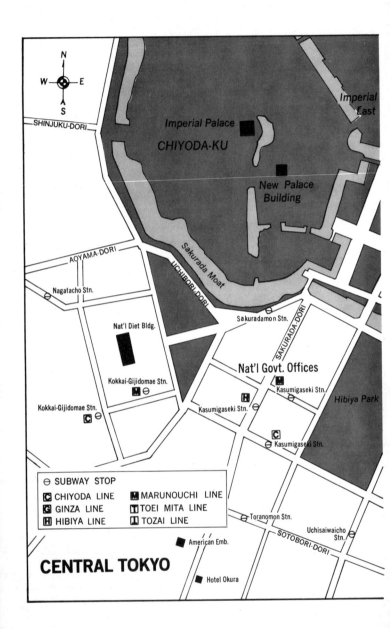

CENTRAL TOKYO

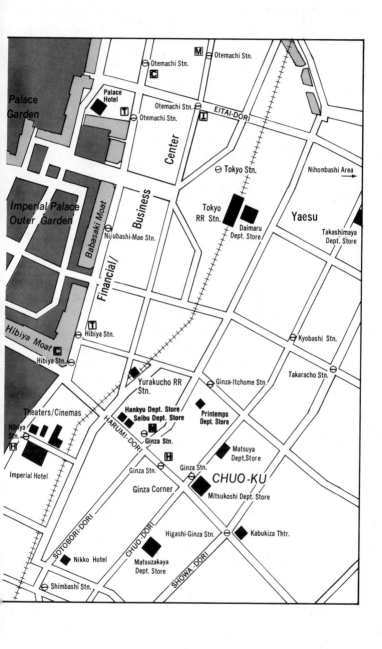

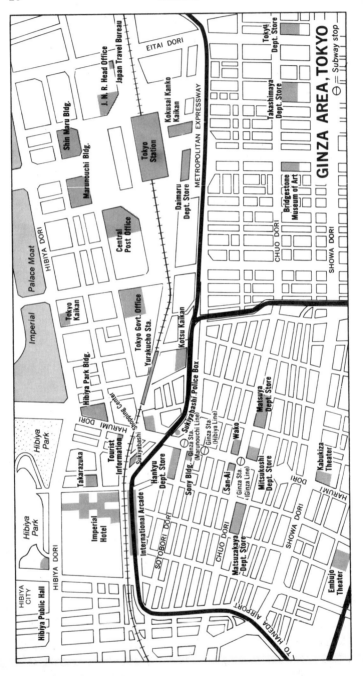

GINZA AREA, TOKYO

① = Subway stop

EITAI DORI

METROPOLITAN EXPRESSWAY

Tokyu Dept. Store

Takashimaya Dept. Store

Bridgestone Museum of Art

CHUO DORI

SHOWA DORI

J. R. Head Office

Japan Travel Bureau

Kokusai Kanko Kaikan

Shin Maru Bldg.

Marunouchi Bldg.

Tokyo Station

Central Post Office

Daimaru Dept. Store

Palace Moat

Imperial

HIBIYA DORI

Tokyo Kaikan

Tokyo Govt. Office Yurakucho Sta.

Kotsu Kaikan

Hibiya Park Bldg.

HARUMI DORI

Shopping Center

Sukiyabashi

Matsuya Dept. Store

Sukiyabashi Police Box

Ginza Sta. (Marunouchi Line)

Ginza Sta. (Hibiya Line)

Wako

San-Ai

Ginza Sta. (Ginza Line)

Mitsukoshi Dept. Store

HARUMI DORI

Kabukiza Theater

Hibiya Park

Hibiya Park

Takarazuka

Tourist Information

International Arcade

Hankyu Dept. Store

SOTOBORI DORI

Sony Bldg.

CHUO DORI

SHOWA DORI

HIBIYA DORI

Imperial Hotel

Matsuzakaya Dept. Store

Embujo Theater

HIBIYA CITY

Hibiya Public Hall

TO HANEDA AIRPORT

Kaikan Building, whose first through fourth floors house the tourist offices of most of Japan's prefectural districts. Maps and information can be obtained here. On the Marunouchi side of Tokyo Station, again a predominantly business district, there is the Tokyo Central Post Office, where English is spoken and international parcels are handled.

One of the most popular temples in Tokyo is Zojoji, located in Minato Ward in the southeastern part of central Tokyo. Onarimon Station on the Toei-Mita subway line exits there, or it's a 10-minute walk from Hamamatsucho station on the Yamanote line. Zojoji Temple is said to date from the 14th century, although the main hall had to be rebuilt after the war. The red-lacquered main gate was originally constructed in 1605.

Nearby is Tokyo Tower—you won't miss it, as it rises 333 meters and dwarfs all else below. In addition to the observation points, there is a waxworks on the third floor. From the tower you can look over Shiba Park, which sprawls below.

Hibiya Park and Kitanomaru Park both border the grounds of the Imperial Palace. The former is on the south side. Because it is near the Kasumigaseki, Shimbashi, and Yurakucho business districts, it is a popular place for office workers to rest during their lunch break. Kitanomaru Park is on the north side of the palace and can be reached on foot from Takebashi Station on the Tozai subway line. Located inside this park are the Science and Technology Museum, the National Museum of Modern Art, the Crafts Gallery, and the Budokan concert hall, while nearby, on the opposite side of Yasukuni-dori Avenue, which runs past the park, is Yasukuni Shrine.

The shrine, which has extensive parklike grounds, is reached in 5 minutes on foot to the west from Kudanshita Station on the Tozai subway line. It is dedicated to the souls of all who fought and died for Japan, and as such is the focus of much debate every time the prime minister attends a memorial service there—is he attending in his capacity as prime minister, and thereby maintaining links with the country's militaristic past, or is he attending in a private capacity?

Yasukuni Shrine boasts some splendid buildings, fine stone lanterns, and handsome *torii* gateways, as well as bronze statues of Yajiro Shinagawa (1843–1900) and Masujiro Omura (1824–1869), both political figures of the 19th century, and a Treasure House of war-related memorabilia.

Akasaka

On the western side of the Imperial Palace is Akasaka, an entertainment district with plenty of clubs, restaurants, and discos. It might also be called a diplomatic village—located in the area are the National Diet building; the Ministry of Foreign Affairs; the embassies of the U.S.A., Canada, and Mexico; and the Geihinkan Akasaka Palace, where foreign dignitaries stay. The Metropolitan Police Department, the National Theater of Japan, and the Suntory Gallery also have addresses in this area. Local hotels include such big names as the Hotel Okura, the Hotel New Otani, the Akasaka Prince, the Akasaka Tokyu Hotel, and the Capitol Tokyu. And right in there with them all is Hie Shrine.

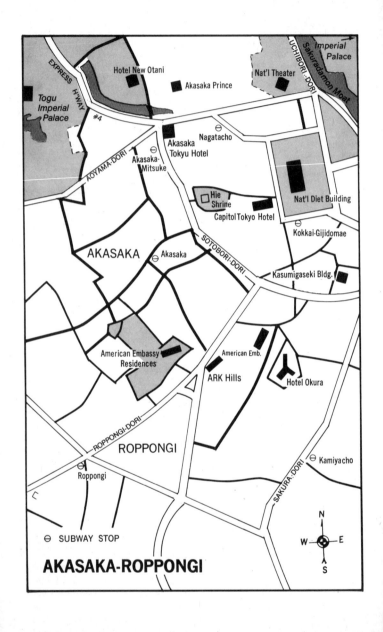

AKASAKA-ROPPONGI

However international it is, a Japanese neighborhood wouldn't be complete without a shrine or temple, after all. If you happen to be in town in June, then be sure to visit the shrine's festival which takes place from the 10th to the 15th of that month every year. It is one of the largest and most colorful annual festivals in Tokyo.

The National Diet Building, which stands on Kasumigaseki Hill in Nagatacho, was completed in 1936. The central tower of the 65.5-meter-high structure has become one of the main landmarks of Tokyo. As you face the building, the right half is taken up by the House of Councillors and the left half by the House of Representatives.

The main entertainment districts in this area are Akasaka-Mitsuke and Roppongi, both of which have convenient subway stations and are well frequented by the foreign resident and tourist communities.

Shibuya

Along with Ginza, Roppongi, Shinjuku, and Ikebukuro, Shibuya, in Tokyo's western quarter, is one of the leading shopping and entertainment districts in the capital. The symbol of the area, however, is neither a main department store nor a nightclub spot, but the bronze statue of a dog called Hachiko that sits outside the north exit of Shibuya Station. Hachiko lived in the Shibuya area from 1923–1935 together with his master. Every day Hachiko would see his master off to work at the station and return again to meet him in the evening. His master died away from home in 1925, and for 10 years after that Hachiko waited at the station for him to return. The dog's loyalty won the hearts of the people of the area, and after his death the statue was erected on the spot in his memory. The statue has become a popular meeting place for people on their way to the many shops, restaurants, bars, and clubs in the area, while Hachiko himself is preserved in stuffed form in Ueno's Science Museum.

From the Hachiko statue, roads fan out in several directions, all of which offer plenty of opportunities for exploration. A good course is to take the street leading away in the direction in which Hachiko is looking. This street passes Seibu Department Store on the left, and beyond this a turning to the left takes you up Shibuya's Park Avenue (Koen-Dori) toward the NHK Broadcasting Center, on the way passing Parco Shopping Complex on the left and the Tobacco and Salt Museum on the right. Adjoining the broadcasting center is Yoyogi Park, a popular spot among joggers and musicians, and it is possible to walk right through the park as far as Harajuku and the Meiji Shrine.

Omote-Sando, the main boulevard linking Harajuku and Aoyama, began as a solemn, stone-lanterned route for pilgrims. During the early postwar years it swarmed with American Occupation Forces families who lived in nearby Washington Heights, which became Olympic Village in 1964 and is now part of Yoyogi Park. Harajuku is a fashionable district and a favorite haunt for Tokyo's young set.

At the big intersection with Aoyama-dori, turn left. This avenue is another that has changed its character over the last few years. Ultra-modern, it still tucks away the oddest little remnants of old Japan in between sophisticated boutiques and fast-food restaurants.

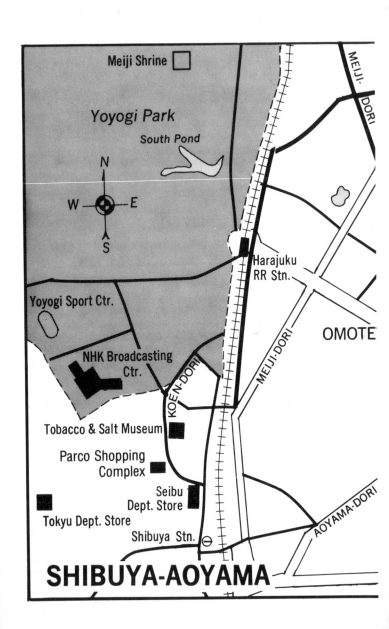

Meiji Shrine

Yoyogi Park

South Pond

N
W · E
S

Harajuku
RR Stn.

Yoyogi Sport Ctr.

NHK Broadcasting
Ctr.

Tobacco & Salt Museum

Parco Shopping
Complex

Seibu
Dept. Store

Tokyu Dept. Store

Shibuya Stn.

MEIJI-DORI

KOEN-DORI

MEIJI-DORI

OMOTE

AOYAMA-DORI

SHIBUYA-AOYAMA

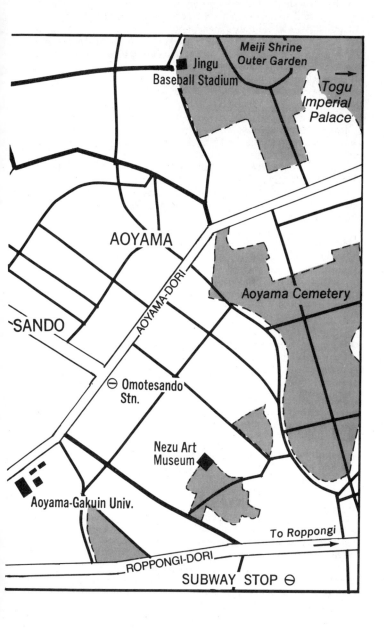

Meiji Shrine
Outer Garden

Jingu
Baseball Stadium

Togu
Imperial
Palace

AOYAMA

AOYAMA-DORI

Aoyama Cemetery

SANDO

Omotesando
Stn.

Nezu Art
Museum

Aoyama-Gakuin Univ.

To Roppongi

ROPPONGI-DORI

SUBWAY STOP

You'll see shops that sell flower bowls, multicolored and multi-shaped. You'll see shops that are stacked to their ceilings with *futon,* the quilts that are not only Japanese bedding but also beds. Next to a shop that sells goldfish is a supermarket. Next to this again is an old-style shop that sells tea, colored tea caddies, blue-and-white Japanese teapots, and handleless Japanese teacups. Then there's a high-class store for kimonos.

Aoyama-dori is fashionable, but younger and breezier and trendier than the Ginza. You can reach this shopping boulevard from Gaienmae or, if you walk far enough, Aoyama-itchome subway station.

Yoyogi Park can be reached directly from Meiji-jingumae Station on the Chiyoda subway line or Harajuku Station on the Yamanote line, and it is in the immediate vicinity of Meiji Shrine, the Yoyogi National Stadium, and the NHK Broadcasting Center in the Shibuya district. Over the past couple of years the road leading from Harajuku Station down to NHK has become an extra tourist attraction itself every Sunday, when it is closed to traffic and young people engage in everything from dancing to 1950s' rock 'n' roll music to roller skating and practicing tennis against the walls of the bridges.

Meiji-jingu is the main shrine in central Tokyo. It is located near Harajuku Station on the Yamanote line or Meiji-jingumae Station on the Chiyoda subway line. Meiji Shrine, as it is often called in English, was dedicated to the Emperor Meiji (1852–1912) and is still one of the main pilgrimage centers in Japan. Crowds of people visit here from quite distant places, especially on New Year's Day. As well as its *torii* gateways marking the various entrances to the shrine, Meiji-jingu has a splendid inner garden of trees and shrubs, and a particularly outstanding display of irises, which blossom in late June. The wooden *torii* gate of the shrine is the largest of its kind in Japan, standing 12 meters high. The shape of *torii* gates, by the way, is said to derive from the shape of a rooster's perch, because of an old legend in which a rooster crowed, waking the sun goddess and bringing light to the world.

Shinjuku

Walk through one of the exits of Shinjuku Station, ride up a short escalator, and you'll probably find yourself, not out on the street, but inside a department store. Old-fashioned stations serving one purpose only have all but disappeared in Tokyo (one exception being Harajuku Station on the Yamanote line, which is a quaint cottage-like structure). Most of the modern station buildings have literally been built right over the railway lines and house stores, shops, restaurants, coffee shops, and even sometimes cinemas. It is now possible to do your shopping, eat a meal, and have your entertainment without ever leaving the station.

In the case of Shinjuku, the west side is taken up by the Odakyu and Keio department stores and the east side by the appropriately named Shinjuku Station Building. If you do seek to venture outside, the west exit takes you to the Shinjuku skyscraper buildings (the KDD Building, NS Building, Keio Plaza Hotel, Century Hyatt Hotel, Hilton Hotel, Daiichi Seimei Building, Sumitomo Building, Mitsui Building, Shinjuku Center Building, Nomura Building, and Yasuda Building).

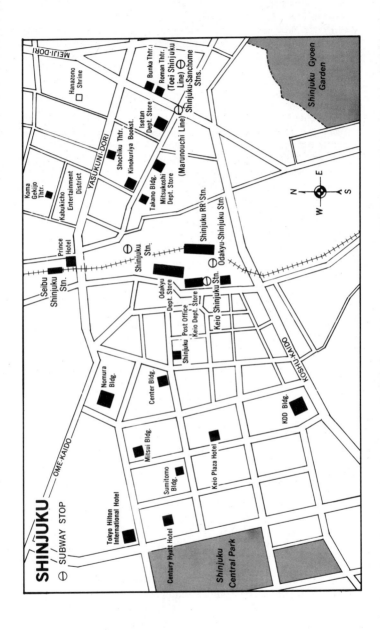

The east exit leads to the Kabukicho entertainment district which, despite its name, has nothing to do with Kabuki. In the area you'll find, on the safer side, scores of coffee shops, restaurants, discos and pubs, as well as the Koma Gekijo Theater where musicals and variety shows are held. On the "be warned" side, there are lots of strip joints, bars, cabarets, and dark alleyways.

Also to be reached from the east exit are Mitsukoshi and Isetan department stores, Kinokuniya Book Store, the Takano building of boutiques and other shops, which is built on the most highly valued piece of land in Japan, and Hanazono Shrine. This shrine is near the crossing where Yasukuni Dori Avenue and Meiji Dori Avenue meet. It is the scene of a cock fair (*tori no ichi*) every November. The fair is held two or three times in the month, but on differing days, so check with the local press if you're in town around that time. Nearby is "Golden Street," a district of small bars frequented by writers, poets, and others connected with the literary world. Once it was a "red-light" area. Many cinemas are located in the two areas near Koma Gekijo and the Isetan Department Store, and Shinjuku Gyoen Garden.

Both the east and west exit areas of Shinjuku have a good selection of smaller stores offering goods at prices cheaper than can be found in the department stores. Discount cameras are a particular attraction. Look for the Sakuraya and Yodobashi stores near the east exit, and the Yodobashi and Doi stores near the west exit.

The Shinjuku district is north of the Shibuya district, and west of the Imperial Palace.

Japan is famous for its parks and landscape gardens, and there are several to be found in Tokyo. One of the best known is Shinjuku Gyoen, which can be reached in 15 minutes on foot from the east exit of Shinjuku Station, or more quickly from Shinjuku-Gyoenmae Station on the Marunouchi subway line. Shinjuku Gyoen has all the attractions of the typical Japanese garden: careful landscaping, artificial hills, ponds, stone lanterns, bridges, plenty of trees and plants, and paths that wind their way throughout. The two main themes of such a garden are serenity and care in arrangement, and after spending a couple of hours inside enjoying the scenery, it comes as quite a shock to step outside again into the crowded and chaotic streets of the capital. Walk through Shinjuku Gyoen as far as the Sendagaya exit, and nearby is the National Stadium, Meiji Shrine Outer Garden, and the Jingu Baseball Stadium.

Two more gardens are located in Bunkyo Ward, in the northern part of central Tokyo. Lying in the shadow of Korakuen, one of the main amusement grounds in Tokyo and also the home of the Yomiuri Giants baseball team, is Koishikawa Korakuen, which can be reached in about 6 minutes on foot from Iidabashi Station on the yellow Sobu line. Like many such gardens, this one was completed in the Edo Period (1603–1868), when Japan enjoyed domestic peace and the shogun demanded that regional lords set up homes in Edo (Tokyo) in order to guarantee their loyalty. Koishikawa Korakuen was planned by Tokugawa Yorifusa of Mito (in today's Ibaraki Prefecture). Mito is the site of one of Japan's three most outstanding landscape gardens, the others being in Okayama and Kanazawa. Such gardens are splendid creations, but more often than not they are full to the brim with groups of tourists following loudspeaker-wielding, flag-waving guides. In this respect, the gardens of Tokyo are what they are intended to be—places of quiet solitude. It is especially advantageous to go on a weekday, but remember that most parks, gardens, zoos, and museums in Tokyo are closed on Mondays.

Also located in Bunkyo Ward is Rikugien, reached in a few minutes on foot to the south from Komagome Station on the Yamanote loop line. Rikugien is a strolling garden set around a central lake; its notable feature is the picturesque view of the lake from whatever angle it is seen. Again, the garden was first landscaped in the 17th century, and like many other such gardens, it consists of artificial recreations of famous scenic spots elsewhere.

Ueno-Asakusa

Ueno Station, to the northeast of the Imperial Palace, is the third largest in Tokyo after Tokyo Station and Shinjuku Station. It is the starting point for railway lines leaving Tokyo for northern Japan, and also the gateway to Ueno Park with all its cultural and natural attractions. It is highly recommended that visitors drop in at the Shitamachi Museum located near Shinobazu Pond, where various exhibits related to the lives of the common people of the area are on display. These include a model of an old tenement house, kitchen and other household utensils, furniture, toys, games that neighborhood children used to play, and photographs.

Tokyo is not a city famous for its statues, but most Tokyoites are well acquainted with at least two, one being the statue of Hachiko the dog outside Shibuya Station and the other being the statue of Saigo Takamori (1827–77), a leading statesman during the period of the Meiji Restoration. The latter is standing in Ueno Park, near Keisei-Ueno Station and not far from Shinobazu Pond.

Ueno Park is located by Ueno Station on the Yamanote and Keihin-Tohoku lines, and includes within its borders Ueno Zoo, Shinobazu Pond, the National Museum of Western Art, the Tokyo National Museum, the National Science Museum, and several other attractions. It is not too much of an exaggeration to say that, while the Imperial Palace is the center of Tokyo, the city's heart is in Ueno. It would be wise to set aside a whole day to see all the attractions of Ueno Park. As well as those mentioned above, there are also Kiyomizu Kannon Temple, which looks over Shinobazu Pond, the five-story pagoda of Kaneiji Temple, which rises 36 meters and dates from 1639, and Ueno Toshogu Shrine, dedicated to the first shogun Tokugawa Ieyasu.

If you don't want to spend the whole day in Ueno Park, one good course for a day's outing would be to visit the park first, then take the special double-decker bus to Asakusa—a 10-minute ride—and after seeing Asakusa Kannon Temple at the end of Nakamise shopping street, take the boat trip down the Sumida River to Hamarikyu Garden, which, in the 17th century, served as the site of a detached palace of the shogun. It is an extensive park, and is a 10-minute walk southeast

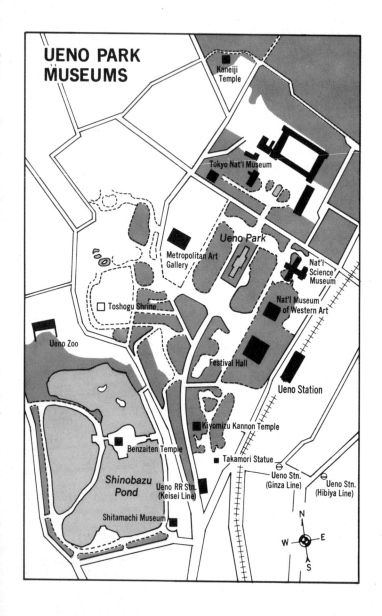

UENO PARK MUSEUMS

Kaneiji Temple

Tokyo Nat'l Museum

Ueno Park

Metropolitan Art Gallery

Nat'l Science Museum

Toshogu Shrine

Nat'l Museum of Western Art

Ueno Zoo

Festival Hall

Ueno Station

Kiyomizu Kannon Temple

Benzaiten Temple

Takamori Statue

Shinobazu Pond

Ueno RR Stn. (Keisei Line)

Ueno Stn. (Ginza Line)

Ueno Stn. (Hibiya Line)

Shitamachi Museum

N
W E
S

from Shimbashi Station on the Yamanote line. The boats leave from near the bridge just along the road from the Kaminarimon Gate.

As well as being a castle town, Tokyo is a city of many temples and shrines. Temples belong to the Buddhist religion, and shrines, which are characterized by their *torii* entrance gateways, are centers of the Shinto religion.

Asakusa Kannon is the oldest temple in Tokyo, located in a district that has retained much of the atmosphere of its past. Asakusa is a large shopping and entertainment area, consisting of dozens of cross-hatched alleys and covered passageways. Asakusa Station is at the southeastern corner of the district, on the Ginza and Toei-Asakusa subway lines. Take the exit for Kaminarimon Gate, the huge and magnificent entrance to the long and narrow Nakamise shopping street, which leads directly into the grounds of the temple. Nakamise Street is full of colorful souvenir shops offering everything from Japanese-style lanterns and talismans to the latest robot toys for children. By reputation, goods tend to be cheaper in Asakusa, and many Tokyoites come here to shop.

The temple, which is also known as Sensoji, is said to have been founded originally in the 7th century after three local fishermen discovered a small image of the goddess of mercy (Kannon) in their nets. The main buildings in the temple's precincts are the main hall, the front gateway, and a five-storied pagoda, all of which were rebuilt after being burned down during World War II. The temple grounds also seem to be a gathering place for pigeons. Located nearby is a small amusement park, called Hanayashiki Yuenchi.

The western end of Asakusa is dedicated to amusement: theaters, burlesque shows, bath houses, restaurants, tea and snack houses. If you walk along the Sumida River south toward Ryogoku, you will come to the New Kokugikan, the headquarters of sumo wrestling. Sumo tournaments are held there, and a sumo museum is open daily within the building. With any luck on your walk you might meet some sumo wrestlers on theirs. You'll never mistake a sumo wrestler when you see one. Huge, his hair worn in the traditional style, dressed in the traditional style, he makes a picture of old Japan all on his own.

In the industrial area of Koto Ward, to the southeast of Asakusa near the Sumida River, is Kiyosumi Garden. The history of this garden reflects the fate of many Edo-Period gardens and of the aristocracy as well. After the Meiji Restoration, Kiyosumi Garden fell into disuse as feudal lords came upon hard times and all energy was spent on modernizing the nation. Then in 1878 it was purchased by a wealthy industrialist, Baron Iwasaki, who at that time was president of the Mitsubishi Steamship Company. Iwasaki's residence on the site was destroyed in the great 1923 earthquake, after which the garden was donated to the capital, restored and opened to the public. The best way to get to the garden, which is closed on Mondays, is to take a short taxi ride from Monzennakacho Station on the Tozai subway line. Ask the driver for "Kiyosumi Teien."

Another oasis of peace and quiet in Tokyo can be found at the Mukojima Hyakkaen garden in Sumida Ward, located a short walk from Tamanoi Station on the Tobu line, which leaves from Asakusa.

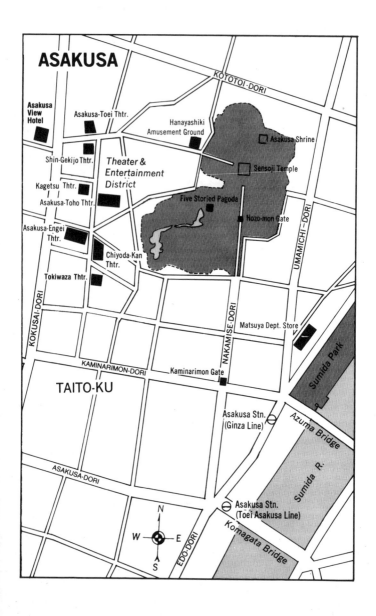

ASAKUSA

KOTOTOI-DORI

Asakusa View Hotel

Asakusa-Toei Thtr.

Hanayashiki Amusement Ground

Asakusa Shrine

Shin-Gekijo Thtr.

Theater & Entertainment District

Sensoji Temple

Kagetsu Thtr.

Asakusa-Toho Thtr.

Five Storied Pagoda

Hozo-mon Gate

UMAMICHI-DORI

Asakusa-Engei Thtr.

Chiyoda-Kan Thtr.

Tokiwaza Thtr.

KOKUSAI-DORI

NAKAMISE-DORI

Matsuya Dept. Store

Sumida Park

KAMINARIMON-DORI

Kaminarimon Gate

TAITO-KU

Asakusa Stn. (Ginza Line)

Azuma Bridge

Sumida R.

ASAKUSA-DORI

N

W E

S

EDO-DORI

Asakusa Stn. (Toei Asakusa Line)

Komagata Bridge

Make sure you get on the train that stops at every station. Mukojima Hyakkaen, which when translated becomes "Garden of a Hundred Flowers," was a meeting place for poets and writers in the Edo Period and one of its striking features is the many stone monuments standing among the trees and plants with verses written by famous haiku poets engraved on them. It is only a short distance from Mukojima Hyakkaen to the bank of the Sumida River.

One more garden to be noted is the Kyu-Furukawa Garden in Kita Ward. This is a Japanese-style garden, with a difference—it was designed by an Englishman, James Conder, who came to Japan at the beginning of the Meiji Period when Japan was just starting on the road to Westernization. Conder is said to have been responsible for educating the first generation of Japanese architects of the Western school. The residence building of the garden, completed in 1917, is Western-style, and the garden is a typical Japanese *teien*. Kyu-Furukawa Garden can be reached in 10 minutes from Kami-Nakasato Station on the pale blue Keihin-Tohoku line which passes through Tokyo and Ueno stations, or by taxi from Komagome if you want to visit it after seeing Rikugien.

Akihabara-Kanda

Between Ueno and Tokyo stations on the Yamanote line lie Akihabara and Kanda stations, the gateways to two very specialized districts. The Akihabara area is the place to go for discount prices on electric appliances, audio/video equipment, tape recorders, radios, and computers. This is said to be the biggest discount center in the country, and over 50,000 shoppers visit the 600 or so stores every day. As well as being on the Yamanote line, Akihabara Station is also on the Sobu line (for those arriving from the Shinjuku direction) and the Keihin-Tohoku line.

Kanda, together with neighboring Ochanomizu and Jimbocho, is a student town, and the streets are lined with secondhand bookshops, many of them dealing in English-language as well as Japanese books. Taken together with Akihabara, this area makes for a pleasant day's outing, with visits to Kanda Myojin Shrine, Nicolai Cathedral, and the Transportation Museum (5 minutes on foot to the west of Akihabara Station) added to stereo- and book-browsing. On the corner of the Jimbocho main crossing is Iwanami Hall, housing the British Council offices and library.

A recommended walking course in this area is one linking Ochanomizu with Ueno, taking in Nicolai Cathedral, Yushima Seido, Kanda Myojin Shrine, Yushima Tenjin Shrine, Shinobazu Pond, and Ueno Park, in that order. Nicolai Cathedral is a splendid structure, dating from 1891 and a 1-minute walk to the south from Ochanomizu Station. From there, return to the station, and follow the signposts to Yushima Seido, or the Yushima Shrine of Confucius, with its fine gateways and sidewalls built in the original Chinese Ming Dynasty-style.

Across the road is Kanda Myojin Shrine, originally founded in 730 and consisting of several interesting buildings. When leaving this shrine through its *torii* gateway, turn right, walk as far as the first crossing with a police box on the opposite corner, and turn right again. This road leads directly to Yushima Shrine, passing numerous glittering "love hotels" on the way.

Yushima Shrine, founded in the 14th century, is dedicated to scholarly advancement, and it's quite likely that during your visit you'll come across young high-school students offering a prayer there and writing their wishes on special wooden tablets in the hope of gaining a place at university. The shrine is also famous for its plum-blossom festival held every year from late February until mid-March. The shrine can be reached directly in 5 minutes on foot to the west of Yushima Station on the Chiyoda subway line.

To the left of Yushima Shrine's main hall, there are some steps leading down to a road. Turn right at the foot of these steps, and follow the road until you reach the second main crossing. Turn left there, and the road leads to Shinobazu Pond in Ueno Park.

Other Notable Temples

Both Sensoji Temple in Asakusa and Zojoji Temple in Minato Ward appear in the list of 100 most popular spots in Tokyo compiled by the Tokyo Metropolitan Government in 1983 on the basis of a public poll. The place that was voted the most scenic was Takahata Fudo Temple in Hino City, to the west of central Tokyo. It can easily be reached by taking the private Keio line from Shinjuku Station and alighting at Takahata Fudo Station—the temple is just a short walk away, its colorful pagoda showing the right direction. Express trains stop at the station, and the journey from Shinjuku takes about 30 minutes. The grounds house several buildings of cultural and historic importance, and there is also a small hiking course laid out on the hill behind the temple.

Jindaiji Temple is another place worth a short trip outside the center of Tokyo, and it, too, is reached by taking the Keio line from Shinjuku. This time get off at Chofu Station (express trains stop there) and take a bus bound for Jindaiji from in front of the station. The bus journey takes about 15 minutes. In contrast with the urban temples to be found in central Tokyo, Jindaiji has a refreshingly rustic appearance, and behind the temple, which was originally founded in 733, is located the Jindai Botanical Garden with its numerous trees and plants from around the world.

Attractions for Children

Unlike adults who find enjoyment in the unusual, children tend to have universal interests. While adults visiting Japan will probably want to explore temples, shrines, and gardens first, children will delight in a trip to a zoo. The most well-known zoo in Tokyo is Ueno Zoo, located in Ueno Park. A 3-minute train ride from Takahata Fudo (on the Keio line from Shinjuku) takes you to Tama Zoo, which is of the safari kind with humans riding around in buses and the lions wandering about in relative freedom. Nogeyama Zoo in Yokohama is reached in 10 minutes on foot from Hinodemachi Station, 4 minutes from Yokohama Station by the Keihin-Kyuko line. These zoos are open every day except Mondays.

Amusement grounds will probably be next on the child's itinerary, and there is certainly no lack of these in the Tokyo area. Korakuen amusement park is a short walk from Suidobashi Station on the Sobu line, two stops from Akihabara, which is famous for its many discount electric appliance stores. There is also the small Hanayashiki Park near Asakusa Kannon (Sensoji) Temple, suitable for the younger and less daring.

Toshimaen amusement park is in the northeastern part of central Tokyo and can be reached by the Seibu line running from Seibu-Ikebukuro Station to Toshimaen Station, which faces the park's entrance. A little farther away is Seibuen, reached via the Seibu line, which runs from Seibu-Shinjuku Station and passes through Takadanobaba on the Yamanote line on the way. Located near Seibuen is UNESCO Village, which children should also enjoy. On display in this large park are a number of folk houses from nations around the world.

Other amusement parks, with similar jet coaster thrills and chills as offered by the above places, are Mukogaoka Yuenchi in Kawasaki (from Mukogaoka Yuenchi Station on the private Odakyu line which leaves Shinjuku Station), Yomiuriland (from Yomiurilandmae Station on the Odakyu-Odawara line), and Tama Tech in Hino City, which is located a 5-minute bus ride from Tama Zoo.

Hanayashiki amusement park in Asakusa is closed on Fridays, Korakuen on Mondays, and Yomiuriland on Tuesdays. The other amusement parks are open every day of the week.

A recent addition to entertainment facilities for children visiting or living in Japan's capital city is Tokyo Disneyland, built on land reclaimed from the sea, in Urayasu, just over the city's eastern border in Chiba Prefecture. Tokyo Disneyland consists of five areas based on separate themes: World Bazaar, Adventureland, Westernland, Fantasyland, and Tomorrowland. It has become enormously popular, not only with children but with adults as well. Advance reservations are recommended for people going on weekends or national holidays. See the Practical Information section for details.

Some other places that children should enjoy are the Goto Planetarium on the 7th floor of the Tokyu Bunka Kaikan, across the road from Shibuya Station on the Yamanote line; the aquarium in the Sunshine 60 skyscraper in Ikebukuro; the National Children's Castle, 5–53–1 Jingumae, the most technologically advanced and creatively designed children's center in the world; the Waxworks Museum on the 3rd floor of Tokyo Tower; and Baji Koen, a horse-riding park in Setagaya Ward that regularly holds special meetings and riding sessions for children (a short taxi ride from Chitose-Funabashi Station on the Odakyu line). Local newspapers usually carry announcements of events scheduled at Baji Koen.

DAY TRIPS

Day trips outside the central Tokyo area can be made by using the suburban rail lines that run from several of the main stations on the Yamanote loop line. Some main lines and day-trip destinations are:

From Shinjuku

Odakyu line. The Odakyu line runs from Shinjuku to Odawara, special express Romance Cars covering the distance in just over one hour with no stops on the way. Odawara is the site of Odawara Castle, and also the base for excursions into the Hakone hills. The Hakone Tozan railway leaves from Odawara Station for spots such as the Hakone Outdoor Sculpture Museum and Mount Sounzan, while buses depart from outside the station for Lake Ashinoko, on the shores of which are the old Hakone Checkpoint Museum, Hakone Shrine, and nearby Hakone Picnic Garden.

Odakyu line express trains stop at Mukogaoka Yuen Station (20 minutes from Shinjuku), near which are located the Mukogaoka Yuenchi amusement park and the Nihon Minkaen park in which traditional rural dwellings from different parts of Japan have been reconstructed. This park is located a short taxi ride or a 20-minute walk from Mukogaoka Yuen Station. Two stops down the line from Mukogaoka Yuen is Yomiurilandmae Station, from where it is a 7-minute bus ride to the Yomiuriland amusement park, a huge recreation center that claims to have something for everybody.

Keio line. The Keio line runs west from Shinjuku to Keio-Hachioji, with branch lines on the way for Tama Dobutsuen Zoo and Takaosanguchi Station, which is located at the foot of the popular and easily conquered Mount Takao. Both the zoo and Mount Takao make excellent day trips, and the former can be visited together with nearby Takahata Fudo Temple, which, as mentioned earlier, was voted Japan's most popular scenic spot in a government poll.

The Keio line also passes through Tsutsujigaoka and Chofu stations, from which buses leave for Jindai Temple and Jindai Botanical Garden.

Seibu-Shinjuku line. The Seibu-Shinjuku line departs from Seibu-Shinjuku Station, which is situated a short walk north from the east exit of the main Shinjuku Station, near the Kabukicho entertainment district. If you're on the Yamanote line, you can also catch a Seibu-Shinjuku line train at Takadanobaba Station, one stop away from Seibu-Shinjuku. The line goes as far as Hon-Kawagoe in Saitama Prefecture, with branch lines on the way for Haijima and Seibuyuenchi stations, and also for Seibukyujomae Station if you're visiting the Seibu Lions Baseball Ground or the UNESCO Village of folk houses from around the world.

Day trips using the Seibu-Shinjuku line include the Seibuen Amusement Ground, a short walk from Seibuyuenchi Station. The amusement ground and UNESCO Village are connected by a special railway line, and the picturesque Lake Sayama and Lake Tama are located nearby. Kitain Temple, with its cluster of about 500 small Buddhist statues, can be reached from Hon-Kawagoe Station. The city of Kawagoe preserves many Edo-style buildings open to visitors on a well-planned walking tour.

From Ikebukuro

Seibu-Ikebukuro line. Seibu-Ikebukuro Station is located a short walk from the main Ikebukuro Station, and under the same roof. This line runs westward out to Seibu-Chichibu, where you can catch the local Chichibu Railway line to popular day-trip destinations such as Nagatoro Gorge. Special Red Arrow express trains reach Seibu-Chichibu in about 1 hour and 20 minutes from Ikebukuro.

Just before Seibu-Chichibu there is Ashigakubo Station, a 20-minute walk from Ashigakubo Orchard.

Nearer to central Tokyo, there is Shakujii Koen Station, a short walk from Shakujii Park, which offers boating facilities on its lake.

Tobu-Tojo line. The Tobu-Tojo line leaves Ikebukuro Station and runs out west toward the Chichibu hills and passes through Kawagoe. Stations to note on the way are Shinrin Koen (1 hour by express train from Ikebukuro) and Ogawamachi, two stops on. The former is the station for Shinrin Park, which includes cycling courses and play-grounds. Bicycles can be rented in front of Shinrin Koen Station. Ogawamachi is a small rural town that has been a home of paper making for many centuries. The craft of making Japanese paper is still carried on, and visitors are welcome to see it.

From Ueno

Keisei line. Several long-distance trains leave from Ueno, but in terms of local suburban lines, only the Keisei line need be noted here. This line runs from Keisei-Ueno Station to Narita, a trip that can be covered in a day from Tokyo if you just want to visit Narita's Shinshoji Temple and the park that adjoins it. Other stations to note on this line are Horikiri Shobuen, from where the Horikiri Iris Garden is a 15-minute walk south, and Takasato Station, where you can pick up a branch line to Sakura, the site of a new museum of Japanese history.

Note: Shinkansen (bullet train) now runs north from Ueno making day trips farther afield possible.

From Asakusa

Tobu-Nikko line. The Tobu-Nikko line from Asakusa reaches Nikko in about 1 hour and 40 minutes by special express, but the number of attractions in Nikko makes it worthwhile for at least a one night's stay. Other stops on the Tobu-Nikko line that are within a day trip's range from Tokyo include Tochigi (2 hours by express), Tobu Zoo (from Tobu Dobutsu Koen Station), and Nishiarai Daishi Temple, reached by a branch line from Nishiarai Station.

The Tobu-Isezaki line from Asakusa also passes through Tobu Dobutsu Koen Station on its way to Isezaki. En route there is Ashikagashi Station, in the town of Ashikaga. The town's attractions include Bannaji Temple, originally established in the 1190s and containing within its precincts several structures of cultural and historic interest; the site of the Ashikaga Gakko school said to have been founded in the 9th century; and Mount Gyodosan, which rises to 400 meters and provides a pleasant hiking course with another temple, Joinji, as the destination. If you want to do the hiking course, it's best to take a taxi from Ashikaga to Joinji Temple, and from there follow the trail, which leads back into the town.

From Tokyo Station

Note: Shinkansen (bullet train) speeds to Nagoya in two hours. Sights include the Tokugawa Castle and Museum, Atsuta Shrine, and the Osu Kannon.

Chuo line. The orange-colored Chuo line starts at Tokyo Station and runs out to the western suburbs of the capital, passing through Shinjuku on the way. Stations to note for day trips are Kichijoji which brings you within a short walk from Inokashira Park; Takao Station, from which it is possible to reach Mount Takao; and Tachikawa Station, where you can pick up the Ome line to places such as Lake Okutama, Mitake Station for Mount Mitake, and Musashi-Itsukaichi Station for Akikawa Keikoku gorge.

Yokosuka line. The Yokosuka line runs from Tokyo Station south to Kurihama at the mouth of Tokyo Bay, passing Yokohama, Ofuna, Kamakura, Zushi, and Yokosuka on the way. All of these places make for excellent one-day-trip destinations from Tokyo. In particular, Yokohama with its strong traces of Western influence as a port city (see the *Yokohama* chapter), and Kamakura, the ancient capital of Japan with its many temples and shrines and domineering Great Buddha statue, are musts. Kamakura can also be reached from Shinjuku by the Odakyu line, with Katase-Enoshima as the final stop. From Katase-Enoshima, take the local Enoden line to Kamakura.

From Shinagawa

Keihin-Kyuko line. The Keihin-Kyuko line runs south from Shinagawa Station down through the Miura Peninsula, ending up at Miura Kaigan Station. Branch lines go to Zushi and to Uraga on the eastern coast of the peninsula. It was at Uraga in 1846 that Commodore Biddle arrived with a letter from the president of the United States asking for the opening of Japan to foreign trade.

The Keihin-Kyuko line also passes through Kurihama, where you can take a ferry across Tokyo Bay to Hama-Kanaya in Chiba. Sea bathing can be enjoyed at several spots on the Miura Peninsula's east coast, within range of a day trip from Tokyo, and also at Zushi.

Keihin-Tohoku line. The Keihin-Tohoku line, which passes through Shinagawa, operates between Ofuna in Kanagawa Prefecture, famous for its statue of the goddess of mercy (Kannon) which can be seen from the train, and Omiya in Saitama Prefecture, which is well known for its village of bonsai plants and for Omiya Park, within which stands Hikawa Shrine. This line also passes through Yokohama, and therefore can be used to visit that port city. To reach the seafront, take the train to Kannai Station.

Hiking Day Trips

Tokyo is a city with many faces. At the same time that it is a modern business capital, it is also a castle town (albeit without a castle any-more), a port city, a town of temples and shrines, and a haven for garden- and park-lovers. Another aspect of Tokyo that is often forgotten is its mountainous district to the west. The city's tallest mountain is Mount Kumotori, which rises to 2,018 meters and stands on the western edge of the capital, with one foot in Tokyo, one in Saitama Prefecture, and another in Yamanashi Prefecture.

Mount Kumotori is out of the range of day-trippers from the Tokyo area, the ascent requiring a stopover in a mountain lodge on the way. There are two other mountains, however, which can certainly be con-quered in day trips. Mount Takao, at 600 meters, is very popular among Japanese people living in the capital. To reach it, take the Keio line from Shinjuku Station to its terminus at Takaosanguchi Station (express trains cover the distance in about 45 minutes). From Takao-sanguchi Station it's a short walk to a cable car station, and the cable car then whisks you up to the mountaintop in a couple of minutes. On the summit of Mount Takao there is Yakuoin Temple, and several short nature trail courses which are well laid out. However, the sign-posts are all in Japanese, so it's advisable not to wander too far off the beaten track unless you are with Japanese friends.

The second mountain that can be easily reached and scaled from Tokyo is Mount Mitake. Take the Chuo line from Tokyo or Shinjuku out west to Tachikawa, and there change to the local Ome line for Mitake Station. It takes about 45 minutes by express train from Tokyo to Tachikawa, and then about 1 hour from Tachikawa to Mitake. A bus leaves from in front of Mitake Station for the foot of the mountain (a 10-minute ride), and then a cable car carries people up to near the top of the 929-meter high mountain. Located a 20-minute walk from the cable car station is Mitake Shrine, the path going through a small mountaintop village of thatched-roof houses.

 TOKYO SIGHTSEEING CHECKLIST. The problem all visitors to Tokyo face is, where to begin? Each person will come up with his or her answer, depending on per-sonal interests, amount of time available, and so on. A recommended starting place, however, is an observation point in one of the city's main hotels or skyscraper buildings. The cluster near the west exit of Shinjuku Station offers your best bet to get a general view of Tokyo from above. Other-wise, try Tokyo Tower in Shiba Park, or the Sunshine 60 building in Ikebukuro, to the north of Shinjuku on the western side of central Tokyo. After enjoying this experience, you can tackle the many parks, gardens, temples, shrines, museums, and shopping areas in the city.

Parks. As many people start a sightseeing tour of Tokyo at the Imperial Palace, the first parks to be visited will be those near there: *Hibiya Park* on the south side and *Kitanomaru Park* on the north. The other parks not to be missed are *Yoyogi Park,* next to Meiji Shrine in the western part of Tokyo, and the immensely popular *Ueno Park* in the northeast. Ueno has it all: fountains, temples, a boating lake, greenery, wild birds, numerous museums—and plenty of tramps as well.

Gardens. Despite its reputation as a concrete jungle, Tokyo has many fine gardens worth seeing. Among them, don't miss *Shinjuku Gyoen* in Shinjuku, in the western part of the city, *Rikugien* in the north (reached from Komagome Station on the Yamanote loop line), and *Hamarikyu Garden* in the south (reached from Shimbashi Station, or taking the stylish route—by boat from Asakusa). These gardens offer tranquility and peace of mind while all else around goes on at a hectic pace.

Temples. To see some of Tokyo's religious architecture, head for the temples. The most famous ones are *Zojoji Temple* in Shiba, near Tokyo Tower, and *Asakusa Kannon Temple,* sometimes called Sensoji Temple, in Asakusa.

Shrines. The main shrines in Tokyo are *Meiji Shrine,* which lies in extensive grounds near Harajuku Station on the Yamanote line, in the western part of the city, and *Yasukuni Shrine,* which is opposite Kitanomaru Park, on the north side of the Imperial Palace.

Museums. There are numerous museums and galleries in Tokyo. Many of them have standing exhibitions (see Tokyo *Practical Information*). For others, refer to the local English-language newspapers, which carry up-to-date details.

Particularly recommended are the *Shitamachi Museum* by Shinobazu Pond in Ueno Park, which has an exhibition of items related to life in the past in downtown Tokyo; the *Mingeikan,* or Folkcraft Museum, in Meguro Ward, with a fine display on Japanese crafts; and the *Tokyo National Museum* in Ueno Park.

Shopping. Department stores such as *Seibu, Mitsukoshi, Takashimaya, Oda-kyu, Isetan,* and so on can be found in the Ginza, Shibuya, Shinjuku, and Ikebukuro districts. *Harajuku* and *Aoyama* are popular shopping districts among the young. But don't rule out the side streets of *Shinjuku, Shibuya, Shimbashi,* and *Asakusa* when hunting for souvenirs—you'll find many small shops and stores where bargains can be found. For electrical appliance goods, the place to go is *Akihabara,* in the eastern part of the city between Ueno and Tokyo stations. For books, try *Maruzen* in Nihonbashi, *Jena* in Ginza, and *Kinokuniya* in Shinjuku, a 5-minute walk from the east exit of Shinjuku Station.

Nightlife. The center of night life in Tokyo is *Ginza,* but this is a very expensive district. Most foreigners frequent the *Roppongi* and *Akasaka* districts, which can be reached from subway stations of the same names in central Tokyo. *Shibuya* and *Shinjuku* are also beehives of entertainment, and although they do not cater to the foreign visitor as directly as Roppongi and Akasaka do, there are still many places that welcome foreigners.

Day trips. Many foreigners tour the sightseeing spots of central Tokyo and then take the next train out to such famous places as Nikko or Kyoto, without realizing that many enchanting spots lie within the range of a day trip from the capital. The most popular of these is *Kamakura* to the southwest, with its giant Great Buddha statue and many temples and shrines. If you have time, pay a visit to the nearby *Enoshima Island* as well.

Another recommended day trip involves a circular tour of *Tokyo Bay.* Take the Keihin-Kyuko line from Shinagawa to Kurihama, then a ferry across the bay to Hama-Kanaya port on the Boso Peninsula, and after visiting the Great Buddha statue on nearby Mount Nokogiri (larger than the Kamakura Buddha but not so old), return to Tokyo by train.

Nearer to Tokyo is *Yokohama*, the international port city to the south, which can be reached in about 30 minutes by the Keihin-Tohoku line from Tokyo Station. Do not get off at Yokohama Station, but at Kannai, from where it is a short walk to Chinatown, Yamashita Park, the harbor, the Yokohama Archives museum, and the Foreigners' Cemetery.

Another popular day trip south takes you to *Odawara* to see the city's castle. Odawara is on the Odakyu line, which leaves from Shinjuku Station, and is the entranceway to the Hakone mountains. A day trip to *Hakone* should include visits to Lake Ashinoko, Hakone Shrine, and Owakudani, the boiling valley.

Children of all ages enjoy *Tokyo Disneyland*, which, despite its name, is located in Chiba Prefecture, not Tokyo. The park can be reached by bus from Urayasu Station on the Tozai subway line or directly by shuttle bus from Tokyo Station.

PRACTICAL INFORMATION FOR TOKYO

WHEN TO GO. Tokyo keeps buzzing year-round, and there will be no season during which you'll find yourself with too much free time on your hands. This is not to say, however, that there are not good and bad times of the year to visit. If you are able to plan your journey, remember Tokyo summers are either rainy or hot and steamy, definitely the months to head north and enjoy Japan's cooler northern districts. The best seasons to visit Tokyo are autumn and spring, although New Year's is also a pleasant time.

HOW TO GET THERE. By air. Tokyo has its main international airport at Narita and its domestic airport at Haneda. *Japan Air Lines* operates air service coordinated with international flights arriving at Narita to Osaka, Fukuoka and Sapporo. Taipei's *China Airlines* is the only international carrier operating air service to and from Haneda, although it is used by planes carrying state guests.

By bus. It is unlikely that international travelers will arrive in Tokyo by bus. It is possible, though, from Osaka, Kyoto, and Nagoya, on a *Japanese Railways Highway Bus*, which arrives at Tokyo Central Station, Yaesuguchi side. The journey from Osaka takes more than 9 hours, from Kyoto less than 9, and 6 hours or so from Nagoya.

By train. *Shinkansen* superexpress bullet trains of the Tokaido line pull in at Tokyo Station from Fukuoka, Osaka, Nagoya, and stations in between. Tokyo Station is in central Tokyo, in the Marunouchi district. Those of the Tohoku line arrive at Ueno, near Tokyo Station, from Morioka, and those of the Joetsu line also come to Ueno, from Niigata.

To reach Tokyo from Osaka or Kobe, the best way is by a *Shinkansen* bullet train. You have a choice of many. From Shin Osaka Station, the *Hikari* type takes 3 hours 10 minutes and costs ¥13,300; the *Kodama* type takes about one hour longer. You could fly from Osaka in about 55 minutes, but if you aren't careful you might land at Narita. You would have to specify Haneda. From there you get to Hamamatsu-cho Station in 15 minutes on the *monorail* for ¥290, and complete your journey either by local train or taxi.

From Yokohama Station, local JR trains take only 30 minutes to reach Tokyo Station.

Be assured that all this sounds more complicated than it will prove to be in fact. All you need to do is survive your arrival and your first day. After that, things will fall into place with surprising ease.

 TELEPHONES. The Tokyo area code is 03, for calls made from outside the city. Within Tokyo, a call anywhere costs ¥10 for three minutes. Insert the coin after picking up the receiver and hearing the dial tone, then dial the number. To keep going, insert another ¥10 coin before the time is up. There are also ¥100 phones.

 HOTELS AND INNS. As new hotels rise one after the other, and old hotels add imposing new towers, there is Tokyo talk of "hotel wars." Steady, annual occupancy rates of 85 to 90 percent continue to encourage fresh, innovative construction, as well as constant refurbishing of older buildings. Each new structure sets out to achieve a new high in style and splendor. The stage has been reached where Tokyo's best hotels are, simply, magnificent. It's difficult to imagine what they could think of next to improve in appearance, facilities, or service.

Tokyo's Western-style hotels are very popular places with local people. They supplement the home. Friends are much more likely to meet each other in a hotel coffee shop or cocktail lounge than to entertain each other at home. Dinner parties and business banquets and wedding receptions are popularly held in the hotels. Even Tokyo department stores are likely to hold bargain sales in hotel public rooms. Since Tokyo qualifies as a safe city, Tokyo hotels do not need to be made into exclusive places. Instead they are important community centers.

Western-style hotels usually have some Japanese-style accommodation as well, commanding prices at the dizzying top end of the scale. Completely Japanese-style inns of exquisite quality are rare in Tokyo. There are many lower-priced establishments that are clean, simple, and convenient, and run along the old lines.

Tokyo, which has never been a planned city in the Western sense, has its many splendid hotels in several different areas. In some cases, a new, grand hotel has done a lot toward brightening up an old, unremarkable neighborhood. In other cases, a more modest establishment has been able to hold its ground in a more affluent and noteworthy district. Not so very long ago, Tokyo's best hotels were thought to be in the Ginza-Marunouchi area. Then new buildings began to pull the hotel district along to Akasaka-Mitsuke and Yotsuya. More recently, Shinjuku has been developing as the region for a concentration of new hotels. In a city with Tokyo's idiosyncrasies, location is less important than price when deciding where to stay. Wherever you are, you're likely to find that wherever you want to go is a long way off across town. Tokyo's facilities are dotted all over this huge city. Fortunately local transport is excellent and you can move about readily.

In our *super deluxe* category for **Western-style** hotels is a small coterie of hotels that have everything, and are still getting more. Special features include sauna, gymnasia, swimming pools, panoramic views of the city and distant mountains, and separate, speedy recognition of executive needs. There also will be English-speaking staff. Guest rooms have refrigerators. Hotels in this class have several different kinds of restaurants, as well as 24-hour room service. Their arcade shops are as elegant as any in town. A couple staying in a super deluxe hotel will pay between ¥25,000 and ¥55,000 for a double room. Tax and service charges will be additional.

Our *deluxe* hotels are more numerous, and are only marginally less outstanding than the supers. But, with some overlapping, the room charge is less. Expect to pay between ¥20,000 and ¥40,000 for a twin or double room.

As we go down the scale, the same things have to be said: accommodation and service normally are excellent throughout Tokyo's hotels. The scaling down occurs in the opulence of the surroundings and the exceptional nature of some of the facilities. A couple could expect to pay between ¥14,000 and ¥30,000 for our next category, the *expensive*.

Hotels falling within our *moderate* group have nothing the matter with them. They are just not grand. They are clean, friendly places without the embroidery. A couple would pay between ¥10,000 and ¥20,000.

Business Hotels have their own listings. They are Western-style, efficient, and low cost, without being fancy. You carry your own bags, amenities available from dispensers, and reasonable meals are provided in coffee-shop–type restaurants. Most business hotels are conveniently located near railway stations.

Hostels include the youth hostels and dormitory accommodations that round out a city's offerings. For a bed in a dormitory, you can pay as little as ¥1,500. The YMCAs and YWCAs cost more: ¥4,000 should do it.

Tokyo's **Japanese-style** accommodation decreases, except in the inexpensive category. In the *expensive* group, overnight charge per person with two meals would fall within the brackets of ¥12,000 to ¥25,000. Everything would be exquisite in small ways. You would be lucky to find any English spoken.

An inn in the *moderate* group would charge, on the same basis, about ¥8,000 to ¥12,000. An *inexpensive* inn charges anything less than this, and is informal and easygoing.

WESTERN-STYLE

Super Deluxe

Akasaka Prince. 1–2 Kioi-cho, Chiyoda-ku, 102; 234–1111. Designed by Kenzo Tange and rising 40 stories, the Akasaka Prince is proud that every one of its 761 rooms in its new Tower commands a wide, spectacular view of all Tokyo. The Tower has 12 international restaurants, as well as a cocktail lounge, a coffeehouse, a lobby, and parlor. A wide range of services are helpful to business guests, and shopping and entertainment are only minutes away.

ANA Hotel Tokyo. 12–33, Akasaka 1–chome, Minato-ku, Tokyo 107; 505–1111. Open since June 1986. 900 rooms: singles, doubles, Japanese- and Western-style suites. Shopping arcade, banquet facilities, garden pool, beauty salon. Eight restaurants offer American, Mediterranean, Chinese, Continental, and, of course, Japanese cuisine.

Hilton International. 6–6–2 Nishi-Shinjuku, Shinjuku-ku, 160; 344–5111. Opened in 1984, the Hilton has shown its confidence in the west of the city by locating itself in Shinjuku. Its special features include a panoramic view of Mount Fuji, a sauna, gymnasium, indoor swimming pool and tennis court. There seems to be no end to what the Hilton offers, from ordinary guest rooms to meeting facilities and equipment; from massage in the room to interpretation in six languages. Overall, the Hilton touch in service personnel is outstanding.

The Imperial. 1–1–1 Uchisaiwaicho, Chiyoda-ku, 100; 504–1111. Near the Imperial Palace Grounds and the Ginza. This Preferred Hotels Association member is the grande dame of hostelry in Japan. As a guest house for foreign visitors, it opened its doors in 1890 and has flown its flag ever since. Now that it has added the 31-story Imperial Tower, the hotel has a total of 1,135 rooms, with twins, doubles, semisuites, double suites, and full deluxe residential suites. Tower rooms have floor-to-ceiling bay windows. In the shopping arcade are 64 high-quality stores. Its handsome 19th-floor pool is open year-round exclusively for hotel guests. Deserving of every accolade, the Imperial regards itself as developing beyond a "city" to a "metropolis."

New Otani and Tower. 4–1 Kioi-cho, Chiyoda-ku, 102; 265–1111. With 2,051 rooms, this is the largest hotel in Asia and the fourth largest in the world. The traditional Japanese garden of 10 acres dates back to the 17th century. The New Otani Golden Spa is a health, sports and beauty culture complex. 32 restaurants including the first Trader Vic in the Orient. Crystal Room is a sophisticated restaurant-theater. Special features: *Blue Sky Lounge* atop the hotel, taking one hour for a complete revolution; rooms for businessmen's daytime use; rooms for the physically handicapped; a Tiny Tots' Room, the only one of its kind in Japan providing 24-hour baby-sitting care; a Christian chapel providing "the world's first 24-hour spiritual guidance service in a hotel"; its own orchestra, *The Joyful;* and an automatic money distributor permitting withdrawals of ¥110,000 at a time. 30 rooms on the 21st floor are for ladies only.

The Okura. 2–10–4 Toranomon, Minato-ku, 105; 582–0111. This hotel is known for its supreme, Japanese kind of elegance. It has a traditional garden and two swimming pools, one for the summertime only, and the second for all year. In the ground is the Okura Art Museum, an old Tokyo fixture. Its 980 rooms, many high-class restaurants and banquet rooms occupy the Main Building and South Wing. Membership of the Okura Club International ensures VIP courtesies; while the Executive Service Salon provides the ultimate for business-people.

Deluxe

Capitol Tokyu. 2–10–3 Nagata-cho, Chiyoda-ku, 100; 581–4511. This used to be the Tokyo Hilton and is now the flagship of the Tokyu Hotel Chain. Nearly 500 rooms. Distinguished by its Japanese elegance.

Century Hyatt. 2–7–2 Nishi Shinjuku, Shinjuku-ku, 160; 349–0111. 28 stories opposite the Shinjuku Central Park. 800 rooms and suites, a heated swimming pool, and an eight-floor lobby.

Keio Plaza. 2–2–1 Nishi Shinjuku, Shinjuku-ku, 160; 344–0111. The tallest in Japan, with 47 stories, 1,500 rooms now that the deluxe annex is open, 20 restaurants, 9 bars and lounges, 800-car garage, 25 elevators, 7th floor swimming pool, 2 wedding halls, all in the middle of Shinjuku. Complimentary Continental breakfast for guests staying in the best rooms.

Miyako Hotel Tokyo. 1–1–50 Shiroganedai, Minato-ku, 108; 447–3111. This Miyako has 5½ acres of beautifully landscaped Japanese garden. There are 500 rooms, a pool, sauna, health club, along with several restaurants and usual facilities. Its location, in a semi-residential area, offers an introduction to local life. It is owned by the famous Miyako of Kyoto.

New Takanawa Prince. 3–13–1 Takanawa, Minato-ku, 108; 442–1111. Near Shinagawa Station. This is a 16-story, white building with more than 1,000 rooms and the nation's biggest banquet hall. Beautiful garden.

Pacific Hotel. 3–13–3 Takanawa, Minato-ku, 108; 445–6711. Near Shinagawa Station. This hotel has 30 stories of 954 well-equipped rooms, restaurants, bars, banquet halls, a swimming pool, and shopping arcade. Its garden is large and beautiful in the Japanese way.

Palace. 1–1–1 Marunouchi, Chiyoda-ku, 100; 211–5211. Just on the edge of the Emperor's palace grounds. Beautiful views of the palace, Tokyo's distinctive skyline, and the Imperial Plaza, the latter especially in the evening. Excellent location for the time-conscious businessman. Arcades and shops, airline offices and all other conveniences. In spite of its central location the surrounding plaza and boulevard keep this hotel in an airy spot. 407 rooms.

Tokyo Prince. 3–3–1 Shiba Koen, Minato-ku, 105; 432–1111. Overlooks Shiba Park and famed Zojoji Temple, a 15-minute walk from Hamamatsucho Station. 510 rooms, well equipped, seven restaurants, four cocktail lounges, and unusually pleasant garden restaurants.

Expensive

Akasaka Tokyu. 2–14–3 Nagata-cho, Chiyoda-ku, 100; 580–2311. 566 small but modern guest rooms. Excellent service.

Ginza Tokyu. 5–15–9 Ginza, Chuo-ku, 104; 541–2411. In the busy heart of Tokyo. 420 rooms; 8 Japanese-style, 4 small apartments. Rooms soundproofed have radio and TV. Several grills, bars, restaurants. Excellent Chinese restaurant. Bus to Narita for Cathay Pacific Airways passengers.

Grand Palace. 1–1–1 Iidabashi, Chiyoda-ku, 102; 264–1111. "An economy-class hotel for businessmen," in the first-class superior bracket. 23 stories, 500 rooms (incl. 131 singles).

Holiday Inn. 1–13–7 Hatchobori, Chuo-ku, 104; 553–6161. 130 rooms, roof-top swimming pool, near Hatchobori.

Kayu Kaikan. 8–1 Sanban-cho, Chiyoda-ku, 102; 230–1111. Near the Imperial Palace. Under Hotel Okura management. 128 guest rooms. Special monthly rates.

Marunouchi. 1–6–3 Marunouchi, Chiyoda-ku, 100; 215–2151. Close to Tokyo Station. Quiet and pleasant, with the atmosphere of a U.S. commercial hotel. Dinner music every night. 210 rooms.

President, Aoyama. 2–2–3 Minami Aoyama, Minato-ku. 107; 497–0111. 212 rooms, a convenient location away from the heart of Tokyo.

Takanawa. 2–1–17 Takanawa, Minato-ku, 108; 443–9251. A pleasant smaller hotel, near Shinagawa Station. 217 rooms on the small side. Swimming pool. A regular bus service connects this hotel with Narita Airport, and another with Shinjuku Station.

Takanawa Prince. 3–12–1 Takanawa, Minato-ku, 108; 447–1111. A British Airways Associate Hotel. Ultramodern facilities are mixed with extensive and charming Japanese landscaping. 2 swimming pools. Arcade shops. 500 Western-style rooms, all with bath. Beautiful garden.

Other Prince Hotels, all recommended, are: **Shinjuku Prince,** 1–30–1 Kabuki-cho, Shinjuku-ku, 160; 205–1111. **Shinagawa Prince,** 4–10–30 Takanawa, Minato-ku, 108; 440–1111. **Sunshine City Prince,** 3–1–5 Higashi Ikebukuro, Toshima-ku, 170; 988–1111. This one has 1,000 rooms in Japan's tallest building.

Tokyo Grand. 2–5–3 Shiba, Minato-ku, 105; 454–0311. In the 15-story Sodo Building, business nerve center for the Sodo Sect of Buddhism. Japanese, Italian and French restaurants, plus Sodo Buddhist vegetarian dinners. Zazen sessions twice a month.

Yaesu Fujiya. 2–9–1 Yaesu 104, Chuo-ku; 273–2111. A 17-story urban resort-type hotel, near the Yaesu exit of Tokyo Station. 377 rooms, deluxe facilities, and warm hospitality.

Moderate

Atagoyama Tokyu Inn. 1–6–6 Atago, Minato-ku, 105; 431–0109. Very conveniently near Kamiyacho on the Hibiya subway line.

City Pension Zem. 2–16–9 Nihonbashi, Kakigaracho, Chuo-ku, 103; 661–0681. A modern, small hotel, family owned and managed. Walking distance to TCAT. A place to make friends.

Dai-ichi. 1–2–6 Shimbashi, Minato-ku, 105; 501–4411. Fairly comfortable, all conveniences. Close to Shimbashi bar, tavern and nightclub section, but claims its own popular restaurants.

Diamond. 25 Ichiban-cho, Chiyoda-ku, 102; 263–2211. Behind the British Embassy. A new annex opened recently. Many Japanese entertain here.

Fairmont. 2–1–17 Kudan-Minami, Chiyoda-ku, 102; 262–1151. Also close to the Palace and British Embassy. Quiet, pleasant air of comfortable restraint. 214 rooms. One of the best places for cherry blossom viewing.

Gajoen Kanko. 1–8–1 Shimo Meguro, Meguro-ku, 153; 491–0111. Near Meguro Station. An old-timer still leading a gaudy life.

Ginza Dai-ichi. 8–13–1 Ginza, Chuo-ku, 104; 542–5311. Sister of the Shimbashi Dai-ichi, this has 817 rooms in a 15-story, H-shaped building near Shimbashi Station.

Ginza International. 8–7–13 Ginza, Chuo-ku, 104; 574–1121. 94 rooms at Shimbashi, adjoining the Ginza. Individual temperature controls in rooms.

Hill-Top. 1–1 Kanda, Surugadai, Chiyoda-ku, 101; 293–2311. 87 rooms in the student district of Kanda. Popular.

Hotel Den Harumi. 3–8–1 Harumi, Chuo-ku, 104; 533–7111. Seven minutes by taxi from the Ginza district, convenient for the Trade Fair complex at Harumi. Swimming pool as well as more expected facilities.

Hotel Toshi Center. 2–4–1 Hirakawa-cho, Chiyoda-ku, 102; 265–8211. Near the Diet and Akasaka. Very popular.

Hotel Universe. 2–13–5 Nihonbashi, Kayabacho, Chuo-ku, 103; 668–7711. Has the big advantage of being near TCAT.

Ibis. 7–14–4 Roppongi, Minato-ku, 106; 403–4411. 200 rooms on the upper floors of the Ibis Kyodo Bldg., in a fun district.

Kokusai Kanko. 1–8–3 Marunouchi, Chiyoda-ku, 100; 215–3281. Next to Tokyo Station, Yaesuguchi side. Occupies eight floors of one side of an office building. Pleasant.

Miyako Inn. 3–7–8 Mita, Minato-ku, 108; 454–3111. 400 rooms at Tamachi. Brightens a bleak neighborhood.

Shiba Park. 1–5–10 Shiba Koen, Minato-ku, 105; 433–4141. Old favorite with a new annex now has 370 rooms and appropriate facilities.

Shiba Yayoi Convention Hall. 1–10–27 Kaigan, Minato-ku; 434–6841. 156 guest rooms on floors 3–10. Tokyo Bay waterfront.

Takanawa Tobu. 4–7–6 Takanawa, Minato-ku, 108; 447–0111. In Shinagawa. 201 rooms. Interesting neighborhood.

Takara. 2–16–5 Higashi Ueno, Taito-ku, 110; 831–0101. Near Ueno Park and the museums. 100 rooms.

Tokyo Kanko. 4–10–8 Takanawa, Minato-ku, 108; 443–1211. Near Shinagawa station. 102 Western rooms, 56 Japanese.

BUSINESS HOTELS

Akasaka/Roppongi

Akasaka Shanpia Hotel. 586–0811. Nearest station: Akasaka on Chiyoda subway line.

Asia Center of Japan. 402–6111. Nearest station: Nogizaka on Chiyoda subway line. Student oriented.

Ginza/Shimbashi

Ginza Capital Hotel. 543–8211. Nearest station: Tsukiji on Hibiya subway line.

Hotel Ginza Daiei. 541–2681. Nearest station: Tokyo on Yamanote, Keihin Tohoku and Chuo lines.

Mitsui Urban Hotel Ginza. 572–4131. Nearest station: Shimbashi on Yamanote and Keihin Tohoku lines or Ginza subway line.

Tokyo City Hotel. 270–7671. Nearest station: Mitsukoshimae on Ginza subway line.

Tokyo Hotel Urashima. 533–3111. Short taxi ride from Ginza subway station.

Kayabacho Pearl Hotel. 553–2211. Nearest station: Kayabacho on Hibiya and Tozai subway lines.

Shinagawa

Hotel Hankyu. 775–6121. Nearest station: Oimachi on Keihin Tohoku line.

Keihin Hotel. 449–5711. Nearest station: Shinagawa on Yamanote and Keihin Tohoku lines.

Shibuya Area

Hotel Sunroute Shibuya. 464–6411. Nearest station: Shibuya on Yamanote line.

Shibuya Tobu Hotel. 476–0111. Nearest station: Shibuya on Yamanote line.

Shibuya Tokyu Inn. 498–0109. Nearest station: Shibuya on Yamanote line.

Shinjuku

Hotel Sun Route. 356–0391. Nearest station: Shinjuku Sanchome on Marunouchi subway line.

Lions Hotel Shinjuku. 208–5111. Nearest station: Shinjuku on Seibu Shinjuku line.

Shinjuku Park Hotel. 356–0241. Nearest station: Shinjuku on Yamanote, Chuo and Sobu lines.

Shinjuku Sun Park Hotel. 362–7101. Nearest station: Okubo on Sobu line or Shin Okubo on Yamanote line.

Shinjuku Washington Hotel. 343–3111. Nearest station: Shinjuku on Chuo and Sobu lines.

Kanda Area

Akihabara Washington Hotel. 255–3311. Nearest station: Akihabara on Hibiya subway line or Yamanote and Keihin Tohoku lines.

Central Hotel. 256–6251. Nearest station: Kanda on Ginza subway line.

Hotel Juraku. 251–7222. Two-minute walk from Ochanomizu Station or five-minute walk from Akihabara.

New Central Hotel. 256–2171. Nearest station: Kanda on Ginza subway line.

Satellite Hotel. 814–0202. Korakuen, neighboring the stadium.

Suidobashi Grand Hotel. 816–2101. Nearest station: Suidobashi on Toei Mita subway line.

Tokyo Green Hotel Awajicho. 255–4161. Nearest station: Awajicho on Marunouchi subway line.

Tokyo Green Hotel Suidobashi. 295–4161. Nearest station: Suidobashi on Chuo and Sobu lines.

Ueno Area

Hokke Club Ueno. 834–4131. Nearest station: Ueno on Yamanote and Keihin Tohoku lines.

Hokke Club Ueno Ikenohata. 822–3111. Nearest station: Yushima on Chiyoda subway line.

Ueno Station Hotel. 833–5111. Nearest station: Ueno on Yamanote and Keihin Tohoku lines.

Hotel Ohgaiso. 822–4611. 3-3-21 Ikenohata, Taito-ku. Nearest station Keisei Ueno Station, Ikenohata exit. Author Ogai Mori (1862–1922) lived here.

JAPANESE INNS

Expensive

Fukudaya. 6–12 Kioi-cho, Chiyoda-ku; 261–8577. Central, just behind Sophia University. 14 rooms, 3 party rooms. Strictly for relaxing. Some Western cooking, but food is primarily Japanese. Price range: ¥17,000 to ¥39,000.

Moderate

Seifuso. 1–12–15 Fujimi, Chiyoda-ku; 263–0681. ¥6,000 lowest rate for one person, excluding meals. A small, family-run, modernized inn with a separate dining room. No room service.

Yaesu Ryumeikan. 1–3–22 Yaesu, Chuo-ku; 271–0971. Small, central, attractive. About ¥12,000 with two meals.

Inexpensive

Chomeikan. 4–4–8 Hongo, Bunkyo-ku; 811–7205. ¥6,500 with two meals.

Fujikan. 4–36–1 Hongo, Bunkyo-ku; 813–4441. Just to stay, ¥3,000. Food and bath extra.

Hongokan. 1–28–10 Hongo, Bunkyo-ku; 811–6236. Basically, ¥4,800 with two meals.

Inabaso. 5–6–13 Shinjuku, Shinjuku-ku; 341–9581. ¥7,000 per person with meals and bath.

Kikaku. 1–11–12 Sendagaya, Shinbuya-ku; 403–4501. ¥12,000 with two meals.

Kimi. 2–1034 Ikebukuro, Toshima-ku, 171; 971–3766. Has a Western-style hotel next door, both run by two young and eager traveled brothers. You're lucky to stay here.

Koshinkan. 2–1–5 Mukogaoka, Bunkyo-ku; 812–5291. ¥4,000 per person, just to stay.

Nagaragawa. 4–14 Yotsuya, Shinjuku-ku; 351–5892. ¥8,000 for two persons, without meals but with bath.

Okayasu. 1–7–11 Shibaura, Minato-ku; 452–5091. ¥3,800 per person, overnight only.

Ryokan Fuji. 6–8–3 Higashi-Koiwa, Edogawa-ku; 657–1062. Only seven rooms; five minutes walk from Koiwa Station.

Sansui-So. 2–9–5 Higashi-Gotanda, Shinagawa-ku; 441–7475. Small (only nine rooms); five minutes walk from Gotanda Station.

Sawanoya. 2–3–11 Yanaka, Taito-ku, 110; 822–2251. Near Ueno Park, in a district redolent of old Edo.

Shimizu Bekkan. 1–30–29 Hongo, Bunkyo-ku; 812–6285. ¥10,000 is the basic charge.

Suigetsu. 3–3–21 Ikenohata, Taito-ku; 822–4611. Single, ¥6,000. Public bath, family bath, showers, coin laundry. Bicycles for rent, cycling and jogging courses nearby.

Yashima. 1–15–5 Hyakunincho, Shinjuku-ku; 364–2534. Every recommendation.

Just for your interest, we're letting you know that Tokyo has "capsule" hotels that are becoming popular for anyone missing the last train home. A capsule is plastic, equipped with a TV set, an intercom, and a radio. Capsules are stacked two or three high in horizontal rows. Patrons crawl in at night and draw a curtain behind them. There's a communal bath or shower, a lounge, and refreshment area as well. For ¥3,000, no one expects much privacy or quiet.

HOSTELS AND DORMITORY ACCOMMODATION

English House. 2–23–8 Nishi Ikebukuro, Toshima-ku; 988–1743. Long-stay arrangements ¥3,000 for two, ¥1,900 for one.

Japan YWCA Hostel. 4–8–8 Kudan Minami, Chiyoda-ku; 264–0661. For women only.

Okubo House. 1–11–32 Hyakunin-cho, Shinjuku-ku; 361–2348. Dormitory beds, men ¥1,400, women ¥2,800.

Shin Nakano Lodge. 6–1–1 Honcho, Nakano-ku; 381–4886. Dormitory accommodation, from ¥4,500.

Tokyo International Youth Hostel. 21–1 Kaguragashi, Shinjuku-ku; 235–1107. Bunk beds. ¥3,000.

Tokyo YWCA Hostel. 1–8 Kanda Surugadai, Chiyoda-ku; 293–5421. For women only.

Tokyo Yoyogi Youth Hostel. Bldg. No. 14, Olympics Memorial Youth Center, 3–1 Yoyogi-Kamizono-cho, Shibuya-ku, Tokyo; 467–9163. ¥1,700, includes sheet. Meals provided, if booked. Members' kitchen.

Tokyo YWCA Sadohara Hostel. 3–1–1 Ichigaya Sadohara-cho, Shinjuku-ku; 268–7313. Has quarters for married couples.

Yoshida House. 1–36 Nishiki, Nerima-ku; 931–6709. ¥1,300 per person.

YMCA Asia Youth Center. 2–5–5 Sarugaku-cho, Chiyoda-ku; 233–0681.

 HOW TO GET AROUND. It may be a shock to airline passengers arriving at the new Tokyo International Airport at Narita to find that they still have 64 kilometers to go to reach central Tokyo. Brace yourself for at least another hour of travel before you get to town. This may prove to be the most trying part of your trip.

FROM THE AIRPORT

By bus. When you have passed Customs inspection and reached the arrival lobby, please look carefully at all the announcements and signs in English. Some 30 major Tokyo hotels are served by direct express buses. If you are booked into one of the listed hotels, you can take this bus for a fare of ¥2,700. The journey will take anywhere between 1 and 2 hours, depending upon the time of day and the volume of traffic.

Your next alternative is to take the airport bus to the City Air Terminal (known as TEE-Cat, TCAT) at Hakozaki-cho. You buy your ticket at the *Limousine Bus* ticket counter in the arrival lobby. This bus fare is ¥2,500, and the time allowance to TCAT is up to 1½ hours. Your baggage is carried in a hold on the bus, and delivered to you at TCAT, in exchange for the claim tag given you. They have a taxi stand here, or you can go to the nearest subway station, Ningyo-cho, on the Hibiya line, an 8-minute walk. You can also take an airport bus to Tokyo Station. Children under 12 and the physically handicapped are carried for half price on the Limousine Bus.

By train. Rail travel aboard the *Skyliner* has much to commend it. The Skyliner offers reserved seats only, baggage space, and temperature control. It leaves Keisei Narita Airport Station at half-hourly intervals between 7:52 A.M. and 10:00 P.M., and reaches Ueno Station in exactly 1 hour. You can buy a combination bus/Skyliner ticket for ¥1,680 at the Skyliner ticket counter between the North and South wings of the airport. (Keisei Narita Airport Station is a 6-minute bus ride from the airport.) The Skyliner ticket counter closes at 9:00 P.M. Late arrivals can buy bus tickets for ¥190 each, and Skyliner tickets for ¥1,490 at the Airport Station, for the 10:00 P.M. train.

The Skyliner stops at Nippori Station for passengers transferring to the Japan Railroad trains and then proceeds to Keisei Ueno Station. A taxi from here to your hotel may take a half hour, depending on traffic.

The fares for slower trains from Keisei Narita Airport Station to Keisei Ueno Station are ¥790. A limited express (*tokkyu*) takes 1 hour 15 minutes. An express (*kyuko*) takes 1 hour 30 minutes.

You can get to Shimbashi in central Tokyo from Keisei Narita Airport Station via the *Toei Asakusa* subway line: From Higashi Ginza Station 1 hour 38 minutes, ¥920. Not every train is direct; you may have to change at Oshiage.

Japanese Railways have a station, called Narita, that is 25 minutes by bus, a ¥350 fare, from the airport. This line is called Sobu Hon-sen Narita line. A JR limited express from Narita to Tokyo Station takes 63 minutes and costs ¥2,300 for an unreserved seat. A JR rapid (*kaisoku*) train takes 75 minutes and costs ¥1,000.

By taxi. Your final option, unless you are being met or planning on not going any farther, is a taxi all the way. This will cost at least ¥17,000; it may take only 1 hour, but, at the mercy of road traffic conditions, it may take longer.

Porter service charges are fixed at ¥200 per piece, and for the longer hauls at ¥300 per piece. Luggage carts are also available. Before leaving Narita you can check your heavy baggage at the Air Baggage Service Company (ABC) counter, and have it delivered to your destination the following day. The charge is ¥2,000 for one item under 30 kilograms, and ¥1,000 for each additional piece.

Passengers **transferring** from Narita to Haneda Airport are taken by the Limousine Bus in, say, 1¾ hours: ¥2,700.

LEAVING BY TRAIN

To leave Tokyo by Shinkansen, you have to go to Tokyo Station. On each of many platforms there is a guide in English, giving a rundown of each line, track number, and the destinations. It points the way also to the JR Expressway Bus. Tokyo Station has a North, a Central, and a South exit. Each one leads down to a main plaza where, again, everything is clearly indicated in English. Shinkansen tracks are from number 14 to number 19 inclusive. Shinkansen directions are given in blue lettering.

It would be helpful if you asked your hotel to buy your Shinkansen tickets in advance. Otherwise you must go to the windows marked for Shinkansen tickets. Make sure of your carriage number and seat number, train name, and departure time. It is simplicity itself to make all the identifications and to get aboard the correct train.

IN TOKYO

Tokyo sprawls inconveniently and has not one but several business, shopping, and entertainment areas. Each one is accessible by public transport.

By train. JR operates several electric train services in Tokyo. The *Yamanote* line loops Tokyo with trains going in both directions. Its coaches are green. Fares are calculated by distance, with the shortest distance costing ¥120. Tickets are bought at machines, which give change. Some machines accept ¥1,000 notes. If you know the fare to the station you want to go to, insert coins to cover the fare and press the appropriate button on the machine. If you need change, you will get it delivered along with your ticket. If you don't know the fare, you can try asking somebody for help. Otherwise, buy a basic fare ticket and pay the excess amount when you leave the train. Look for the fare adjustment window, which is usually somewhere near the exit gate, or pay as you exit. The attendant will tell you how much you owe. Hold on to your ticket. You must surrender it when you exit or buy a full-fare replacement.

Another above-surface JR line is the *Chuo.* Its coaches are orange, and its trains begin from Tokyo Station and travel west out to Shinjuku and beyond. The *Sobu* line, with yellow coaches, also runs between Shinjuku and Ochanomizu, but then goes off on a different route.

By subway. Tokyo's subway system has 10 lines that cover the city underground. Some are private lines, some are run by Tokyo City Government. With the use of a subway map, you should be able to get around with a minimum of difficulty and a maximum of speed. Again, we recommend your coping with the ticket machines in the manner described above. Some stations have subway maps and fares posted in English.

By bus. Buses crisscross the city. Fares begin at ¥160. Buses are not easy to use unless you have familiarity with both language and routes.

By taxi. Taxi basic fare is ¥470 for the first two kilometers, and ¥80 for each additional 405 meters. There is also a time charge, when traffic holds you up, registered automatically on the meter. After 11:00 P.M., the total fare increases by 20 percent. You can flag down a cruising taxi in the street, or go to a taxi stand. In Tokyo's central district, between 10:00 P.M. and 1:00 A.M., cabs stop at eleven designated taxi stands.

By car. More expensive and more comfortable than taxis are the big *haiya cars.* The word "haiya" is how the Japanese say "hire." Cost is about ¥5,000 per hour within Tokyo. They will call for you if summoned by phone. Their drivers are especially careful and polite.

By special arrangement you can hire chauffeured cars for longer trips (ask at any hotel) or self-drive cars. You'll need an operator's permit for the latter. International licenses are valid in Japan. If you do not have one, take your own national licence to the Samezu Test Center, and after a sight test you can get a Japanese license. Otherwise, you have to take the same practical and theoretical tests as the Japanese.

Hire taxis: *Anzen,* 404–6361; *Daiwa,* 201–7007; *Eastern Motors,* 438–1666; *Fuji,* 571–6411; *Green Cab,* 202–6011; *Hinomaru,* 584–0080 and 580–8338; *Kokusai,* 585–5931 and 583–7161; *Nihon,* 231–4871; *Odakyu Kotsu,* 453–6711 and 453–3911; *Seibu,* 432–7581; *Takara,* 403–7931/2; *Teito,* 214–2021 and 571–6146.

Rent-a-car: *Isuzu,* 452–3097; *Japaren,* 354–5531; *Mitsubishi,* 213–8071; *Nippon,* 468–7101; *Nissan,* 587–4123; *Nissan Kanko,* 587–4100; *Tokyo,* 407–4431; *Toyota,* 263–6321.

 TOURIST INFORMATION. Most major hotels in Tokyo have information corners where pamphlets can be picked up and the weekly *Tour Companion* obtained, so it's worth popping in to the nearest one even if you're not staying there. The other essential place to know about is the *Tourist Information Center,* at Kotani Building, 1–6–6 Yurakucho, Chiyoda-ku. It is operated by the Japan National Tourist Organization and located near Yurakucho Station. The TIC is open from 9:00 A.M. until 5:00 P.M. on weekdays and from 9:00 A.M. until noon on Saturdays. It is closed on Sundays. The center also operates a telephone information service daily from 9 A.M. to 5 P.M.; phone 502–1461. Outside Tokyo, use the toll-free Travel-Phone. Dial 106 from a yellow or blue phone, and say, "Collect Call T.I.C." An *airport office* is located

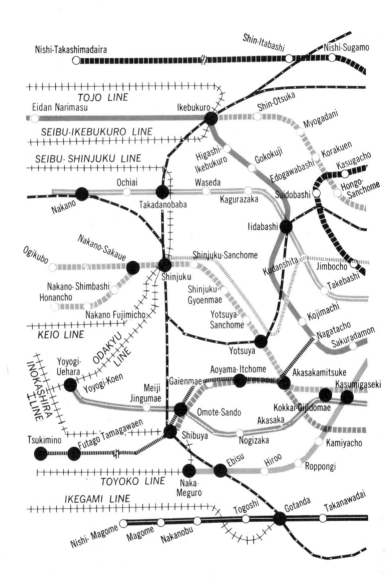

TOKYO SUBWAYS

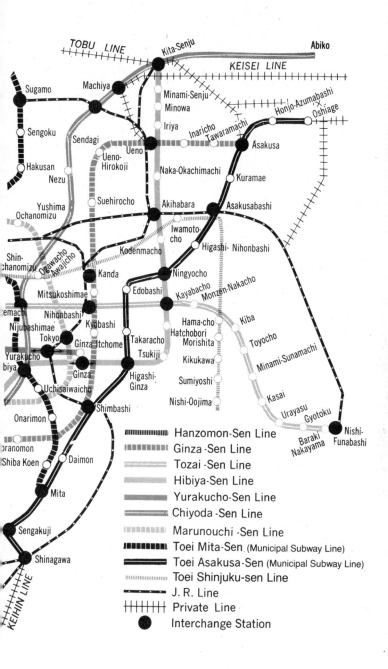

in the New Tokyo International Airport, Narita. There is a *Kyoto office;* phone 371–5649.

Japan Travel Bureau will also be glad to help you. Some of their offices: Narita (0476–32–8805); *Foreign Tourist Department,* Nittetsu-Nihonbashi Bldg., 1–13–1, Nihonbashi, Chuo-ku, 276–7777; and in several hotels. JTB's headquarters are next to the Hotel Marunouchi, Otemachi.

Japan National Tourist Organization, 10th floor, Tokyo Kotsu Kaikan in Yurakucho, 216–1901, will assist you with any particular problems. Dial 503–2911 (for English) or 503–2926 (for French), for information on current exhibitions, entertainment, and events in and around Tokyo.

RECOMMENDED READING. There are five daily English-language newspapers in Japan, all of them available at hotels and newsstands around Tokyo. The *Japan Times,* the *Mainichi Daily News,* the *Daily Yomiuri,* and the *Shipping and Trade News* are morning papers, and the *Asahi Evening News* comes out in the afternoons. Other publications include *Tokyo Business Today* and *The Magazine,* both monthly magazines, and *Tokyo Journal,* which is a monthly information paper. *Tour Companion* is an information weekly for tourists which can be obtained free of charge at most major hotels. *Time* and *Newsweek* publish weekly English editions in Tokyo. All hotels catering to foreigners have them on sale each Wednesday.

The larger hotels all have stands and bookstores where English-language magazines and books can be purchased. The main bookstores in Tokyo are **Kinokuniya** in Shinjuku and Shibuya, **Biblos** in Takadanobaba (opposite Takadanobaba Station), **Kitazawa, Sanseido,** and **Maruzen** in the Kanda-Jimbocho district. Maruzen also has shops in Nihonbashi, the World Trade Center Bldg., Isetan Dept. Store, and Tokyo University shop. **Jena** is near Yurakucho Station in Ginza.

$P£

MONEY. Banks, and most well-equipped hotels have licensed money-changing facilities. Our advice is to use traveler's checks. Your yen is reconvertible into dollars at official counters. Tokyo's foreign banks can give you direct service and further information. They are:

American Express, Toranomon-Mitsui Bldg., 3–8–1 Kasumigaseki, Chiyoda-ku. *Bank of America,* Tokyo Kaijo Bldg., 1–2–1 Marunouchi, Chiyoda-ku. *Bank of India,* Mitsubishi Denki Building, 2–2–3 Marunouchi, Chiyoda-ku. *Banque de l'Indochine,* French Bank Bldg., 1–1–2 Akasaka, Minato-ku. *Barclays Bank International,* Mitsubishi Bldg., 2–5–2 Marunouchi, Chiyoda-ku. *Chartered Bank,* Fuji Bldg., 3–2–3 Marunouchi. *Chase Manhattan Bank,* AIU Bldg., 1–1–3 Marunouchi, Chiyoda-ku. *First National Bank of Chicago,* Time-Life Bldg., 2–3–6 Ote-machi, Chiyoda-ku. *Grindlays Bank Ltd.,* 303 Palace Bldg., 1–1–1 Marunouchi. *Hongkong & Shanghai Banking Corp.,* Chiyoda Building, 2–1–2 Marunouchi, Chiyoda-Ku. *Manufacturer's Trust,* 21st Floor, Asahi Tokai Bldg., 2–6–1 Otemachi Chiyoda-ku. *Algemene Bank Nederland,* Fuji Bldg., 3–2–3 Marunouchi, Chiyoda-ku. *Bank Negara Indonesia,* Kokusai Bldg., 3–1–1 Marunouchi, Chiyoda-ku. *Bangkok Bank,* 2–8–11 Nihombashi, Muromachi, Chuo-ku. *Lloyds Bank International,* Yurakucho Denki Bldg., 1–7–1 Yurakucho. Chiyoda-ku. *Mellon Bank, N.A.,* 242 Shin-Yurakucho Bldg., 1–12–1 Yurakucho. *Midland Bank,* Togin Bldg., 1–4–2 Marunouchi, Chiyoda-ku. *Morgan Guaranty Trust Co. of New York,* New Yurakucho Building, 1–12–1 Yurakucho, Chiyoda-ku. *Wells Fargo Bank,* N.A., Fuji Building, 3–2–3 Marunouchi, Chiyoda-ku. *National Westminster Bank,* Mitsubishi Building,

2–2–5 Marunouchi, Chiyoda-ku. Many foreign banks have representative offices in Tokyo, but do not carry out banking transactions.

BUSINESS AND COMMERCIAL INFORMATION.

The *Tokyo Trade Center* can give the foreign businessperson any information concerning Japanese industry and trading affairs. The Trade Center has a showroom where you can see almost any kind of product made in the country. Open 9:00 A.M. to 5:00 P.M., daily except Sundays. 3F. World Trade Center Bldg. Annex, Hamamatsucho; 435–5394.

The *Japan Export General Merchandise Show Center* is located at the *Tokyo International Trade Center,* Harumi Pier, the site of Tokyo's international trade fairs. The address of the Trade Center is 2, 6-chome Harumicho, Chuo-ku. The Merchandise Center is open from 10:00 A.M. to 5:00 P.M. daily, except Sunday.

Major hotels have business centers with services most business travelers need: secretarial and translator services, the use of office equipment, services to print business cards in English and Japanese, etc. Check the American Embassy Commercial Section, 583–7141 and/or JETRO at 582–5511 for information on doing business in Japan. The *Tokyo Chamber of Commerce and Industry* has offices in Marunouchi; 283–7867. The *American Chamber of Commerce* is at 4–1–21 Toranomon, Minato-ku; 433–5381.

Useful Hints. For name cards, English one side Japanese the other, you can get quick printing at *Iwanaga Inc.* (209–3381); and at *Wakabayashi,* (255–7909). Hotel newsstands have business directories in English. Ask your hotel for document copy service, or call *Fuji Xerox Co.,* (585–3211). Interpreters and secretaries are supplied by *I.S.S.* (265–7101), and *E.S.S.* (251–5755). *JAL* also has an "Executive Service," from 747–3191.

COMMUNICATIONS.

All good hotels will handle your communications problems for you. Tokyo's *Central Post Office* is on Tokyo Station Plaza, but there are branch post offices all over the city. The Central Post Office is open around the clock daily.

The overseas telegraph office foreign visitors will be most likely to use is: *K. D. D. (International Telegraph & Telephone Center),* 3–2–5 Kasumigaseki, Chiyoda-ku. It issues credit cards for "credit-card calls."

Book your overseas calls at your hotel through the operator. For the international operator, dial 0051. Major hotels operate a direct dialing system.

USEFUL ADDRESSES. Embassies and Consulates.

American Embassy and Consulate, 1–10–5 Akasaka, Minato-ku. The Consular hours (Passport and Citizenship branch): 8:00 A.M. to 4:00 P.M.; closed Saturdays (583–7141).

British Embassy and Consulate, 1 Ichiban-cho, Chiyoda-ku. Consular hours: 9:00 A.M. to noon, 2:00 to 4:00 P.M.; closed Saturdays and holidays (265–5511).

Canadian Embassy, 7–3–38 Akasaka, Minato-ku. Hours: 9:00 A.M. to 12:30 P.M., 2:30 to 4:30 P.M.; closed Saturdays and holidays (408–2101).

New Zealand Embassy, 20 Kamiyama-cho, Shibuya-ku. Consular hours: 9:00 A.M. to 12:30 P.M., 2:00 to 5:00 P.M.; closed Saturdays and holidays (460–8711).

Australian Embassy, 2–1–14 Mita, Minato-ku. Consular hours: 9:00 A.M. to noon, 2:00 to 4:00 P.M. Closed Saturdays and holidays (453–0251).

Imperial Household. If you have any business with the Imperial Household agency (for example, if you wish to view part of the palace grounds normally not open to the public), you may telephone them at 213–1111, ext. 485. The office of the Imperial Household Agency Visitors' Department is at the Saka-shitamon across from the Palace Hotel. If you wish to write, the address is 1–1 Chiyoda-ku, Tokyo.

MEETING PLACES. The following coffee shops serve as English conversation lounges where Japanese students of English and native speakers can meet and chat together: **English Inn.** 470–0213. One minute from Meiji-Jingumae subway station in Harajuku. **International Pacific Club.** 358–1681. Seven minutes from Yotsuya Station on the Chuo line. **E.S.S.** 498–2056. Five minutes from Shibuya Station. **Com'inn.** 793–3371. Three minutes from Ebisu Station on the Yamanote line, 5th floor Arai Bldg.

ESCORT SERVICE. The **Tokyo Escort Service,** 358–7322, offers English-speaking female companions for dining, dancing, shopping, and sightseeing.

MEDICAL SERVICE. The following hospitals are ac-customed to dealing with foreigners, and many of their staff members are foreign-trained. *International Catholic Hospital* (Seibo Byoin) in Naka-Ochiai, Shinjuku Ward; 951–1111. *St. Luke's International Hospital* in Akashicho, Chuo Ward; 541–5151. No emergency service. No entry Sundays and holidays. *Tokyo Medical and Surgical Clinic* in Shiba-Koen; 436–3028. No emergency service. No entry Sundays or holidays. *International Clinic* in Roppongi area; 582–2646 or 583–7831. Accepts emergencies.

EMERGENCIES. If you wish to report a fire or accident, and if you speak Japanese or if you want to take a chance that somebody at the other end will understand you, you can dial the following numbers from any telephone: *Fire,* 119; *Ambulance,* 119; *Police,* 110. There may be someone at the other end who understands English if you speak slowly.

TELL, Tokyo English Life Line. A telephone service for anyone in distress needing a listener and counselor, and also for assisting in emergency telephone calls in Japanese. TELL-a-phone, 264–4347.

LOST AND FOUND. The Central Lost and Found Office of the Metropolitan Police is at 1–9–12 Koraku, Bunkyo-ku; 814–4151. If you leave something on a train, report to the Lost and Found Office at any station. If you leave anything in a taxi, report to *Tokyo Taxi Kindaika Center,* 33 Shinanomachi, Shinjuku-ku; 355–0300.

ELECTRIC CURRENT. The electric current in Tokyo is 100 volts and 50 cycles, AC (American current is 110 volts and 60 cycles and British is 220 volts). You can use most American appliances, such as electric shavers, ra-dios, irons, etc., on this current, but delicate machines such as record players require adjustment because of the difference in cycles.

CHURCHES. There are many churches of all denomi-nations in Tokyo, although very few of them are English-speaking. The main ones where services are held in English are as follows:

Catholic. *Franciscan Chapel Center* in Roppongi; 401–2141. *St. Mary's Cathedral* in Bunkyo Ward; 941–3029. *St. Ignatius Church* near Yotsuya Station; 263–4584. *German-Speaking Catholic Church* in Meguro Ward; 712–0775. *French-Speaking Catholic Church* in Chiyoda Ward; 446–9594.

Christian (other). *Church of Jesus Christ of Latter-Day Saints* in Shinjuku; 952–6802. *Keio Plaza Chapel Service* in Shinjuku; 344–0111. *New Otani Garden Chapel* in Chiyoda Ward; 265–1111. *Ochanomizu Church of Christ* in Chiyoda Ward; 291–0478. *Tokyo International Church* in Ebisu, Shibuya Ward; 464–4512. *Tokyo Union Church* near Omotesando Subway Station; 400–0047.

Christian Science Church in Shibuya; 499–3951. *Church of Christ* in Ochanomizu; 291–0478. *German-Speaking Protestant Church* in Shinagawa; 441–0673. *Tokyo Lutheran Center* near Iidabashi Station; 261–3740. *Tokyo Baptists Church* in Shibuya Ward; 467–7829. *St. Alban's* in Shiba-Koen; 431–8534.

Muslim. *Tokyo Mosque* in Shibuya Ward; 469–0284. *Japan Muslim Association* in Yoyogi; 370–3476.

Russian Orthodox. *Russian Orthodox Church* in Shinjuku Ward; 341–2281. *Nicolai Cathedral* in Kanda; 291–1885.

Others. *Bahai Center* in Shinjuku; 209–7521. *Jewish Community* of Japan in Hiroo, Shibuya Ward; 400–2559. **Buddhist.** English lectures on Buddhism are given every Sunday at 10:30 A.M. at the *Tsukiji Honganji Temple,* on Harumi Avenue, by Japanese missionaries. This is not a Zen temple.

Zen Buddhist. Regularly scheduled services are not part of Zen, but instruction in English may be obtained at the following temples, a short distance from downtown Tokyo (from 25 to 45 minutes by train): *Sojiji Temple,* 128 Tsurumi, Tsurumi-ku, Yokohama, 045–581–6021; *Enkakuji Temple,* 478 Yamanouchi, Kamakura, 0467–22–0478; or *Kenchoji Temple,* 8 Yamanouchi, Kamakura, 0467–22–0981. In Tokyo, contact *Eiheiji,* a 15 minute walk from Roppongi, 400–5232.You should telephone and make arrangements to visit these places well in advance so that they can have English-speaking preceptors on hand.

 BEAUTY PARLORS AND BARBERS. All the leading hotels have good beauty salons, in which imported beauty preparations are widely used. Also excellent, the shops run by Japan's leading cosmetic maker, Shiseido. *André Bernard of London* is on the 4th floor, Horaiya Bldg., Roppongi (404–0616). Other beauty salons where English is spoken include: *Maroze,* above the National Abazu Supermarket at Hiroo (444–4225); *Sweden Center House of Beauty* at Roppongi (404–9730); and *Peek-a-Boo,* Omotesando, 409–9654. *Yamano* has shops in ten locations (main one in the Ginza; 561–1200). Cosmetic plastic surgery is performed by highly skilled doctors at *Jujin Hospital,* 1–12–5 Shimbashi, Minato-ku, Tokyo (571–2111).

The barbershops in the major hotels usually are best for the foreign visitor, as they have had experience cutting non-Japanese hair, and you can get your instructions across to them in the English language. Haircuts and shampoo will cost you about ¥4,000 in these places, and all of the side services, such as manicure, scalp massage, shoeshine, and facial treatment are available. In addition to the shops in the hotels, *Nisshin Barbers* in Yurakucho's Sanshin Building (591–1839) and *Yonekura* in the Asahi Building, 6–6–7 Ginza (571–1538), more expensive, but highly recommended. *Andre Bernard* at Roppongi (address above) accepts men as well as women customers, as indeed do many others.

CLOSING DAYS AND HOURS. To the casual observer, it seems that the shops and restaurants of Tokyo never close. Generally, establishments in the Ginza area open around 10:00 A.M. and close about 7:00 P.M. Department stores are usually open on Sundays, but close on Mondays, Wednesdays, or Thursdays. (Each store has its own closing day.) Smaller shops remain open seven days a week, as do restaurants. Dining out can be a problem sometimes, because many fine restaurants close at 8:00 or 9:00 P.M. A special law seems to govern the restaurants in the Roppongi and Akasaka areas, however, where you can eat Chinese, Italian, or American food until 2:00 or 3:00 A.M. Some hotel arcade shops close on Sundays. It is a 5½-day week for banks, business houses, and government offices. From Monday to Friday banks are open from 9:00 A.M. to 3:00 P.M., and on Saturday until noon. They do not open on the second Saturday of each month. From Monday to Friday business and government offices are open from 9:00 A.M. to 5:00 P.M., and on Saturday until noon. Some business houses enjoy a five-day week. In liaison with the banks, post offices are not handling money nor insurance transactions on the second Saturday of each month.

 SEASONAL EVENTS AND FESTIVALS. Most festivals and fairs are held in honor of local deities and are religious in nature. Often portable shrines and decorated floats, in which dancers and musicians entertain, are carried around the districts. Often people of the neighborhood join in street parades. These are occasions especially for children to wear their brightest kimono, helping to make festivals and fairs colorful and convivial. Usually shopkeepers sell trinkets, flowers, and snacks at streetside stalls along the approaches to temples and shrines.

Although we try to be as up-to-date as possible, dates of festivals are subject to change and should be verified through the local press or the Tokyo Tourist Information Center.

The following are markets and fairs that can be enjoyed every month:

Every morning except Sundays and national holidays. Fish market at Tsukiji, held in the Tokyo Central Wholesale Market from early morning until about 11:00 A.M. From Tsukiji station on the Hibiya subway line.

First Sunday. Antique market at Araiyakushi Temple in Nakano Ward. From Araiyakushimae station on the Seibu-Shinjuku line.

Second Sunday. Antique market at Nogi Shrine in Akasaka. From Nogizaka station on the Chiyoda subway line.

Third Saturday and Sunday. Antique market on 1st floor of Sunshine 60 building in Ikebukuro. From Ikebukuro station on the Yamanote line or Higashi-Ikebukuro subway station on the Yurakucho line.

Fourth Thursday and Friday. Antique market at the Roi Building in Roppongi. From Roppongi Station on the Hibiya subway line.

Fourth Saturday. Antique market at Yushima Shrine. From Yushima Station on the Chiyoda subway line.

Fourth Sunday. Antique market at Togo Shrine in Shibuya Ward. From Shibuya Station on the Yamanote line.

On the 1st and 21st. Local fair at Nishiarai Daishi Temple in Adachi Ward. From Daishimae Station on the Tobu line from Asakusa, changing onto a branch line for the temple at Nishiarai.

On the 4th, 14th, and 24th. Local fair held by the Togenuki Jizo Temple in Sugamo, Toshima Ward. From Sugamo Station on the Yamanote line.

January. Daruma doll festival at Kitain Temple in Kawagoe on the 3rd, on the western outskirts of Tokyo. This is a red, legless doll that, because its bottom is weighted and rounded, always returns to the upright position no matter how much it is pushed around. The doll symbolizes buoyancy and resilience. At New Year, Japanese people buy new daruma dolls to ensure good fortune for the coming year. The left eye of the doll is colored in as a wish is made, and the right eye when that wish is fulfilled.

Demonstrations of traditional skills and acrobatics by firemen along Chuo-dori Ave. in Harumi district, from 10:00 A.M. until noon on the 6th.

From the 15th to 16th is the famous flea market called the Setagaya Boro Ichi. Held along Daikan Yashikimae Ave. in Kamimachi, Setagaya Ward. Take bus 1, 3, or 34 from the south exit of Shibuya Station and get off at Kamimachi bus stop.

February is the month for plum blossoms in Tokyo. Good places to view them are *Shinjuku Gyoen* park in Shinjuku, from Shinjuku Gyoenmae Station on the Marunouchi subway line or from Sendagaya Station on the Sobu line; *Ume Yashiki Park* in Ota Ward, from Keihin-Kyuko line Ume Yashiki Station; *Koishikawa Korakuen Garden,* from Iidabashi Station on the Sobu line; *Koishikawa Botanical Garden,* from Shireyama Station on the Mita subway line; and *Yushima Tenjin Shrine* in Bunkyo Ward, from Yushima Station on the Chiyoda subway line. Yushima Tenjin Shrine holds a plum blossom festival from mid-February until mid-March.

Annual bean-throwing festival is held on the 3rd at shrines and temples across the country to herald the coming of spring. In Tokyo, the most popular (but also most crowded) places are Asakusa Kannon Temple in Asakusa and Zojoji Temple in Shiba.

March is the month of tulips, and while most parks have at least some in their collections, the most colorful spot is *Hibiya Park,* reached from Yurakucho Station on the Yamanote line or Hibiya Station on the Hibiya subway line.

Daruma doll fair is held from the 3rd to 4th at Jindaiji Temple, reached by bus from Chofu Station on the Keio line.

On the second Sunday in March a fire-walking ceremony is held at Mount Takao. Priests, and anyone else who wants to, walk barefoot over burning ashes.

April is the month for cherry blossom viewing, accompanied by much song, drink, and dance, in parks across the capital. Perhaps the most popular spot, especially for cherry blossom parties in the evenings, is *Ueno Park,* but others include *Shinjuku Gyoen; Yasukuni Shrine,* from Kudanshita Station on the Tozai subway line; *Ikegami Honmonji Temple,* from Ikegami Station on the Ikegami line from Gotanda; *Kinuta Park,* from Yoga Station on the Shin-Tamagawa subway line from Shibuya; *Yoyogi Park;* the *Outer Garden of Meiji Shrine* in Harajuku; and *Mukojima,* now linked to Asakusa by a footbridge across the Sumida River, popular since Edo days and now part of a city rebeautification program.

April is also the month for peonies, and *Nishiarai Daishi Temple* (from Daishimae Station on the Tobu line) has an excellent peony garden in its grounds.

The best azalea festival of April is held at *Nezu Shrine* (Nezu Station is on the Chiyoda Line). Besides the banks of flowers, scheduled events include drum performances and open-air tea ceremonies.

Annual spring festival of Yasukuni Shrine is held on the 22nd.

From April 25–May 5 is the annual plant fair, said to be the biggest in Kanto, at Ikegami Honmonji Temple in Ota Ward. Also held during this period is the wisteria festival, at Kameido Tenjin Shrine in Koto Ward (from Kameido Station on the Sobu line).

Late April–early May is the annual spring festival at Meiji Shrine in Haraju-ku.

May is the month of camellias, and good places to view them include *Komazawa Olympic Park,* from Komazawa Daigaku Station on the Shin-Tamagawa subway line from Shibuya; *Yoyogi Park; Shinjuku Central Park,* located near the Shinjuku skyscrapers; and *Nezu Shrine,* from Nezu Station on the Chiyoda subway line.

May 12–15. Kanda Festival, a huge affair with many local shrines taking part in street processions in the Kanda area.

May 16–18. Sanja Festival, the annual festival of Asakusa Shrine in Asakusa, located near the Asakusa Kannon Temple.

June brings the irises, and fine displays can be seen at several places in Tokyo, including *Meiji Shrine's Iris Garden, Jindai Botanical Garden* in Chofu, *Yasuku-ni Shrine,* and *Horikiri Iris Garden,* near Horikiri Shobuen Station on the Keisei line from Ueno.

In mid-June is the annual Sanno Festival of Hie Shrine in Akasaka, a few minutes' walk from Akasaka-Mitsuke Station.

The Fuji Festival from June 30–July 2, marking the opening of Mount Fuji for the climbing season, takes place at Fuji Shrine near Komagome Station on the Yamanote line. Snakes made of scrolls are sold. These are believed to protect people from evil. Many open-air stalls selling potted plants, trinkets, and food are set up around the shrine.

July. A morning glory fair is held from the 6th–8th in the grounds of *Kishibojin Temple* near Iriya Station on the Hibiya subway line.

A ground cherry fair is held in the grounds of *Asakusa Kannon Temple* in Asakusa from the 9th–10th.

From the 13th–16th is the *Mitama* (spirit of the dead) *Festival of Yasukuni Shrine.* Memorial service for the enshrined deities. Demonstrations of the mar-tial arts and ancient Imperial Court music and dances.

Plum fair of *Okunitama Shrine* in Fuchu, near Fuchu Station on the Keio line from Shinjuku. Takes place on the 20th.

At the end of July is the grand evening fireworks display on the Sumida River. This fireworks display originated in the 18th century, when a Buddhist mass was held for the souls of famine victims. It also marked the opening of the river for sweet trout fishing.

From July 11–Aug. 11 is the summer evening festival by Shinobazu Pond in Ueno Park. Stalls are set up and various forms of entertainment held to help people forget the heat of the day.

September. Annual festival of *Nogi Shrine* is held on the 12th–13th in Akasa-ka.

October. From the 11th–13th is Oeshiki pilgrimage with lighted lanterns at *Ikegami Honmonji Temple,* commemorating the anniversary of the death of Priest Nichiren in 1282.

Annual autumn festival of *Yasukuni Shrine* runs from the 17th–19th.

From October 30–November 4 is the annual autumn festival of *Meiji Shrine.*

From mid-October–mid-November chrysanthemum displays can be seen at *Meiji Shrine, Shinjuku Gyoen, Yasukuni Shrine, Tsukiji Honganji Temple,* and other places around the city.

November. Ornamental rakes said to bring good luck and prosperity are sold at Otori (cock) fairs. The fairs take place two or three times during the month at Otori Shrine in Asakusa, from Minowa Station on the Hibiya subway line; Otori Shrine in Meguro, from Meguro Station on the Yamanote line; and Hanazono Shrine in Shinjuku, from the east exit of Shinjuku Station on the Yamanote line. The dates of these fairs vary from year to year.

December. Year-end fair at Suitengu Shrine on the 5th. Near Ningyocho Station on the Hibiya subway line.

The 14th is the festival at Sengakuji Temple in memory of the 47 loyal retainers, who, in the feudal past, took their own lives after avenging the death of their master. From Sengakuji Station on the Toei Asakusa subway line.

Boro Ichi flea market is held from the 15th-16th along Daikan Yashikimae Av. in Kamimachi, Setagaya Ward. Also held on **Jan. 15–16.**

From the 17th-19th the annual hagoita (battledore, an early form of badminton) fair is held at Asakusa Kannon Temple in Asakusa. Very ornate battledores are sold. They are used in New Year displays in the home.

From Dec. 31st-Jan. 1st people make New Year visits to shrines and temples to pray for health, happiness, and fortune in the coming 12 months. Meiji Shrine is the biggest crowd-puller.

TOURS. All the travel agents listed in the *Facts at Your Fingertips* section earlier in this book have Tokyo offices and can arrange private tours to your specifications. In addition, there are regularly scheduled bus tours with English-speaking guides offered by JTB (276–7777) and private agencies such as **Fujita Travel Service** (573–1417); **Tobu Travel** (281–6622), **Hankyu Express** (508–0129), and **Japan Gray Line** (436–6881). Their precise itineraries change somewhat from year to year, according to what proves popular, but the main places of interest are well established. A recent and typical JTB listing included 10 different tours: *Tokyo Morning, Tokyo Afternoon,* different full-day *Tokyo* tours and *Night Life* tours. Prices range from ¥3,500 to ¥12,000. The *Tokyo Bright Night* course, for example, starts with a sukiyaki dinner at a top-class restaurant, then goes to see part of a kabuki performance at the Kabuki Theater, and finishes with geisha entertainment at a restaurant in Asakusa. The cost is ¥12,000. The *Tokyo Morning Tour* takes about 4 hours and includes Tokyo Tower, Keio University, Happo-en Garden, the National Diet Building, Imperial Palace and Ginza. The price is ¥4,000 for adults, ¥2,500 for children.

JTB is now offering three full-day tours of *Industrial Tokyo.* Each one visits various industrial plants, with the most popular proving to be the Japan Air Lines maintenance center at Tokyo's Haneda Airport. Visitors are shown the B747 hangar and the airline's power plant overhaul center, where jet engines are stripped and repaired. Industrial Tokyo tours cost ¥9,000 for adults and ¥7,000 for children, including lunch. The tour is made on Tuesday, Thursday, and Friday, and occupies about 9 hours. The Tuesday tour is the one that takes in the airline maintenance base.

DO-IT-YOURSELF TOURS. The independent-minded can see a lot of Tokyo on their own and at minimal cost. Here are some suggestions:

The Diet Building and the Parliamentary Museum. At Kasumigaseki, near Kokkai-Gijidomae Station, which is on both the Marunouchi and the Chiyoda subway lines. To enter the Diet Building and see the chambers where the governing of this country goes on, applications have to be made to your embassy and permission awaited. The Parliamentary Museum, that is directly opposite the Diet Building at Kasumigaseki, is the next best thing. Admission is free. The Museum is open from 9:30 A.M. to 3:30 P.M. every day except Sundays, National Holidays, and the last day of each month. On the second floor is a large model of the Diet Building. The model is equipped with an audio/color-slide system, operated by push-button, and giving pictures on a screen and a narration in English. Here you can learn about the development of Parliamentary conduct in Japan and its survival through earthquakes and war. Next to the Museum is the Ozaki Memorial Hall, revering Yukio Ozaki, who was a member of the Diet for more than 60 years.

Japan Broadcasting Corporation (NHK) Center. Follow the map (your first purchase in Tokyo) from either Shibuya or Harajuku stations on the Yamanote line. NHK's broadcasting center was built over a period of several years, is thought to be the "world's best," and at a total cost of ¥31,700 million is also probably the world's costliest.

The center is open for public inspection any weekday, between 8:30 A.M. and 6:00 P.M. There's no need to make a reservation for a tour, as you go right in and proceed unescorted. If you would prefer to have an English-speaking guide, call 465–1111. You walk past control rooms, see what is going on under the lights in the studios, inspect elaborate sets that are the actual ones used in screening long-running serial dramas. Studio 101 is NHK's famed and largest studio. If you want to probe deeper into NHK's complexities, call 464–0114 or 464–0115 to make special arrangements.

Through the **Japan National Tourist Organization,** you may receive names, addresses, telephone numbers and details of several enterprises willing to receive individual tourists. Usually no charge is made. Often English-speaking guides are available. Sometimes just to see, without explanations, is enough. These enterprises include car manufacturers; makers of optical instruments (cameras, lenses); producers of beer and whiskey; makers of electrical goods; makers of musical instruments, of cloisonné, chinaware; a slaughterhouse; a dyeing factory; the stock exchange; makers of confectionery and glassware. In most cases, the head offices are in Tokyo, but the factories in different parts of the country. Those factories in Tokyo, or within reasonable distance from Tokyo, include Honda Motor Co.; Nikon, Asahi Pentax and Konica; Suntory and Sapporo Beer; Sony and Toshiba; Mashiko ware; the slaughterhouse; the stock exchange; Morinaga Confectionery; Hoya Crystal. JNTO is also able to introduce tourists interested in gardens to some of Japan's most outstanding garden designers.

Newspaper Plants. For an example of an immense and complex operation, go on a tour of one of the newspaper plants in Tokyo. The Asahi Shimbun (545–0131) and the Mainichi Shimbun (212–0321) arrange guided tours daily, without charge. Reservations should be made in advance, as each group is limited in size.

These Japanese enterprises manufacture daily papers, weeklies, monthlies, quarterlies, and annuals. English-language dailies, special publications, and books. They have thousands of employees, airplanes and helicopters, affiliated radio and television stations, and other companies handling clipping services, sound recording and real estate. Their daily editions roll off presses simultaneously in different major cities. English-speaking guides are available, if you make your arrangements well in advance.

State Guest House. Formerly the Akasaka Detached Palace, the State Guest House has been renovated and splendidly decorated. It is not open to the public, but can be seen from the road near Yotsuya station and the Hotel New Otani.

The Sumida River. Walk, or take a short taxi ride, from Shimbashi Station to the waterfront gardens of Hamarikyu, a beautiful city park where there was once a detached palace. Take the path that runs parallel to the canal until you reach a ramshackle landing stage. A "water bus" is timed to leave the landing stage every day except Tuesday. The boat is comfortable with an enclosed cabin and an outside deck. For ¥480, you cruise along the Sumida River as far as Asakusa, getting a different view of the city. Near Azuma-bashi are tilting wooden waterfront houses with washing hanging outside. Logs float on the river. Bobbing pink lanterns decorate the landing stage. From Azuma-bashi, famed Asakusa Kannon Temple is only a block away, and downtown Tokyo is all around you. Your return route can be underground, on the Ginza subway line back to Shimbashi.

Tokyo Bay. In summer, the *Tokai Steamship Co.,* (432–4551) operates a 2-hour evening cruise on a ship that puts on variety shows and that has a beerhall. Departures nightly from Takeshiba Pier, fares from ¥500 to ¥2,500.

Walkaholics International. For the foot-loose in Tokyo. You are invited to join half-day walking tours that make use of both JR and subway trains. Call Mr. Oka, 0422–51–7673.

HOME VISIT PROGRAM. In 1968, the Tokyo government in cooperation with the Japan National Tourist Organization inaugurated a Home Visit program. To apply, go in person to the JNTO Tourist Information Center at 1–6–6 Yurakucho, Chiyoda Ward (502–1461) at least one day before the visit, to get your instructions. (No mail or telephone applications.) You usually visit the family after dinner, stay for an hour or two. No charge, but it's gracious to take a small gift, such as flowers or cakes.

TEA CEREMONY. Several places in Tokyo welcome visitors from abroad to see and take part in Japan's traditional tea ceremony. These include: *Sakura-kai.* 3–2–25 Shimo-Ochiai, Shinjuku-ku; 951–9043. Near Meji-ro Station, on the Yamanote line. Fee ¥600. For a lesson, lasting 40 mins., ¥1,200. A lesson in flower arrangement may be added: one hour, with tea: ¥2,500. From 11:00 A.M. TO 4:00 P.M. Thursdays and Fridays. Reservations necessary.

Toko-an. Imperial Hotel 4th floor; 504–1111. Fee ¥1,100. From 10:00 A.M. to 4:00 P.M.; except Sundays and national holidays.

Chosho-an. Hotel Okura 7th floor; 582–0111. Fee ¥1,000. From 11:00 A.M. to 5:00 P.M., with a noon lunch break.

Seisei-an. Hotel New Otani Tower 7th floor; 265–1111, ext. 2567. Fee ¥1,000. From 11:00 A.M. to 4:00 P.M. Open Thursdays, Fridays, and Saturdays.

LESSONS. Flower Arranging. If you have time for lessons, try the following: *Ikenobo Gakuen* in Kanda Surugadai, Chiyoda Ward; 292–3071; lessons for tourists on Wednesday mornings. *Ohara School of Ikebana* in Minami Aoyama, Minato Ward; 499–1200; lessons every morning (¥2,000). *Sogetsu School of Ikebana* in Akasaka, Minato Ward; 408–1126; Tuesday mornings (¥3,000). Reservations are necessary.

Yoga. Contact the *Ghosh Yoga Institute* in Shinjuku (352–1307), the *Yoga College of India* in Shibuya (461–7805), or the *Tokyo Yoga Center* in Shinjuku (354–4701). The *Tomonaga Yoga School* in Ogikubo (393–5481) offers classes in both yoga and Zen.

Japanese Cooking. *Akabori Cooking School* in Mejiro (953–2251) offers two-hour lessons for foreigners three times a month on Mondays. ¥3,500. Reservations necessary.

There are schools in Tokyo for just about everything you could imagine. If you want to try your hand at something other than those mentioned above, such as doll making, weaving and other handicrafts, how to wear a kimono, and, of course, Japanese language, ask for up-to-date information on classes and prices at the Tokyo Information Center in Yurakucho (see the *Tourist Information* section).

PARKS AND GARDENS. Nearly all the parks mentioned below are open from 8:30 A.M. to 4:00 P.M. daily, including holidays. **Hibiya Park.** Across from the Imperial Hotel. A small but pleasant spot in the heart of the city. About 40 acres. Hibiya Hall features frequent concerts and there are shows and exhibitions in the park from time to time. In November, Japan's biggest chrysanthemum show is held here. Among the trees are dogwoods sent by the United States in return for the famous Washington cherry trees.

Ueno Park. Across from Ueno Station. On Keihin Tohoku or Yamanote JR train lines, or on Hibiya or Ginza subway lines. This huge park is full of attractions; you can easily spend a day exploring the area. It contains a popular zoo; various museums of art, science and natural history, temples, pagodas, shrines, and a monument to Ulysses S. Grant. A tree he planted on his visit to Japan still stands. In Ueno Park you can also take a short ride on Japan's first monorail train.

Hamarikyu Park. Just south of the center of Tokyo and on the harbor. 60 acres with lovely walks, lawns, foliage, and a pond with an island. On reclaimed land, it had once been a shogunate palace, later transferred to the Imperial Household. Visiting former president Ulysses S. Grant was housed here.

Oi Bird Park. For birds and bird watchers. On Tokyo Bay, and a 15-minute walk from Ryutsu Center Station on the monorail line from Hamamatsu-cho to Hareda.

Imperial Palace East Garden. At the east end of the Imperial Palace grounds. Opened in 1968 to commemorate construction of the new palace. One of the best examples of modern Japanese gardening.

Kiyosumi Garden. Just east of the center of Tokyo, and everything you've imagined an exquisite Japanese garden ought to be. Ponds, rock stepping stones, stone lanterns and winding walks. Highly photogenic.

Tama Zoological Park. On the southwest edge of Tokyo, in the Tama district. Large, sylvan grounds and displays of animals behind moats and in naturalistic habitats. Amusement facilities nearby: merry-go-rounds, roller coasters, etc.

Shinjuku Gyoen. Certainly one of Japan's loveliest gardens. Huge grounds, exquisitely landscaped. Botanical displays from all over the world. In west central Tokyo, not far from Shinjuku Station. Cherry blossoms in April and chrysanthemum displays throughout October.

Rikugien Garden, perhaps the most beautiful and most typical Japanese garden in Tokyo, is located near the Komagome Station on the Yámanote Line (the loop around central Tokyo). A favorite resort of the *shogun* and other officials, it includes a large pond, a teahouse, and some magnificent, twisted trees. Dates back to early 18th century.

Meiji Shrine Inner Gardens are particularly beautiful during the last two weeks of June when the iris are at their best. An amazing display of varieties in a lovely setting. The gardens are inside the shrine, which is at Harajuku Station on the Yamanote loop. Open from 8:30 A.M. to 4:30 P.M. daily. In the fall, usually the entire month of October, displays of chrysanthemums are held here.

National Park for Nature Study is just what it says it is, and is an oasis in Shirogane. An insectarium is open from April to November.

Yoyogi Park, near Harajuku station, is the site of Olympic Village in 1964, and of an American housing area before that. It has now reverted to nature, a delightful green area close to Tokyo's beating heart.

Tokyo Metropolitan Medicinal Plants Garden, Kodaira City, Tokyo, is a representative herb garden. Open daily, 9:00 A.M. to 5:00 P.M. No entrance fee. On the Seibu Shinjuku line from Shinjuku to Omebashi.

Hoshi Pharmaceutical College, Ebara, Shinagawa-ku. Visits by appointment. Tel. 786–1011.

Tokyo Shobu-en (Iris Garden) is also a fine place for viewing the gorgeous Japanese iris in June. Located near Tamagawa Station on the Keio Teito private railway line from Shinjuku Station.

Odaiba (Kaihen), a waterfront park built on reclaimed land in Tokyo Bay is near an oceanographic museum that has the shape of a 60,000-ton passenger liner. The *Soya,* a former Antarctic expedition ship, is now moored there.

ZOOS. Ueno Zoo, which is in Ueno Park, stars two very popular pandas, gifts from China. In the Children's Zoo, small children may ride ponies. Open 9:00 A.M.– 4:30 P.M., Closed Mondays, Dec. 29–31. **Tama Zoo** allows its animals to live in as natural a setting as possible. A Lion Bus drives visitors through the area where lions roam freely. Take a Keio line express train from Shinjuku Station to Takahata-fudo Station, and change there for a local train to Tama Dobutsu-koen. Open 9:00 A.M.–4:30 P.M.; closed Mondays.

BATHHOUSES. Tokyo Onsen. 6 Ginza; 541–3021. This is a five-story emporium dedicated to hedonistic cleanliness. You can spend about ¥3,000 here and enter the large public baths (segregated), or you can hire a private room, where you will find a steam cabinet, small pool, and a massage team of two women, one of whom will probably walk up and down your spine as the high point of your massage. The top floor boasts a "human dock" where battered wrecks are presumably repaired. The fee up here is about ¥7,000 for which you can enjoy (or suffer) a Finnish sauna, a whirlpool bath, a massage by the usual light-fingered women or the bone-breaking masseurs, and end your experience with a fast shakedown on the torture rack known as the Swedish electrical massage machine. (The masseurs are alleged to be apprentice sumo wrestlers, and presumably they are building their muscles at the expense of yours.) Sauna baths are being installed for tired executives in many business buildings and hotels. No hanky panky in these high-priced establishments. Neighborhood public bathhouses are a vanishing institution, but there are still 2,700 of them left in Tokyo. ¥220 per adult, all the hot water you want and no time limit. Americans Hatch and Wilson run a Fitness Center in **Azabu Towers,** next to the Soviet Embassy. The **Swedish Health Center for Ladies,** in the Sweden Center Building, Roppongi, has sauna baths and massage. Another ladies-only is the **Tarner,** at Myogadani, ¥2,500 with sauna. **Ginza Steam Bath,** at 1 chome, has a 70-minute service for ¥3,500, daily from noon to midnight.

THEME PARKS AND AMUSEMENT CENTERS. There can be only one leader among Tokyo's many amusement centers. That is **Tokyo Disneyland,** far and away the winner in its field, the first Disney theme park outside the United States. Some folks who have been to all three say that Tokyo Disneyland is better than Disneyland in California and Walt Disney World in

Florida. In every way, Tokyo Disneyland is faithful to the original concepts, with that little bit extra: the Japanese touch.

JTB runs a daily *Sunrise Tokyo Disneyland and City Tour,* except on the days when Tokyo Disneyland is closed. The tour lasts about 8½ hours. It costs ¥8,500 for adults, ¥7,500 for the 12–17 year olds, and ¥5,000 for ages 4–11. These prices include Tokyo Disneyland and individual attraction tickets. The tour also takes in the Imperial Palace plaza and the Asakusa Kannon Temple and district.

The Hato Bus Company also offers a visit to Tokyo Disneyland. Its 4½-hour tour costs ¥6,300 for adults. Its 4-hour tour includes Tokyo Tower together with Tokyo Disneyland, and costs ¥7,400 for adults.

Admission tickets to Tokyo Disneyland are sold by reservation. They are available by category:

1. Passport—usable on weekdays except for holidays, Golden Week, and summer. Admission Passport includes unlimited use of all attractions except the Shooting Gallery. Adults, ¥4,200; 12–17 years old, ¥3,800; 4–11 years old ¥2,900.

2. Guided Tour Passport aboard Disney vehicles with English speaking guide, 3½-hour course. ¥4,700 adults, 4,200 high-school and junior-high students, 3,200 children.

3. Gate tickets are also available at the Tokyo Disneyland Main Entrance on a space available basis, however, foreigners showing their passport will be allowed to buy a ticket even if the day is sold out. General admission day tickets cost: Adults, ¥2,700; 12–17 years old, ¥2,300; 4–11 years old, ¥1,600.

Starlight tickets are good for summer evenings from 5 P.M. when the park is open until 10:00 P.M. Starlight tickets are made up of an admission ticket and five attractions tickets.

Reservations for individual visitors and groups may be made through major travel agents in Japan, and directly from the Tokyo Disneyland Reservation Center, (0473) 51–1171. Tokyo Disneyland Information Center is (0473) 54–0001, or, within Tokyo, 366–5600.

Adjustments in the park's hours are continuously being made, and vary from month to month, so it is advised that you call for information concerning the time you wish to visit.

From either Nihonbashi or Otemachi Stations, the train to Urayasu, Tozai subway line, takes 15 minutes. A nonstop shuttle bus from Tokyo Disneyland bus terminal (5-minute walk from Urayasu Station) takes 20 minutes. ¥200 for adults, ¥100 for children, one way. On peak days, a bus leaves the terminal every minute. Direct shuttle bus between Tokyo Station and Disneyland operates at 15-minute intervals. ¥600 adults, ¥300 children one way.

UNESCO Village and Murayama Reservoir. Almost directly west of Tokyo and about 25 miles from the center is a huge reservoir with several lakes. It is surrounded by picnic grounds, has a nearby amusement park, and adjoins a village of cottages in the styles of all nations, built as a United Nations project. A quaint narrow gauge train runs from the park to the village. Official name of the reservoir is Lake Tama.

The area may be easily reached by automobile, though in this case you'll need a guide of some sort. By train, from Tokyo Station, take a subway to Ikebukuro (about 15 minutes), change to the Seibu-Ikebukuro line and go to Nishi-Tokorozawa (about 40 minutes), then change to the Seibu-Sayama line and ride to the terminal—Seibu Kyujomae Station. The terminal is but a few hundred feet away from UNESCO Village.

Toshimaen Amusement Park. This is a large, well-equipped amusement park in the northwest corner of Tokyo proper. It is about 45 minutes from the center by automobile. You can also ride there by subway from Tokyo Station to Ikenbukuro, where you change to a special train, that runs often, from Seibu-Ikebukuro Station to Toshima-en, the end of the line.

Yomiuriland. This is a huge recreation center on the outskirts of Tokyo, and is billed as "the world's first religious, cultural, sports, and recreation center." Golf courses, aquariums, artificial ski runs, a parachute tower and other amusement facilities, plus a pagoda housing relics of Buddha. On Tamagawa River near Kawasaki.

Toyama Traffic Park. Located at Nishi-okubo, Shinjuku-ku, this park is designed to teach children traffic safety. Those between the ages of eight and 16 may drive go-carts along roads that simulate real ones, and must obey regular rules of the road. Outdoor play equipment is available, too.

 CHILDREN'S ACTIVITIES. Tokyo, with its busy air of make-believe, can be one vast toyland for children. There are, of course, the parks, zoos, and gardens. In the city itself there are toy shops on all the main shopping streets and in many out-of-the-way areas. Tokyo's fabulous department stores also have huge toy sections, guaranteed to provide several hours' diversion for any youngster.

Some big department stores have miniature amusement rinks on their roofs. Sometimes these include small zoos of birds and monkeys. There are slides and rides of various kinds for the smaller youngsters.

Surprisingly, many children enjoy eating out with the grown-ups at Tokyo's restaurants. Eating places are often interestingly decorated, especially Japanese or Chinese restaurants, where there may be gardens with rocks and pools and where there are enough colorful shapes and gadgets such as miniature waterfalls to keep interest at a high level. Restaurant people are apt to be fond of children and anxious to help keep them amused. High chairs are nearly always available.

Baby sitting can be a problem if you're on a short visit. Most of the better hotels can arrange for a maid or someone to take care of children.

If the youngsters can stand movies all day you might take them to the **Tokyu Kaikan Building** across from the Shibuya Station, in a large shopping section about 20 minutes west by southwest of the center. There are five motion picture theaters in this one building.

Bicycling. Try the Yoyogi Park Cycling Course, where free bicycles are provided for children 15 years and younger, between the hours of 9:00 A.M. and 4:00 P.M. daily. Near Harajuku station. Other possibilities: Ichinohashi Traffic Park (taxi from Roppongi;) Kitanomaru Cycling Course, near Takebashi station. Palace Cycling Course, on Sundays and holidays.

Fishing. No standing around in the cold with never a bite, but waters full of rainbow trout that you catch as fast as you can cast your line. Artificial, but fun. Attendants clean your fish for you, and you can cook and eat them on the spot. For Akikawa River, go to Tachikawa on the Chuo line and change for Musashi Itsukaichi on the Itsukaichi line; ask for the fishing pond. For Ohtaba-gawa International Trout Fishing Ground, go from Tachikawa on the Ome line, get off at Kawai and ask for the fishing ground.

Planetarium. Easy to reach, in Tokyu Bunka Kaikan on the seventh floor at Shibuya. The performance lasts one hour, with narration in Japanese except for large groups making arrangements in advance.

Rowboating. Several sites in Tokyo have rowboats for rent. Some of the most central are: Ueno Park; the Imperial Moat at Chidorigafuchi; Akasakamitsuke.

Tokyo Tower. The Waxworks Museum on the third floor has tableaux appealing to children, as well as horror scenes better avoided. Adventure World, a Disney-type animation show on the ground floor, can keep children entertained for half a day. Taxi there from Kamiyacho subway station on the Hibiya line, or from Hamamatsu-cho station on the Yamanote line.

PARTICIPANT SPORTS. Don't expect a lot of opportunities to indulge in your favorite sport. Facilities in Tokyo are cramped, and often limited to club membership.

Several of the super deluxe hotels—but by no means all of them—have pools, outdoor for summer swimming, indoor for year-round use. Several have gymnasia. If your concern is to keep fit, take advantage of the jogging courses that exist. Again, the super deluxe hotels will help, with jogging outfits and joggers' maps.

Japan Gray Line offers a **golf** tour, daily from Tuesday to Friday. It means a full day's outing, but you do play on one of Japan's finest private golf courses, the Fuji Ace Golf Club. The cost is ￥24,000. Contact a travel agent, a hotel information desk, or telephone 433–5745 or 433–5746.

Quite satisfactory **skiing** can be enjoyed on a man-made run about an hour by train west of Tokyo, at the *Seibuen Park* adjacent to Yamaguchi and Murayama reservoirs. In winter, spring, and fall, the three major **ice skating rinks** are: *Ikebukuro Skating Center* (Ikebukuro, northwest part of Tokyo); *Korakuen Ice Palace* (near Suidobashi Station on Chuo Line) (north-center); *Tokyo Skating Rink* (near west entrance of Shinjuku Station). The Gold Rink at Shinagawa Sports Land is the nation's first exclusively for figure skating.

Bowling is available at the *Korakuen Bowling Arena,* near the Ice Palace and the baseball stadium. There are 62 AMF lanes and you can bowl from 7:00 A.M. to midnight in air-conditioned comfort. Shoes and balls can be rented here, as well as at the other lanes listed below. One game will cost you ￥300. You can try to make a reservation. The *Tokyo Bowling Centre,* in Meiji Park, now has 46 Brunswick automatic alleys, and a few of Japanese manufacture. ￥300 per game. Snack bar and restaurant. Open daily 7:00 A.M. to 11:30 P.M. The *Tower Bowl,* located in Shiba Park under the Tokyo Tower, charges ￥300 per game. It has 78 automatic alleys.

For **cyclists**, there is good news. Rent-a-bike facilities are increasing. Consult the *Japan Cycling Association* in Tokyo (582–3311), or the *Tokyo Cycling Association* (832–6895). 500 cycles are available free of charge for Sunday cyclists at Tokyo's 4.6-mile-long course round the Imperial Palace; closed to cars 10:00 A.M.–5:00 P.M. Inquiries on cycling or bicycles are handled in English at the *Bicycle PR Center* (586–0404), between 10:00 A.M. and 4:00 P.M. (2:00 P.M. on Saturdays) except on Sundays and national holidays.

For **field athletics** such as running and jumping (over a simple obstacle course setup), approach the Japan Field Athletics Ass., YH Bldg., 1–36–1 Higashi Ikebukuro, Toshima-ku.

The Tourist Information Center will give you a complete rundown on **fishing** facilities near Tokyo. About 150 species of fish are available.

The *YMCA* in Kanda, 293–1911, provides a variety of sports and games for members who pay a registration fee of ￥5,000 and a monthly fee of ￥3,000. Other sports facilities, including those for T'ai Chi, are available at reasonable rates at the *Tokyo Taiikukan,* opposite Sendagaya station (408–6191); in the bleacher basement of the *Kokuritsu Kyogijo* (National Stadium), left from Sendagaya station (403–1151); in the *Do Sports Plaza,* Sumitomo Building Annex, Nishi-Shinjuku (344–1971); and at *Tokyo Athletic Club* in Nakano (384–2131).

SPECTATOR SPORTS. Japanese **sumo** tournaments are held in Tokyo at New Year's time, in May and in September. They last 15 days. Two sides, or leagues, called *East* and *West,* compete with each other. Sumo takes place in a huge arena just beyond central Tokyo; the *New Kokugikan,* by Ryogoku Station on the Sobu line. With a taxi driver you need no other address than its name-Kokugikan.

Tickets are hard to come by, since blocks are bought up in advance by firms and organizations. Your Japanese friends will have to help you here. It is possible, sometimes, to buy tickets at the box office, but they'll be fairly distant from the ring. Complete television coverage is given.

Rabid fans attend the long daily sessions from late morning till 6:00 P.M. Food boxes and baskets are served, along with beer and sake. The lesser wrestlers start the day; the grand champions come later.

Tokyo is dotted with smaller **judo** halls and clubs, but the big center-almost the shrine of judo-is the *Kodokan* in north-central Tokyo. (1–16 Kasugacho, Bunkyo-ku—tel. 811–7151—near the Suidobashi Station on the Chuo Line.) Best hours for watching are from 5:00 to 7:00 P.M. on Tuesdays and Wednesdays, when the more advanced foreigners practice. Regular practice hours are 3:00 to 7:30 P.M. weekdays; 9:00 to 12:00 noon on Sundays.

You may be interested too in **Aikido:** at Wakamatsucho, Shinjuku (203–9236); in **Karate:** at 1–6 Ebisu, Shibuya-ku (462–1415); and in *Nippon Budokan,* the martial arts hall where judo events were held in the Olympic Games, and where many martial arts are now practiced: 2–3 Kitanomaru Koen, Chiyoda-ku, 216–0781). The nearest station is Kudanshita on the Tokyo Municipal Subway Shinjuku line and the Tozai subway line. For **T'ai-Chi Ch'uan,** Chinese exercises, approach Asahi Culture Center in the Shinjuku Sumitomo Building; or the Tokyo YMCA Athletic Gymnasium in Kanda.

If you are a **baseball** fan you'll find Tokyo a paradise. The long season breaks only for year's end and the dead of winter. There are often two major games in town and the brand of ball played is first rate. The big baseball center is at *Korakuen Stadium* in Bunkyo-ku, an amusement area that includes several arenas; a few minutes from the center of Tokyo. About once a year a major league American team visits Japan and plays a series with a Japanese all-star team. Five or six of these games will be in Tokyo. Consult your English-language newspapers for daily baseball schedules.

There are two major **racetracks** in the Tokyo area: *Tokyo Race Course,* Fuchu (about 20 miles west); and *Oi Race Course,* Samezu-machi, Ota-ku (about 6 miles south). Meets are held year-round. Excellent thoroughbreds are raced clockwise around the track. There is government controlled betting but the system is complicated, involving multiple bets something like the daily double, and you have to work with immensely long odds.

HISTORICAL SITES. Twice destroyed in modern times—once by the 1923 earthquake, once by wartime bombing during the 1940s—Tokyo doesn't have a lot to offer along the lines of ancient monuments. The **Emperor's Palace** is a new building, built in 1968, although the grounds were also the site of Edo Castle (also known as Chiyoda Castle) built by Dokan Ota (1432–1486). The Tokugawa shoguns lived in the castle for 265 years, but the palace was destroyed during World War II. The present Imperial Palace is on the site of the old western keep. It is Japanese in style, but of ferro-concrete, one story. The grounds are encircled by moats and high stone walls.

As the seat of government, the **National Diet Building** warrants attention. Visitors are admitted to the gallery when the Diet (legislature) is in session. The building, 18 years in construction, was opened in 1936. It is at Kasumigaseki near Kokkai-Gijidomae Station, which is on both the Marunouchi and Chiyoda subway lines. **Asakusa Kannon Temple** has to be on everyone's itinerary. With its traditional architecture, enormous temple gate, and giant paper lanterns, it represents feudal times in today's modern city. The main hall is a replica of the one built in 1651 and destroyed in World War II. Asakusa is the name of the nearest station on the Ginza subway line.

Honganji Temple is at Tsukiji, south of the Ginza district in Chuo Ward. The nearest station is Higashi Ginza on the Hibiya subway line. The temple is on an historical site, though the present building dates from only 1935. Honganji Temple was founded in 1630 and destroyed repeatedly by fires. It is a branch of Nishi-Honganji, headquarters of the Jodo-Shinshu sect of Buddhism in Kyoto. **Zojoji Temple** was founded in 1393 and is the headquarters of the Jodo sect of Buddhism. Main Hall was destroyed in World War II, but a new ferro-concrete building was completed in 1974. The Main Gate, an "Important Cultural Property," was built in 1605.

Yasukuni Shrine honors the memory of the war dead, and comes the closest to being a national monument. Shrine buildings, in themselves, are usually quiet, austere, dignified places, not always striking in appearance. Shrine grounds, however, with trees and stone lanterns, conjure a special atmosphere. Yasukuni is on Kudan Hill, a few minutes walk from Kudanshita station on both the Tozai subway line and the Tokyo Municipal Shinjuku line.

Meiji Shrine, dedicated to Emperor Meiji, who died in 1912, and to his consort, was completed in 1920. It's a holy pilgrimage center. Main shrine, oratory, and some other buildings were destroyed in 1945, restored in 1958. The nearest station is Harajuku on the Yamanote line. **Hie Shrine** is another that has a sense of grandeur and nobility. Dedicated to Oyamakui-no-Mikoto, an ancient Shinto deity, the shrine was very popular during the Edo Period (1603–1867). Main shrine and other structures were burned during the war; the new main shrine was constructed in 1959 and the gate in 1962. Hie Shrine is on a hilltop in Akasaka, near the Capitol Tokyu Hotel. Near Akasaka-Mitsuke Station on both the Ginza and the Marunouchi subway lines, and Kokkai Gijidomae Station on the Chiyoda and Marunouchi lines.

 LIBRARIES. There are several libraries in Tokyo that have English-languages books available. The following are the main ones: **American Center.** ABC Kaikan, 6–3 Shiba-Koen 2-chome, Minato Ward; 436–0901. **British Council.** Iwanami Hall, 1 Kanda Jinbocho 2-chome Chiyoda Ward; 264–3721. **The Japan Foundation.** Park Bldg., 3–6 Kioicho, Chiyoda Ward; 263–4504. **National Diet Library.** 10–1 Nagatacho 1-chome, Chiyoda Ward; 581–2331. **Tokyo Metropolitan Central Library.** 7–13 Minami-Azabu 5-chome, Minato Ward; 442–8451.

 MUSEUMS. Of course, museum riches emphasize Orientalia, but Tokyo has astonishing wealth in Western treasures also. Insatiable curiosity has long been a characteristic of Tokyo citizens. Those who haven't been able to travel to America or Europe have wanted to see all they can of other countries at home. Those museums that put on shows brought in from abroad are assured of record crowds.

As well as the establishments that show their own collections, department stores and galleries often stage special exhibitions. Several department stores also have sections where they have antiques on sale.

Please note that **Ueno Park** is the center for Tokyo's principal museums. The *Tokyo National Museum* is there, with the finest and most extensive collection of Japanese art and architecture. The *Tokyo Metropolitan Art Museum* is there, with permanent displays including many familiar masterpieces. The *National Museum of Western Art* is there, featuring the famous Matsukata colection of masterpieces with original pieces by Rodin and works of Matisse, Cézanne, and Picasso. And the *National Science Museum* is there, with displays of unfamiliar Japanese flora and fauna.

Other museums and galleries are to be found all over this vast, spreading city of Tokyo. For what is on each week, see Tokyo's English-language newspapers and, especially, *Tour Companion.*

CULTURE AND HISTORY

Calligraphy Museum. Materials related to the art of calligraphy. From Uguisudani Station on the Yamanote line; 872–2645. Closed Mondays.

Communications Museum. Everything from early postal services to the next generation of telephones. Also a good stamp display. From Otemachi Station on the Marunouchi subway line; 270–3841. Closed Mondays.

Constitution Museum. Materials on constitutional government, the Diet, and so on. From Kokkai-Gijidomae Station on the Marunouchi subway line; 581–1651. Closed Sundays and holidays.

Daimyo Clock Museum. Private collection of old Japanese-style clocks. From Nezu Station on the Chiyoda subway line; 821–6913. Closed Mondays.

Earthquake Museum. Materials on the Great Kanto Earthquake of 1923. From Ryogoku Station on the Sobu line; 622–1208. Closed Mondays.

Furniture Museum. Display of old Japanese furniture. Take bus from Tokyo Station to Harumi, alighting at Harumi Post Office bus stop; 533–0098. Closed Sundays and holidays.

Haiku Museum. Materials on haiku poetry and poets. From Okubo Station on the Sobu line; 367–6621. Closed Thursdays.

Iwasaki Chihiro Picture Book Museum. Gallery and reading room of children's books, including some English ones. From Kami-Igusa Station on the Seibu-Shinjuku line from Seibu-Shinjuku Station; 995–0612. Closed Mondays.

Japan Calligraphy Museum. Materials on the art of calligraphy. From Tokiwadai Station on the Tobu-Tojo line from Ikebukuro; 965–2611. Closed Mondays and Tuesdays.

Japan Toy Museum. Toys of the postwar period on display. From Minami-Senju Station on the Hibiya subway line; 871–3171. Closed Mondays, Tuesdays, and Wednesdays.

Kite Museum. Exhibition of kites from around Japan and around the world. From Nihonbashi Station on the Ginza subway line; 275–2704. Closed Sundays, holidays.

Meiji University Penal Museum. Materials on the history of crime and punishment; From Ochanomizu Station on the Chuo line; 296–4431. Closed Sundays.

Museum of Industrial Safety Techniques. How to prevent accidents at work. From Tamachi Station on the Yamanote line; 453–8441. Closed Sundays and holidays.

Musical Instruments Museum. Belonging to Musashino University of Music. Instruments from around the world on display. From Ekoda Station on the

Seibu-Ikebukuro line from Ikebukuro; 992–1121. Open on Wednesdays only, from 10:00–3:00 P.M. Closed during vacation.

NHK Broadcasting Museum. Materials related to the history of broadcasting. From Kamiyacho Station on the Hibiya subway line; 433–5211. Closed Mondays.

Paper Museum. Materials related to Japanese-style and Western-style paper. From Oji Station on the Keihin-Tohoku line; 911–3545. Closed Mondays and holidays.

Printing Museum. Take a look at how stamps and banknotes get made. From Ichigaya Station on the Sobu line; 268–3271. Closed Mondays.

Shitamachi Museum. A museum about the life of the common people in the Edo Period, including homes, lifestyles, and games. From Ueno Station on the Yamanote line; near Shinobazu Pond; 823–7451. Closed Mondays, holidays.

Sugino Gakuen Costume Museum. Materials on women's fashion both old and new, national and international. From Meguro Station on the Yamanote line; 491–8151. Closed Sundays, holidays and in August.

Sword Museum. Collection of Japanese swords. From Sangubashi Station on the Odakyu line from Shinjuku; 379–1386. Closed Mondays.

Tobacco and Salt Museum. Standing displays on these two items, plus special exhibitions of ukiyoe prints. From Shibuya Station on the Yamanote line; 476–2041. Closed Mondays.

Tokyo Modern Literature Museum. Materials on modern Japanese literature. From Komaba Todaimae Station on the Inokashira line from Shibuya; 466–5150. Closed Mondays.

Transportation Museum. Materials on the history of transport. Children will love it. From Akihabara Station on the Sobu line; 251–8481. Closed Mondays.

Waseda University Theatrical Museum. Materials on national and international theater. From Waseda Station on the Tozai subway line; 203–4141. Closed Sundays and holidays.

World Bag Museum. Over 300 bags on display from 28 countries. From Asakusa Station on the Toei-Asakusa or Ginza subway line; 843–8141. Open the 1st–15th of every month; closed Saturdays, Sundays, and holidays.

SCIENCE

Goto Planetarium. If there's too much smog in the air outside, view the stars from inside. From Shibuya Station on the Yamanote line; 407–7409. Closed Mondays.

Kokugakuin University Archeological Museum. A look at what Japan's Stone Age was like. From Shibuya Station; 409–0111.

Meguro Parasitological Museum. Plenty of fascinating specimens here. From Meguro Station on the Yamanote line; 716–1264. Closed Mondays and holidays.

Museum of Maritime Science. Housed in a building shaped like a ship. Good for children. Located in Tokyo Bay. Take bus from Monzennakacho Station on Tozai subway line, or boat from Takeshiba Wharf in Hamamatsucho; 528–1111. No holidays.

National Science Museum. All the sciences under one roof. In Ueno Park; 822–0111. Closed Mondays.

Science and Technology Museum. Keeps up to date with all the latest inventions. From Takebashi Station on the Tozai subway line; 212–8471. No holidays.

Sunshine Planetarium. In Ikebukuro's Sunshine 60 skyscraper; 989–3466. No holidays.

Telecommunications Museum. For the latest in computers. From Tokyo Station; 241–8080. Closed Mondays.

Toshimaen Insect Museum. Inside Toshimaen amusement ground. From Toshimaen Station on the Seibu-Ikebukuro line; 990–3131. No holidays.

ART MUSEUMS

All have changing exhibitions and are closed Mondays. Museums also sometimes close on national holidays, sometimes on the day following.

Ancient Orient Museum. On the 7th floor of Sunshine City Culture Center at Ikebukuro; 989–3491. Prehistoric items excavated in Syria by a research team from Tokyo University. Nearest station: Ikebukuro on JR Yamanote line and Marunouchi subway line. Open 10:00 A.M. to 4:30 P.M.

Bridgestone Art Museum. 1–1 Kyobashi, on the main Chuo-dori, Ginza district; 563–0241. Traditional and modern paintings, both Japanese and Western, and some Greek and modern sculpture. Nearest station: Kyobashi on the Ginza subway line. Open 10:00 A.M. to 5:00 P.M.

Crafts Gallery, National Museum of Modern Art. 3 Kitanomaru Koen, Chiyoda-ku; 211–7781. Exhibits dyed cloths, porcelain, lacquerware, metal works. Nearest station: Takebashi on the Tozai subway line. Open 10:00 A.M. to 5:00 P.M.

Goto Art Museum. 3–9–25 Kaminoge, Setagaya-ku; 703–0661. Features stone Buddhas in the hillside garden, many old mirrors, paintings, Buddhist sutras and books, ceramics. Scrolls illustrating the Heian Period story *Genji Monogatari* are exhibited for only one week in May. Nearest station: Kaminoge on the Denen Toshi line. Open 10:00 A.M. to 4:00 P.M.

Hara Museum of Contemporary Art. 4–7–11 Kita Shinagawa, Shinagawa-ku; 445–0651. Concentrates on the very modern, and often holds temporary exhibitions. Nearest station: Shinagawa on JR Yamanote line and Keihin line. Open 10:00 A.M. to 4:00 P.M.

Hatakeyama Collection. 2–10–12 Shiroganedai, Minato-ku; 447–5787. A very select collection that emphasises tea ceremony ceramics, some of them having belonged to the original tea master Sen Rikyu. Nearest station: Takanawadai on the Tokyo Municipal Subway Asakusa line. Open 10 A.M. to 4 P.M. Closed Mondays, and the last two weeks of March, June, September, and December, and the first week of January.

Idemitsu Art Museum. 9th floor, Imperial Theater Building, 3–1–1 Marunouchi, Chiyoda-ku; 213–3111. The private collection of a Japanese oil king comprises Chinese and Japanese pottery, prints, and screens. Nearest station: Hibiya on the Hibiya subway line, the Tokyo Municipal subway Asakusa line, and the Chiyoda subway line. Open 10:00 A.M. to 5:00 P.M.

Matsuoka Museum of Art. 5–22–10 Shimbashi, Minato-ku; 431–8284. Houses 20,000 international items of a family collection. Nearest station: Onarimon, on the Tokyo Municipal subway Mita line. Open 10:00 A.M. to 5:00 P.M.

National Museum of Modern Art. 3 Kitanomaru Koen, Chiyoda-ku; 214–2561. A mixed collection reflecting what has been going on in Japanese arts since the Meiji Period. Nearest station: Takebashi on the Tozai subway line. Open 10:00 A.M. to 5:00 P.M.

National Museum of Western Art. Ueno Park; 828–5131. Le Corbusier designed the main building, which was opened in 1959. See Museums introduction. Open 9:00 A.M.–4:00 P.M.

Nezu Art Museum. 6–5–36 Minami Aoyama, Minato-ku; 400–2536. Features Chinese bronzes, lacquerware, ceramics, and some really exquisite scrolls, the latter being displayed only by appointment. The garden here is also a work of art. Nearest station: Omote-sando on the Chiyoda subway line, the Hanzo-mon subway line, and the Ginza subway line. Open 9:30 A.M. to 4:30 P.M., except September to November when it opens and closes 30 minutes earlier.

Nippon Mingeikan. (Museum of Folk Crafts), 4–3–33 Komaba, Meguro-ku; 467–4527. A fine display of many Japanese handicrafts, mostly of wood, pottery, and straw, in a rustic old building. Special folkcraft sales during November, in time for Christmas shopping. Nearest station: Komaba on the Inogashira line from Shibuya. Open 10:00 A.M. to 4:00 P.M. Closed throughout January and February.

Okura Shukokan Museum. 3 Aoi-cho, Akasaka, Minato-ku; 583–0781. In the garden of the Hotel Okura, this museum contains a wide range of items, both European and ancient Oriental. Nearest station: Toranomon on the Ginza subway line. Open 10:00 A.M. to 4:00 P.M.

Ota Memorial Ukiyoe Museum. Harajuku; 403–0880. Collection of ukiyoe woodblock prints. Open 10:30 A.M. to 5:30 P.M. Closed Mon. and from 25th to end of each month.

Riccar Museum. 2–3–6, Ginza; 571–3254. Specializes in ukiyoe prints. Near-est station: Ginza on the Ginza subway line, the Marunouchi subway line, and the Hibiya subway line. Open 10:00 A.M. to 6:00 P.M.

Seibu Art Museum. Seibu Department Store, 12th fl., Ikebukuro; 981–0111.

Seiji Togo Museum. Nishi Shinjuku; 349–3080.

Striped House Museum. Roppongi; 405–8108.

Suntory Art Museum. 1–2–3 Moto Akasaka, Minato-ku; 470–1073. In the Suntory Building, this museum features articles from the Edo and Muromachi periods. Nearest station: Akasaka-Mitsuke, on the Ginza subway line, the Marunouchi subway line, and the Hanzomon subway line. Open 10:00 A.M. to 5:00 P.M.

Tokyo Central Museum of Arts. Ginza, Boeki Bldg., 5th fl.; 564–0711.

Tokyo Metropolitan Art Museum. Ueno Park; 823–6921. The museum often stages temporary exhibitions of contemporary art. See also Museums introduc-tion. Open 9:00 A.M. to 4:00 P.M.

Tokyo Metropolitan Teien Museum. Meguro-dori, Meguro-ku; 265–2111. Opened as a museum in 1983, the building used to be the mansion of a prince. Designed by a French architect, it is in art-deco style and still has many original fittings. Since the war it has been used as a guest house for foreign dignitaries. Now it features changing exhibitions, many of them brought for limited periods from overseas. Sculptures in the garden. Nearest station: Meguro on JR Yama-note line. Hours and closing dates are irregular. Call for information.

Tokyo National Museum. Ueno Park; 822–1111. Houses more than 86,000 items, many of them designated National Treasures. It is the largest museum in Japan. See also Museums introduction. Open 9:00 A.M. to 4:00 P.M.

Ueno Royal Museum. (Ueno no Mori Bijutsukan) Ueno Park; 833–4191.

Yamatane Art Museum. 2–30 Kabuto-cho, Nihonbashi, Chuo-ku. The only museum in the world dedicated specially to Japanese paintings, including pastel-type Nihon-ga, of the last 100 years. Art Academy member Architect Taniguchi designed the interior. Nearest station: Kayabacho, on the Hibiya subway line and the Tozai subway line. Open 11:00 A.M. to 5:00 P.M.

PHOTO GALLERIES

Canon Salon. Ginza; 571–7358. Closed Sunday.

Contax Salon. Harajuku; 400–2651. Closed Sunday.

Fuji Photo Salon. Sukiyabashi; 571–9411. Closed Sunday.

Konishiroku Photo Gallery. Shinjuku, 320–4460. Closed Sunday.

Nikon Salon Ginza. 562–5756. Closed Monday.
Nikon Salon Shinjuku. 344–0565. Closed Monday.
Pentax Forum. Shinjuku; 348–2941. Open daily.
Photo Gallery International. Toranomon; 501–9123. Closed Sunday and holidays.
Polaroid Gallery. Toranomon; 434–5201. Closed Saturday, Sunday, and holidays.
Zeit Foto Salon. Nihonbashi; 246–1370. Closed Sunday.

DEPARTMENT STORE GALLERIES

Daimaru. Tokyo Sta.; 212–8011. Closed Wednesdays.
Isetan. Shinjuku; 352–1111. Closed Wednesdays.
Keio. Shinjuku; 341–2111. Closed Thursdays.
Matsuya. Ginza; 567–1211. Closed Thursdays.
Matsuzakaya. Ginza; 572–1111. Closed Thursdays.
Matsuzakaya. Ueno; 832–1111. Closed Wednesdays.
Mitsukoshi. Nihonbashi; 241–3311. Closed Mondays.
Odakyu. Shinjuku; 342–8416. Close Thursdays.
Printemps. Ginza; 567–0077. Closed Wednesdays.
Seibu. Ikebururo; 981–0111. Closed Thursdays.
Shibuya Seibu. Shibuya; 462–0111. Closed Wednesdays.
Takashimaya. Nihonbashi; 211–4111. Closed Wednesdays.
Tobu. Ikebukuro; 981–2111. Closed Wednesdays.
Tokyo Nihonbashi. 211–0511. Closed Thursdays.
Tokyu Toyoko. Shibuya; 477–3111. Closed Thursdays.

STAGE. The following are Tokyo's principal theaters for traditional shows: **Ginza Nohgakudo.** 6–5–15 Ginza, Chuo-ku; 571–3872 or 571–0197. Noh and Kyogen. **Hosho Suidobashi Nohgakudo.** 1–5–9 Hongo, Bunkyo-ku; 811–4843. Noh and Kyogen. **Kabuki-za.** 4–12–15 Ginza, Chuo-ku; 541–3131. Usually stages Kabuki. **Kanze Kaikan.** 1–16–4 Shoto, Shibuya-ku; 469–5241. Stages Noh and Kyogen. **Kita Nohgakudo.** 4–6–9 Kami-osaki, Shinagawa-ku; 491–7773. Noh and Kyogen. **Kokuritsu Gekijo.** The National Theater, 4–1 Hayabusa, Chiyoda-ku; 265–7411. Stages shows of different types, including dances and Bunraku. **Umewaka Nohgakudo.** 2–16–14 Higashi-Nakano, Nakano-ku; 363–7748. Noh and Kyogen. **Yarai Nohgakudo.** 60 Yarai-cho, Shinjuku-ku; 268–7311. Noh and Kyogen. The new *National Noh Theater* is at 4–18–1 Sendagaya, Shibuya-ku; 423–1313. Reached from Sendagaya Station on the Sobu line.

MUSIC. Scarcely a night passes in Tokyo without a concert somewhere, and nearly all are well attended. Japan's own soloists and ensembles vie for attention with visiting foreign performers. There are several symphony orchestras of varying degrees of excellence in Tokyo. Best known are the following. Give them a call if you wish to have a seasonal program mailed to you, or to reserve seats for a single concert or a series. Usually someone at the other end of the phone speaks English. The **Japan Philharmonic Orchestra,** 354–9011; the **New Japan Philharmonic,** 501–5639; the **Tokyo Metropolitan Symphony,** 822–0726; the **Tokyo Philharmonic,** 591–6742; the **Yomiuri Nippon Symphony,** 270–6191; the **NHK Symphony Orchestra,** 443–0271. Individual tickets cost from ¥2,000 to ¥5,000. Prices will be very much higher in the case of distinguished visiting foreign artists.

Foreign orchestras, opera companies, ballet troups, ensembles, and solo artists are constantly coming to Tokyo, usually in the fall and winter seasons. Leading American and European organizations, including Soviet groups, make frequent tours. There are also famed jazz, popular, and novelty performers from time to time. Occasionally, foreign artists work as guest performers or conductors with Japanese musical groups.

Tickets to the best concerts are quickly sold out. The best method is to get them about two weeks in advance at any of Tokyo's several *Play Guides*—ticket offices that handle reservations for every imaginable sort of event. Many of the major department stores have *Play Guides* on the first floor or in the basement.

Tokyo's best concert halls are the following: **Bunka Kaikan.** Tokyo Festival Hall, 5–45 Ueno Park, Daito-ku; 828–2111. There is a small hall on the second floor of the same building. It has the same telephone number. **Hibiya Kokaido.** Hibiya Public Hall, 1–3 Hibiya-Park, Chiyoda-ku; 591–6388. **Iino Hall.** 7th floor Iino Building, 2–1–1 Uchisaiwai-cho, Chiyoda-ku; 506–3251. **Koseinenkin Kaikan.** 19 Banshu-cho, Shinjuku-ku; 356–1111. The small hall, with the same telephone number, is in the basement. **NHK Hall.** 2–2–1 Jinnan, Shibuya-ku; 465–1111. **Nihon Seinenkan.** 15 Kasumigaoka-machi, Shinjuku-ku; 401–0101. **Toranomon Hall.** 3–2–3 Kasumigaseki, Chiyoda-ku; 580–1251. **Yubinchokin Hall.** 13, Shiba Park, Minato-ku; 433–7211. **Suntory Hall.** 1–13–1 Akasaka; 505–1001. Tokyo's newest, in Ark Hills.

 TOKYO SHOPPING. Shopping in Tokyo can be either delightful and fruitful or bewildering to the tourist. The trick is to know about yourself—what you want to buy and how much time you have at your disposal. Does your shopping list contain the names of specific items or does it just have names of persons for whom you want to buy "something" as a gift? Does your schedule allow for shopping only a couple of hours on just one day or do you have two or three days or a week? And, how much confidence do you have in moving around Tokyo? Plan your shopping foray in accordance with your answers to these questions and you can be sure of a successful expedition.

The person who has little time should stick to the hotel arcades or department stores and one-stop shopping centers. These are easy to locate, so you won't waste hours finding them. And, they stock a fair variety of items, ranging from folkcraft items and tourist souvenirs to the latest electronic products. If you don't have anything specific on your mind, these are the places to browse around to look for something that would be suitable as a gift for any person on your list.

If you have little time but you have one or two specific items you want to buy, such as lacquerware or a camera, you should head straight for one of the many specialty shops mentioned below, where the range of choice is wide.

If you have plenty of time and want to make the best buy possible, whether you are looking for a specific article or just something suitable, it might be a good idea to spend the first couple of hours browsing through a department store or a one-stop shopping center, noting the choices, quality, and prices. Then, go to a specialty store or one of the many centers where store after store specializes in the same product and where some bargaining is possible, such as *Akihabara* for electric appliances and electronic gadgets, *Asakusabashi* for dolls, *Harajuku* for boutiques and fashion goods, *Kanda* for books, or *Asakusa* for a slice of old Japan and articles that are out-and-out Japanese.

To go to stores outside your hotel, the most efficient and least time-consuming means of transport is generally the subway or the Japanese Railways (JR) trains. Taxis could be frustrating because roads are congested and sometimes traffic crawls slower than you can walk. (For information on Tokyo's transport system, pick up "Tour Companion," a giveaway weekly, at the counter of your hotel or airline.)

One final note: Most of the small stores do not have anyone who can speak English. If you need to call for information, have someone who can speak Japanese do it for you.

HOTEL ARCADES

Most of the hotels have shopping arcades, which have a number of obvious advantages. For one, the stores offer the range of articles that tourists usually purchase. You don't have to worry about transportation and waste time walking around the streets with a map in hand. The clerks speak English and the shops are branches of reputable and well-established stores, not only of Tokyo but also of Kyoto and other places. The prices in an arcade shop are the same as in its main store.

The **Imperial Hotel Arcade,** for example, in the basement of the Imperial Hotel, has *Mikimoto* and *Uyeda,* both big names in pearls, *Hanae Mori* boutique, and *Suga Camera,* in addition to stores dealing in antiques, ceramics, toys, ukiyo-e woodblock prints, watches, electronic products, and stationery, including Japanese-style greeting cards. The latest addition to the hotel is the **Imperial Plaza,** which houses 64 world-famous shops and boutiques, not only of Japan but also of France, Britain, Switzerland, Italy, and West Germany, including *Lanvin, Gucci, Celine,* and *Cartier.*

Hotel arcades invariably have a bookstore where foreign magazines and books on Japan are available. Many hotel arcade shops are open throughout the year, including Sundays.

ONE-STOP SHOPPING

International Arcade (591–2764), one of Tokyo's biggest bargain centers, is only a few steps from the Imperial Hotel. It houses a number of tax-free shops, most of which are stores of well-established Tokyo companies and all of which specialize in Japanese products that are proven favorites of tourists. They deal in quality name brands.

Tax-free prices and, in some cases, additional discounts are available. Clerks are multilingual and communication is no problem. A great variety of items from pearls and cameras to sophisticated electronic gear, kimono, and small souvenirs for the youngsters is available. The International Arcade is open from 9:30 A.M. to 7:00 P.M. daily. Two of the shops are:

Hayashi Kimono (501–4014). Has a huge stock of kimono, both for men and women, plus obi and items such as happi coats and tablecloths made of kimono and obi fabric to suit the Western taste. Used, but clean and good-as-new, high quality obi and gorgeous wedding kimono can be had at a fraction of what they cost new.

Sundry Camera (501–5774). Specializes in electronic goods, name brand cameras, lenses, filters, tripods, and other camera equipment as well as pocket calculators. Overseas shipping service is available from 9:30 A.M. to 7:00 P.M. daily.

Japan Taxfree Center, 5–8–6 Toranomo, Minato-ku (432–4351), is conveniently located—within walking distance of Hotel Okura and about 50 meters from the Kamiya-cho Station on the Hibiya subway line. Its eight-story building catches the eye as soon as you surface from the subway. It has pearls and accessories on the 1st floor, kimono and dolls on the 2nd, watches and china-ware on the 3rd, handicrafts and gift items on the 4th, electric appliances and toys on the 5th, and cameras and a one-hour photo printing service on the 6th. There is also a cozy cafeteria on the 7th floor to rest your tired feet. Open 9:30 A.M.–5:30 P.M. daily throughout the year except on Wednesdays between December 1 to February 28.

Sukiyabashi Shopping Center (571–0495), across the road from the International Arcade, houses many stores selling apparel, fabrics, sporting goods, cameras, jewelry, pearls, Japanese sweets, books, etc. The center also has coffee shops, restaurants, and snack stands under its roof. Patronized almost entirely by ordinary Japanese consumers. Open 10:00 A.M.–8:30 P.M. daily throughout the year.

Nikkatsu Shopping Arcade, in Hibiya Park Building at a corner of the Hibiya intersection, is small but has a number of attractive stores selling popular tourist items. Most store hours in the arcade are 9:00 A.M. to 7:00 P.M., although some stores close at 6:00 P.M.

TOC (Tokyo Oroshiuri Center) is about 10 minutes walk from Gotanda Station of JR Yamanote Loop Line or of the Toei Asakusa-sen subway line. Surfacing from the subway station you will come out on wide Sakurada Dori. Take that wide road, using the overhead passageway and crossing Meguro River. You will soon find a giant sign "TOC" on top of a big building ahead on the right-hand side. TOC is a consumer's heaven, housing what seems like hundreds of wholesale dealers, many of whom sell directly to individuals. There is not much glamour in the merchandise available, but TOC is one of the few places in Tokyo where you can drive a hard bargain on already discounted merchandise. Shops here sell furniture, furs, accessories, watches, jewelry, Chinese fans, ready-to-wear apparel for men, women, and children, and a lot more.

DEPARTMENT STORES

If your shopping time is limited and if your shopping list contains a variety of items or if you are undecided about what to buy, the most convenient place to go is a department store. Big department stores are found in all the subcenters of Tokyo.

Ginza-Nihonbashi Area

Ginza is Japan's most celebrated quality shopping district. There are almost a dozen big department stores in this area, all fronting Chuo-dori Ave., popularly called Ginza Street.

Mitsukoshi in Nihonbashi (241–3311), the oldest in Japan, is at Mitsukoshi-mae Station of the Ginza subway line. It is *the* prestige store. A number of big-name boutiques are located here, such as *Balenciaga, Givenchy, Celine, Chanel, Bartolo Bartolomei, Oscar de la Renta,* and *Dunhill.* The store is noted for its stock of kimono and obi materials and fine selection of ceramics, lacquerware, and chinaware. Open 10:00 A.M.–6:00 P.M. Closed on Mondays.

Takashimaya (211–4111), a short distance from the Ginza-side exit of Nihonbashi Station on the Ginza subway line, is modern and one of the largest in Japan, famous for its high quality merchandise, especially its excellent kimono section. It boasts a floor layout that makes shopping very easy. The folkcraft section on the 7th floor offers both Japanese and imported articles and is a must for tourists. Its fashion section features *Chanel, Laroche, Courreges, Givenchy, Lanvin, Celine, Boucheron, Dunhill, Louis Vuitton, Gucci,* and *Salvadore Ferrogamo.* It also features famous Japanese fashion designers such as Jun Ashida,

Yuki Torii, Issey Miyake, Kansai Yamamoto and Kenzo Takada. The curio section in the 1st basement is one of the most popular haunts of Tokyo's foreign residents. There is a special corner devoted to old textiles. This is the only department store in Japan that sells Rosenthal chinaware. Open 10:00 A.M.–6:00 P.M. daily; 10:00 A.M.–6:30 P.M. on Fridays and Saturdays. Closed on Wednesdays.

Tokyu (211–0511), located between Takashimaya and Mitsukoshi and closer to Nihombashi Station, has a popular image and is preferred by the ordinary housewife. Prices are moderate. Its furniture section has a good stock of Swedish furniture of Ikeya brand. Open 10:00 A.M.–6:00 P.M.; 6:30 P.M. on Saturdays, Sundays, and national holidays. Closed on Thursdays.

Mitsukoshi (562–1111), at a corner of the Ginza 4-chome intersection of Chuo-dori and Harumi-dori. One of the branches of Mitsukoshi, this one is oriented to young people. Open 10:00 A.M.–6:00 P.M. Closed on Mondays.

Matsuzakaya (572–1111), located one block toward Shimbashi from Ginza 4-chome intersection, is one of the oldest department stores in Japan and has a good kimono fabric section. Open 10:00 A.M.–6:00 P.M. daily; 6:30 P.M. on Sundays. Closed on Wednesdays.

Matsuya (567–1211), located one block toward Nihonbashi from Ginza 4-chome intersection and just above Ginza Station of the Ginza subway line. A very popular store among male and female salaried workers. Prices are moderate and store layout makes shopping easy. It is known for its good stock of household accessories as well as folkcraft items and play things native to various parts of Japan. Open 10:00 A.M.–6:00 P.M. daily, but until 6:30 P.M. on Saturdays and Sundays. Closed on Thursdays.

Wako (562–2111), at a corner of Ginza 4-chome intersection opposite Mitsukoshi. Strictly speaking this does not fall in the category of either department store or specialty store. It has a high-class image like Saks Fifth Avenue in New York. Specializes in quality, high-priced, luxurious fashion items and accessories, including clothing. The glassware section is famous. It has what is probably the widest selection of Seiko-brand timepieces. Open 10:00 A.M.–5:30 P.M. Closed on Sundays and national holidays.

Yurakucho-Tokyo Station Area

Hankyu (573–2231), at the Sukiyabashi intersection over the Ginza Station of the Marunouchi subway line and opposite the Sony Building, is popular with young office girls working in the Ginza area. Large stock of medium-priced fashion goods and accessories. Open 10:00 A.M.–6:00 P.M. Closed on Thursdays.

Sogo (284–6711), adjacent to JR Yurakucho Station, is the Tokyo branch of Sogo Department Store of Osaka. Popular with salaried men and women. Open 10:00 A.M.–6:00 P.M. daily, but until 6:30 P.M. on Fridays and Saturdays. Closed on Thursdays.

Daimaru (212–8011), in JR Tokyo Station Building, is the Tokyo branch of the famous chain originating in the Kansai region surrounding Osaka. Popular with men because it has a good men's wear section. Open 10:00 A.M.–6:00 P.M. Closed on Wednesdays.

Printemps Ginza (433–9300/9301), two minutes from Yurakucho Station, specializes in French products. Open 10:00 A.M. to 6:00 P.M. daily except Wednesday.

Mullion, housing both **Seibu** and **Hankyu,** in twin buildings across from Yurakucho Station, Ginza's newest. Open 10 A.M.–6 P.M. Closed on Thursdays.

Shinjuku Area

Shinjuku is one of Tokyo's many subcenters and is a city in itself. It is the terminal of three interurban private railways lines—Odakyu, Keio, and Seibu.

Isetan (352–1111), less than 5 minutes walk from JR Shinjuku Station and just above Shinjuku Sanchome Station of the Marunouchi subway line, is contemporary and Western-oriented, which makes it popular with the young people. Its atmosphere is more casual than that of the dignified Mitsukoshi or the sophisticated Takashimaya. It has one building exclusively for men's goods and a very good furniture and interior section. Open 10:00 A.M.–6:00 P.M. daily, but until 6:30 P.M. on Saturdays, Sundays, and national holidays. Closed on Wednesdays.

Mitsukoshi (354–1111), across the street from Isetan, is a branch of Mitsukoshi in Nihonbashi and is good for casual shopping. Open 10:00 A.M.–6:00 P.M. Closed on Mondays.

Odakyu (342–1111) is conveniently located in the Shinjuku Station building and a short distance from Shinjuku Station of the Marunouchi subway line. It is known for its cosmetics section on the 1st floor where special cosmetics for delicate and sensitive skin are available. A separate building known as Odakyu Halc building specializes in furniture and interior goods. Open 10:00 A.M.–6:00 P.M. daily, but until 6:30 P.M. on Saturdays, Sundays, and national holidays. Closed on Thursdays.

Keio (342–2111) is conveniently located in the Shinjuku Terminal Bldg. Its policy is "simple life," and it sells only the essentials of life. Open 10:00 A.M.–6:00 P.M. daily, but until 6:30 P.M. on Fridays, Saturdays, and national holidays. Closed on Thursdays.

Shibuya Area

Considered a notch above Shinjuku in class, the Shibuya area is accessible by JR Yamanote loop line, and the Ginza and Hanzomon subway lines.

Tokyu (477–3111) is about 10 minutes walk from the JR Shibuya Station and Shibuya terminal of the Ginza subway line. This is an elegant store selling high-class merchandise. Spaciously laid out, the store makes shopping a leisurely pleasure. It offers attractive imported goods. Open 10:00 A.M.–6:00 P.M. daily, but until 6:30 P.M. on Saturdays, Sundays, and national holidays. Closed on Thursdays.

Toyoko (477–3111), in the Shibuya Terminal Building, is the sister store of Tokyu, and caters to the masses. Open 10:00 A.M.–6:00 P.M. daily, but until 6:30 P.M. on Saturdays, Sundays, and national holidays. Closed on Thursdays.

Seibu (462–0111), several minutes walk from JR Shibuya Station, has a good stock of fashion apparel. Open 10:00 A.M.–6:00 P.M. daily, but until 6:30 P.M. on Saturdays, Sundays, and national holidays. Closed on Thursdays.

Parco (464–5111), several minutes walk from JR Shibuya Station and near Seibu Department Store, is a department store housing fashionable specialty shops very popular with the young and Western-oriented. Open 10:00 A.M.–8:30 P.M. daily throughout the year.

Tokyu Hands (476–5461), near Parco, about 10 minutes walk from JR Shibuya Station, is a specialty store and a paradise for do-it-yourself enthusiasts. It has a complete stock of handicraft, needlework, and sewing tools, gadgets, and materials as well as of paints, and carpentry tools and materials. The electronics parts section, the audio workshop, and the video center are musts for audiophiles. The store is known for its wide stock of scale models of trains, planes, ships, etc. Its fabric section is a must for those looking for fabrics, particularly indigo Chinese cotton fabric. Open 10:00 A.M.–8:00 P.M. Closed on the second and third Wednesdays of each month.

Ikebukuro Area

Seibu (981–0111), conveniently located in the Ikebukuro Terminal Building, has the largest floor space among all the department stores in Tokyo. Each floor is so long that a section has been set up in the middle of each floor where chairs are available for a short rest. Seibu has very good furniture and interior sections besides a good collection of chinaware, pottery, and lacquerware. Its Sports Center satisfies the equipment needs of enthusiasts of any sport. Open 10:00 A.M.–6:00 P.M. daily, but until 6:30 P.M. on Saturdays, Sundays, and national holidays. Closed on Thursdays.

Tobu (981–2211), located on the opposite side of Seibu in the Ikebukuro Terminal. It has a large stock of merchandise like a supermarket. Open 10:00 A.M.–6:00 P.M. daily, but until 6:30 P.M. on Saturdays and Sundays. Closed on Wednesdays.

Mitsukoshi (987–1111), a short distance from JR Ikebukuro Station facing Seibu Department Store, is a branch of Mitsukoshi in Nihonbashi. Open 10:00 A.M.–6:00 P.M. Closed on Mondays.

Parco (981–2111), located next to Seibu Department Store, houses boutiques, apparel shops, accessory shops, and many other attractive stores. Open 10:00 A.M.–8:30 P.M. daily throughout the year.

Kichijoji Area

Kichijoji on the JR Chuo Line is a newly emerging shopping and entertainment town very popular with young people. Many department stores have set up branches here: **Isetan** (0422–21–1111; closed on Wednesdays), **Tokyu** (0422–21–5111; closed on Thursdays), **Kintetsu** (0422–21–3331; closed on Tuesdays), and **Parco** (0422–21–8111, open 10:00 A.M.–8:00 P.M., may be closed on some Thursdays).

ELECTRONICS CENTERS—AKIHABARA, NISHI-GINZA

Akihabara is unexcelled for electronic goods. Store after store is packed to the ceiling with every imaginable article connected with electrical appliances. Here you get a panoramic glimpse of the entire range of Japanese electronics products—at greatly discounted prices. When you get off at Akihabara Station of the JR Yamanote loop line or the Sobu line, you get the feeling of being in the middle of an electronics jungle.

In most of the smaller shops, very little, if any, English is spoken but that is not much of a problem because all the goods are there before your eyes, the prices are listed, and you can bargain with the aid of pencil and paper. The bigger shops housed in buildings several stories high are authorized to sell duty free and have clerks to attend to tourists. These include *Yamagiwa, X-One, LAOX, Onoden, Nishikawa Musen,* and *Hirose Musen.* You can't miss them because they are big and display their names prominently.

Wholesalers and retailers deal in anything from the tiniest screws and bolts for electrical appliances to audio/video components, TVs, tape decks, video equipment and computers at prices that are apt to make the hungry addict from abroad lose his head.

Although it is probable that some of Japan's electronic goods can be bought in Hong Kong at somewhat lower prices, that colony has nothing like Akihabara's selection. Many of the items you'll find in Akihabara are sold in America under their importer's brand name, at much higher prices. Some of the equipment on sale in Akihabara may need adjustment for frequencies, voltage, and cycles in other countries. If you shop at a store offering duty-free goods, they will be able to tell you.

Nishi Ginza Electric Center (501–5905/5910), located across the road from the International Arcade, which is near the Imperial Hotel, houses a number of tax-free shops that specialize in audio/video equipment as well as electric and electronic appliances.

If you are a fan of a particular maker, you can go straight to the service shop or showroom maintained by the manufacturer. At most places, you can audition equipment in relative calm. *Matsushita Showroom,* Technics Ginza, Ginza Core Bldg., 7th Floor, 572–3871; *Sony Showroom Tokyo,* Sony Bldg., Sukiyabashi intersection, Ginza, 573–2371; *Sharp Showroom,* 8–8 Ichigaya, Shinjuku-ku (near JR Ichigaya Station), 260–1161; *Hitachi Showroom,* Hotel New Otani, 261–1701; *Toshiba Showroom,* Toshiba Tourist Corner, Dowa Bldg., 2–22 Ginza, Chuo-ku, 572–2331. For computers, Shinjuku NS Bldg., 5th floor.

TOYS

Japan is one of the great toy manufacturing nations of the world. Mechanical toys are an especially good buy. The department stores all have large toy departments. *Kiddy Land,* on Omote Sando between Aoyama-dori and Meiji-dori, is a wonderland of toys, paper kites, Christmas and party decorations of all sorts. Electric trains are another good buy. Kiddy Land is open 10:00 A.M.–7:00 P.M. on weekdays, 10:00 A.M.–8:00 P.M. on Saturdays, Sundays, and national holidays. Closed on third Tuesday of each month. Address: 6–1–9 Jingumae; Shibuya-ku; 409–3431/5.

Tenshodo, on Harumi-dori between Chuo-dori and Sotobori-dori Ave., is famous for its HO gauge equipment. Tenshodo is open 10:30 A.M.–7:00 P.M. and closed on Thursdays. Address: 4–3–9 Ginza; Chuo-ku; 561–0021/3. *Toy Park,* on Chuo-dori near Shinjuku Station, is the largest toy shop in the country. Open daily 11 A.M.–8 P.M. Hakuhinkan; 8–8–11 Ginza; Chuo-ku; 571–8008.

Japanese folk toys are more popular with the old than the young these days, and make wonderful small, inexpensive presents to bring back home.

DOLLS CENTER—ASAKUSABASHI

You'll find doll shops in all the arcades and shopping centers, but for a much bigger selection try the department stores or, best of all, the area near Asakusabashi Station of the JR Sobu Line where there are numerous stores specializing in dolls of a great variety. Among the biggest are Kyugetsu and Shugetsu at 1 Yanagibashi, Taito-ku, practically in front of Asakusabashi railway station. *Kyugetsu* (861–5511) is open from 9:00 A.M. to 5:00 P.M. and *Shugetsu* (861–8801) is open daily from 10:00 A.M. to 6:30 P.M.; both year round.

A small but charming doll shop in the Ginza area is *Kabuki-ya,* just next to the Kabuki-za theater (543–4297). This shop specializes in Ichimatsu-ningyo—little-boy and little-girl dolls. The store is open every day, Sundays and national holidays included, from 10:30 A.M. to 7:00 P.M.

HARAJUKU FOR YOUTHFUL FASHION

Harajuku is the classy district centering around the intersection of Meiji-dori and Omote-sando avenues near JR Harajuku Station. The district has a tradition of being Western-oriented because of the close proximity of what was once a huge family housing complex of the American occupation forces and later the

Olympic Village during the Tokyo Olympic Games. Thus, there are many shops here designed to satisfy foreign tastes in souvenirs, chinaware, brass, lamps, lanterns, furniture, toys, and silverware. Always keeping a step ahead of the times, Harajuku today caters to the most progressive sector of Japanese youth. Takeshita-Dori is one trendy boutique after another. Numerous boutiques in this section include *Hanae Mori Boutique* (400–3301), which occupies the 1st and 2nd floors of Hanae Mori Building at 3–1–6 Kita-Aoyama. The boutique is open 11:00 A.M.–7:00 P.M. daily.

BOOKS—KANDA-JIMBOCHO

No book lover should leave Tokyo without taking a stroll along Yasukuni-dori, the famous street in the Kanda-Jimbocho district of Chiyoda ward, where close to 100 secondhand bookstores are packed eave to eave. You'll find books from all over the world here, and the determined bibliophile will often unearth a real find.

Many of the secondhand bookstores specialize in a particular discipline ranging from art and history to technology and medicine. Below is a listing of some of the notable stores:

Sanseido, 1–1 Kanda-Jimbocho, Chiyoda-ku; 233–3312. This store does not sell secondhand books, but it is the centerpiece of this district. On its seven floors, Sanseido has Japan's largest stock of current books and magazines, both Japanese and foreign. Located on Yasukuni-dori Ave. near the Surugadai-shita intersection, it is 2 minutes walk from Jimbocho Station of the Toei (municipal) Mita and Shinjuku subway lines. Open 10:00 A.M.–6 P.M. daily from December to end of May. Closed on Tuesdays from June to November.

Isseido, 1–7 Kanda-Jimbocho, Chiyoda-ku; 292–0071/6. This store has art books new and old, and out-of-print Orientalia. Open 9 A.M.–6:30 P.M. Closed on Sundays.

Kitazawa, 2–5 Kanda-Jimbocho, Chiyoda-ku; 263–0011. This store has new foreign books, old books, and rare books. Open 10:00 A.M.–6:00 P.M. Closed on Sundays.

Matsumara, 1–7 Kanda Jimbocho, Chiyoda-ku; 291–2410. This store has many secondhand foreign books on Japan. Open 10:00 A.M.–6:00 P.M. daily. Closed on Sundays and on rainy national holidays.

Ohya Shobo, 1–1 Kanda-Jimbocho, Chiyoda-ku; near Sanseido bookstore; 291–0062. This is a reputable store dealing in old Japanese illustrated books, Ukiyo-e prints, Nagasaki-e prints, Yokohama-e prints, old maps, and Japanese graphic art books. The store has its name written in English and has a large Kabuki picture board above its entrance. Can't be missed. Open 10:00 A.M.–6:30 P.M., closed on Sundays and national holidays.

Shogakudo Shoten, at the far end of the secondhand bookstore row from Sanseido; 262–0908. You can buy foreign language books published in Japan in this store. Open 10:00 A.M.–7:00 P.M. on weekdays. Closed on Sundays.

Major bookstores selling new books, besides Sanseido, are:

Charles E. Tuttle, 1–3 Kanda Jimbocho, Chiyoda-ku; 291–7071/2. An old Vermont firm that runs a publishing house in Tokyo. Current books on Japan at their shop near Sanseido. Open 10 A.M.–6 P.M. Closed on Sundays and national holidays.

Shosen Grande, a multistory bookstore, a few steps from Sanseido, sells only current volumes; 295–0011. Open 10:30 A.M.–6:50 P.M. on weekdays and 10:30 A.M.–6:20 P.M. on Sundays and weekdays. Closed on some Mondays depending on the month. About 50 meters away is its sister store, **Shosen Book Mart**

(294–0011), whose business hours are the same as Shosen Grande, but it may be closed on some Wednesdays.

For new foreign-language books and magazines, **Maruzen** in Nihonbashi 2-chome across Chuo-dori from Takashimaya Department Store in the Ginza district; 272–7211. Open 10:00 A.M.–6:00 P.M., closed on Sundays. Maruzen has a branch near JR Ochanomizu Station in Chiyoda district; 295–5581. Open 10:00 A.M.–6:00 P.M., closed on Sundays. **Jena** is on Harumi-dori near the Ginza 4-chome intersection; 571–2980. Open 10:30 A.M.–7:50 P.M.; closed on national holidays. **Yosho Biblos,** 4th floor, F.I. Bldg., in front of Takadanobaba Station; 200–4531. Open 10:30 A.M.–7:30 P.M. on weekdays; 11:00 A.M.–6:30 P.M. on Sundays and national holidays; closed on the third Sunday of each month. and **Kinokuniya** in Shinjuku, between JR Shinjuku Station and Isetan Department Store. (10:00 A.M.–7:00 P.M. Tel: 354–0131, closed 1st and 3rd Wednesdays).

CAMERAS AND OPTICAL GOODS

Camera shops are all over the city. The best places to buy are the tax-free shops and the huge discount stores that specialize in cameras, including the products of the top names in the industry.

Camera manufacturers' showrooms are *Asahi Kogaku (Pentax), Service Center,* 8 Ginza Nishi, Chuo-ku; 571–5621. *Canon,* behind Matsuzakaya Department Store, 5 Ginza Chuo-ku; 571–7388, open 9:00 A.M.–5:30 P.M. *Minolta,* Kawase Bldg., 3rd Floor, Shinjuku-ku; 356–6281, open 10:00 A.M.–6:00 P.M. *Nihon Kogaku (Nikon),* Mitsubishi Bldg. opposite Central Post Office, 2 Marunouchi Chiyoda-ku; 215–0561, open 9:00 A.M.–5:00 P.M. *Olympus Kogaku,* Ryumeikan Bldg., 6th Floor, Kanda-Ogawacho, Chiyoda-ku; 255–2425, open 9:00 A.M.–6:00 P.M.

Convenient and representative camera shops that are accustomed to dealing with tourists are, in the Ginza district, *Sundry Camera* in International Arcade (501–5774), *Igarashi Camera* in Sanshin Building not far from Imperial Hotel (591–4919), *Hero Camera* inside Sony Building at Sukiyabashi intersection (561–8361), and *Ginza Orient Camera Center* in Ginza 8-chome (574–6121). *Ohba Camera* is in Shimbashi 1-chome (591–0070).

Yodobashi Camera and Doi are huge discount stores on Nishiguchi (west entrance) side of JR Shinjuku Station.

Yodobashi Camera, Nishi-Shinjuku, Shinjuku-ku; 346–1010. The biggest discount store in Japan, it has a stock of about 30,000 kinds of camera and accessories, representing about 100 leading makers. It sells 500 to 600 cameras daily on weekdays and about 1,000 on Sundays and national holidays. It has small cameras on the 1st floor, medium and large-sized cameras on the 2nd floor, and films on the 3rd floor. Open 10:00 A.M.–8:00 P.M. daily throughout the year.

Doi, Dai-ni Seiko Bldg., Nishi-Shinjuku, Shinjuku-ku; 344–2310. Near Keio Plaza Hotel, this store has compact cameras, exchangeable lenses, strobes on the 1st floor and darkroom equipment, medium-sized and large cameras on the 2nd floor. Open 9:00 A.M.–8:30 P.M. daily throughout the year.

Contact lenses figure among Japan's bargains. A specialist who makes appointments with foreigners by telephone (241–6166) is *Hoya Contact Lens Clinic,* 1–6 Nihonbashi-Muromachi, Chuo-ku; Amano Shika (dental clinic) Bldg., 9th floor, which is open 10:00 A.M.–7:00 P.M. on weekdays, 10:00 A.M.–6:00 P.M. on national holidays. Closed on second and third Sundays. Another such specialist is *International Vision Center,* 3 Kita-Aoyama, Minato-ku; 497–1491. Open 10:00 A.M.–7:00 P.M. on weekdays and closed on Sundays and some national holidays.

WATCHES

Wako, Ginza 4-chome intersection of Chuo-dori and Harumidori and nearby Nippondo; 562–2111. This store carries a selection of the best watches of both Japanese and foreign makes, and most of the hotels have a *Seiko* store in their shopping arcades. Wako is open 10:00 A.M.–5:30 P.M. on weekdays and closes on Sundays and national holidays. Tel: 562–2111. *Nippondo,* 5–7 Ginza, Chuo-ku; 571–5511. Open 10:00 A.M.–9:00 P.M. daily throughout the year.

PEARLS

The list below is by no means exhaustive, and there are many other fine pearl dealers in Tokyo.

K. Uyeda is one of Tokyo's leading jewelry and silver dealers. Japanese and South Sea pearls. In the Imperial Hotel Arcade and in his own shop opposite the Imperial Hotel; 503–2587/9. In business since 1884, and absolutely reliable, as are the other shops in our very selective list. The Imperial Hotel Arcade shop is open from 10:00 A.M. to 7:00 P.M. on weekdays, but from 10:30 A.M. to 5:30 P.M. on Sundays and national holidays.

Mayuyama, noted jeweler. Some of the finest pearls find their way to Mayuyama, then to distinguished customers throughout the world. Very elegant. In the Imperial Hotel Arcade; 591–6655. Open 10:00 A.M.–7:00 P.M. on weekdays but 10:00 A.M.–5:00 P.M. on Sundays and national holidays.

Kuki, owned by Mr. Kuki, former New York manager of Mikimoto, is one of Tokyo's reliable pearl jewelers. In the International Arcade; 501–5675. Open 10:00 A.M.–7:00 P.M. daily, but 10:00 A.M.–6:00 P.M. on Sundays and national holidays.

Mikimoto, 4–5–5 Ginza, Chuo-ku; 535–4611. The great Mikimoto Kokichi is the "Pearl King" who discovered the secret of making cultured pearls. The main Mikimoto store, the first in the world to deal exclusively in pearls, is on the Chuo-dori several buildings away from Wako at Ginza 4-chome intersection and diagonally opposite Matsuya Department Store. Open 10:30 A.M.–6:00 P.M. Closed on Wednesdays.

Takashima Shinju specializes in giant South Sea pearls cultivated in the tropical waters of Southeast Asia. Opposite Atago police station near Shiba Park; 432–1601. Open 9:30 A.M.–5:30 P.M. on weekdays; closed on Sundays and national holidays.

Okubo, in Imperial Hotel Arcade; 504–0088. One of the oldest dealers in Japan. Open 9:30 A.M.–7:00 P.M. daily, but 9:30 A.M.–5:00 P.M. on national holidays.

H. Ono, 6–5–10 Ginza, Chuo-ku; 571–6788. Within walking distance from the Imperial Hotel, this store keeps a selection of unusually designed brooches and bracelets.

Matoba and Co., main store in the Nikkatsu Arcade; 271–2170. Has a good variety and will accept mail orders. Shop here for tins of oysters with cultured pearls inside—fun souvenirs. Open 9:30 A.M.–6:00 P.M. on weekdays but 9:30 A.M.–5:00 P.M. on national holidays. Closed on Sundays.

Tasaki Shinju, 1–3–3 Akasaka, Minato-ku; 584–0904/5. Halfway between NCR Building and Tameike intersection in Akasaka, this store has a large selection of cultured pearls, freshwater pearls, etc. Open 9:00 A.M.–6:00 P.M. daily throughout the year.

SILVER

K. Uyeda in the Imperial Hotel Arcade, and Uyeda's own shop, opposite Imperial Hotel Annex; 591–8501. The oldest and best known silver dealer in Tokyo. A reliable firm, all work guaranteed. (See also Pearls.) *Miyamoto Shoko* is another old, well-established firm. Located in Asahi Building at Ginza 6-chome on Namiki-dori street near Mikasa Kaikan restaurant complex; 573–3011. Open 9:30 A.M.–5:30 P.M. on weekdays; closed on Sundays and national holidays.

CLOISONNÉ AND DAMASCENE

Ando, 5–6–2 Ginza, Chuo-ku; 572–2261. The largest and best known cloisonné dealer in Tokyo in Ginza 5-chome on Harumi-dori, one block west of Chuo-dori from Ginza 4-chome intersection. Open 9:00 A.M.–5:30 P.M. daily except Sundays and national holidays.

Inaba Kogei Katsura, branch shop of the noted Kyoto manufacturer Inaba Kogei, is on the second floor of Sukiyabashi Shopping Center; 571–8071. Open 10:00 A.M.–7:30 P.M. daily throughout the year, but it may be closed on some Sundays.

Amita is Japan's leading damascene maker on the second floor of the Sukiyabashi Shopping Center; 571–3274. Cigarette lighters, compacts, jewelry, and a fine selection of pearls. Open 10:00 A.M.–6:00 P.M. daily.

IVORY

(Note: It is prohibited to bring ivory into the States.)
Hodota in the Imperial Hotel Arcade; 580–6056. *Kitagawa,* on Omote-sando opposite the entrance to Meiji Park; 504–1111. Open 9:30 A.M.–7:00 P.M. weekdays; 10:00 A.M.–5:00 P.M. Sundays and national holidays. *Sunamoto,* opposite the Imperial Hotel's newly opened Imperial Tower; 591–5610. Sunamoto is open 9:45 A.M.–6 P.M. on weekdays and 10:30 A.M.–6:00 P.M. on Sundays and national holidays. To see ivory carvers at work, visit the salesroom/factory of *Makino,* a short walk from Nippori Station on the Yamanote line; 6–2–32 Yanaka, Taito-ku; 821–4787. Open 10 A.M.–5 P.M., daily except Sundays.

LACQUER

Yamada Heiando, 3–10–11 Nihonbashi, Chuo-ku; 272–2871. Makes lacquer by appointment to the Imperial Household, and ranks as tops in the field. On street behind Takashimaya, a block north of Yaesu-dori Ave. Open 9:00 A.M.–6:00 P.M.; closed on Sundays and national holidays.

Kuroeya, 1–2 Nihonbashi, Chuo-ku; 271–3356. An old Ginza firm where discerning Japanese have shopped for years. It sells everything from lacquer furniture to chopsticks. On Chuo-dori between Eitai-dori Ave. and Nihonbashi bridge.

Inachu Japan, 1–5–2 Akasaka, Minato-Ru; 582–4451. A newly opened store specializing in Wajima-nuri lacquerware. On sale is a vast range of high-quality lacquerware from such decorative items as jewelry boxes and flower stands to kitchenware and tableware. At Tameike intersection on Sotobori-dori St. on the same side as NCR Bldg. Open daily from 10:00 A.M. to 7:00 P.M. throughout the year.

BAMBOO

Department stores are a good place to find bamboo products, both in the household tableware department (trays, baskets, etc.) and in the flower-arranging sections (bamboo vases). *Nippon Craft Corner* on the 7th floor of Takashimaya Department Store in Nihonbashi is recommended.

PAPER AND PAPER PRODUCTS

Haibara, 2–7 Nihonbashi, Chuo-ku; 272–3801. In Nihonbashi opposite Tokyu Department Store is a venerable old firm dating back to 1803. Sells all kinds of handmade papers, wall paper, Christmas cards, fans. Open 9:30 A.M.–5:30 P.M. on weekdays, but closes at 5:00 P.M. on Saturdays. Closed on Sundays and national holidays.

Isetatsu, 2–18–9 Yanaka, Taito-ku; 823–1453. Founded in 1864. Top shop for lovely, reasonable paper things. (Sendagi stop on the Chiyoda subway line; walk up hill opposite the exit. Isetasu is 200 yards up on the right.) Open daily.

Takumi for wonderful folkcraft papers, in sheets or made up into all sorts of fetching boxes, calendars, and placemats. Shimbashi, near Hotel Nikko; 571–2017. Closed on Sunday.

Matsuya is a small tatami-floored shop that hides a wealth of glorious papers, both for Western walls and Japanese *fusuma* (sliding paper doors). Located on the willow-lined street one block west of Chuo-dori.

Washikobo, Roppongi, on the first floor of Yoshikawa Bldg., 1–8–10 Nishiazabu, Minato-ku; 405–1841. Paper craft in all its diversity. Open 10:00 A.M.–6:00 P.M. Closed on Sundays and national holidays. About 7–8 minutes walk from Roppongi Station on Hibiya subway line or about 10 minutes from Nogizaka Station on Chiyoda subway line.

The Gifu lanterns, handpainted with summery pastoral scenes, are daintier than other Japanese paper lanterns. If you have time to explore, a fun way to lantern shop is to make a trek out to the lantern and paper decoration wholesale shops in the Asakusa area. The shops below are easier to get to than those in Asakusa, and all specialize in lanterns and other typically Japanese products popular with foreigners.

Kiddy Land, 6–1–9 Jingumae, Shibuya-ku; 409–3431/5. On Omote Sando between Meiji and Aoyama Streets, store is well stocked with paper lanterns as well as toys. Open 10:00 A.M.–7:00 P.M. on weekdays, 10:00 A.M.–8:30 P.M. on Saturdays, Sundays, and national holidays. Closed on third Tuesday of every month.

Shimura (turn left on the narrow street after Kiddy Land) 6–3–2 Jingumae, Shibuya-ku; 400–6322. They have kites, big fireplace fans, butterfly paper, bamboo and shoji screens, other household accessories. Paper umbrellas for the hand and the giant processional umbrellas, about 7 feet in diameter, ideal for garden or beach. Open 9:30 A.M.–8:00 P.M. Closed on Thursdays.

Wafudo, first floor of the Marubiru Arcade. (See Folkcraft.)

Wataroku, 2–5–9 Shinjuku, Shinjuku-ku; 354–3658. Store has been in business since 1918, specializing in writing family names and store names on *chochin* paper lanterns, and making small flags. It sells a great variety of paper lanterns, flags, and *tenugui* cotton towels. Open 8:30 A.M.–6:30 P.M. every day except Sunday and national holidays. One traffic signal toward Yotsuya from Isetan Department Store in Shinjuku.

FANS

There are many small fan shops along the Ginza and in the arcades. One of the leading Ginza fan shops is *Haibara,* 2–7 Nihonbashi, Chuo-ku; 272–3801. Noted for its fine paper products, it's located on Eitai-dori, opposite Tokyu Department Store. Haibara is open from 9:30 A.M. to 5:30 P.M. on weekdays, but from 9:30 A.M. to 5:00 P.M. on Saturdays. It is closed on Sundays and national holidays. Another shop is *Eiraido,* 1–3 Nihonbashi, Chuo-ku; 271–8884. On Chuo-dori opposite Tokyu Department Store, it specializes in dance and Noh fans. It is open from 10:00 A.M. to 5:30 P.M. on weekdays, from around 1:00 P.M. to 5:30 P.M. on Sundays and national holidays.

STATIONERY

If you need a writing pad and envelopes to write letters to your friends at home, the best place to go is the stationery counter of any department store or to a stationery shop in your hotel arcade. For a great variety of stationery goods, both domestic and imported, go to *Ito-ya* in Ginza 2-chome near Matsuya Department Store; 2–7–15 Ginza, Chuo-ku; 561–8311. The multistory store on Chuo-dori opens from 9:30 P.M. to 6:00 P.M. on weekdays but from 10:00 A.M. to 6:00 P.M. on Sundays and national holidays.

Maruzen 2–3–10 Nihonbashi, Chuo-ku; 272–7211. Famous for its comprehensive book section, it has a good stationery section, too. Open 10:00 A.M.–5:30 P.M. on weekdays; closed on Sundays.

Bunshodo, 3–4–12 Ginza, Chuo-ku; 563–1511. Established in 1912, store deals principally in office supplies and business equipment. Bunshodo is behind Sumitomo Bank, which is diagonally across the Chuo-dori (Ginza Street) from Matsuya Department Store. Open 10:00 A.M.–5:00 P.M. from Monday through Friday, closes earlier at 4:00 P.M. on Saturdays. Closed on Sundays, national holidays, and first and third Saturdays.

Kyukyodo, next to the circular San-Ai Building at Ginza 4-chome intersection; 571–4429. A very old stationery shop doing business for more than 300 years. It sells Mt. Fuji picture postcards, writing implements, washi handmade paper and folkcrafts (inexpensive and packable), fans, ukiyo-e woodblock prints, prints by contemporary artists, miniature folding screens, photo albums, and much more. Open 10:00 A.M.–8:00 P.M. from Monday through Saturday and 11:00 A.M.–7:00 P.M. on Sundays and national holidays.

MASKS

Old Noh masks, and other dance masks dating further back into Japan's history, are prized works of art. The mask still plays an important role in Japanese theater, dance, and shrine festivals. Craftsmen have discovered that masks are also popular as decorative items in the home, and now turn them out in all sizes as well as in bizarre shapes. A shop that specializes in masks is *Ichy's,* 11–14, Minami-Aoyama 2-chome, Minato-ku; 401–2247. Open 10:30 A.M.–5:00 P.M., closed on Sundays and national holidays. In front of Meiji Memorial Hall wedding hall. Halfway between Aoyama-Itchome Station and Gaien-mae Station on Ginza subway line.

FURNITURE AND HOME FURNISHINGS

Department stores are the best place to shop for new tables and rattan furniture; antique and curio shops for old pieces.

Oriental Bazaar, 5–9–3 Jingumae, Shibuya-ku; 400–3933. A large establishment catering to Westerners. There is something here for everyone including souvenirs, antiques, and lamps. On Omote-Sando, between Aoyama-dori Ave. and Meiji-dori Ave. About 10 minutes walk from JR Harajuku Station. Oriental-style building painted in vermilion. Open 9:30 A.M.–6:30 P.M. Closed on Thursdays.

An appealing shop is *Onoya* at 5–12–3 Ginza, diagonally across the road from Kabuki-za.

Fujiya, 2–2–15 Asakusa, Taito-ku; 841–2283. One of the very few shops specializing in *tenugui* Japanese-style cotton towels and *noren* divided curtains of varying lengths. Stocks more than 100 varieties of decorative towels of its own creation and design. Open 10:00 A.M.–8:00 P.M. every day except Thursday. One street to the right of the famous Nakamise shopping alley.

Bamboo window blinds, called *sudare,* are another interesting item of strictly Japanese home furnishing. They come in a wide range of styles, and ingenious decorators can often find a use for them in the Western home. Visit the department stores for *zabuton* and *sudare* shopping.

The shops and design centers listed in the Good Design section below, are also good places to shop for the latest in up-to-date home furnishings.

STONE LANTERNS

If you want to create your own Japanese garden, and are ambitious enough to cart a lantern home, the best place to go is *Ishikatsu,* 3–4 Minami-Aoyama, Minato-ku; 401–1677. Stone lanterns and other garden ornaments. They will handle packing and shipping. Open 9:30 A.M.–5:00 P.M. except Sundays.

GOOD DESIGN, MODERN CRAFTS

Japan Industrial Design Center, a showroom for products of good design. On the 4th floor of Boeki (trade) Center Building at Hamamatsucho railway station; 435–5633. Open 10:00 A.M.–5:00 P.M. on weekdays, 10:00 A.M.–12 noon on Saturdays. Closed on Sundays and national holidays.

Also *Craft Center Japan,* third floor of Maruzen bookstore, on the Ginza. *Living Arts,* on Aoyama-dori Ave. between Omote-sando and Gaien-Higashi-dori Ave. *Matsuya Department Store,* the Good Design Corner on the 7th floor and the New Crafts Section on the 6th floor. (See Ginza-Nihonbashi Department Stores.) *Takashimaya Department Store,* Rosier Corner on the 7th floor. (See Ginza-Nihonbashi Department Store.)

TEXTILES

The most convenient may be the *Tokyo Kanebo* store, on the 5th floor of the Ginza Cygnas Bldg., at 3–5–2 Ginza; 562–2751. Open 11:00 A.M.–7:30 P.M.; closed third Wednesday of every month. In Ikebukuro, *Kinkado,* 1–24–5 Minami Ikebukuro, Toshimaku; 971–1211. Open 10 A.M. to 7 P.M. Closed Sundays.

Tokyu Hands in Shibuya (see "Department Stores") has an excellent textile section on the fourth floor-A, with stress on cotton fabrics, including indigo dyed cotton from China.

Kyoto Silk, in International Arcade; 501–4757. Store has one of the richest stocks of silk material in Tokyo. The fabrics on display are brought from its main store in Kyoto (established in 1895) and are less expensive than at other stores in Tokyo. Open 10:00 A.M.–6:00 P.M., year-round.

Teoriya, 2–8 Kanda-Ogawacho, Chiyoda-ku; 294–3903. Hand-dyed and handwoven fabrics made from natural materials are sold here. Open 11:00

A.M.–6:00 P.M. every day except Sunday, Monday, and national holidays. On the 2nd floor of Ogi Building close to Ogawacho Station of Shinjuku subway line and Shin-Ochanomizu Station of Chiyoda subway line.

SILK

A department store kimono department is a dazzling place, counter after counter piled high with rolls of material, no two alike. *Mitsukoshi Nihonbashi* and *Takashimaya* have the best kimono and obi materials. Kimono fabric comes in 13-inch widths.

The shops listed below all sell material in standard Western widths.

Kanebo is the Tokyo outlet for Japan's leading silk manufacturer where you can find almost any kind of silk in your mind. Kanebo has the Japan license for Dior. Also has branch shops in Okura, Palace, Capitol Tokyu, Imperial. See above for hours and address.

Moh Long, Imperial Hotel Arcade; 591–4012. Open 10:00 A.M.–7:00 P.M. on weekdays, 10:00 A.M.–5:00 P.M. on Sundays and national holidays.

Kawamura, 8–9–7 Ginza, on Chuo-dori, opposite Shiseido Parlor. Open 10:00 A.M.–7:30 P.M. daily throughout the year.

Yamatoya, on the first floor of the Sukiyabashi Shopping Center. Open 10:00 A.M.–8:30 P.M. daily throughout the year.

Kogei, Sotobori-dori Ave., same block as Hotel Nikko. One of the most interesting little shops in Tokyo. It sells cottons and wools as well as silk, and all its fabrics are hand-woven and hand-dyed. The atmosphere is definitely *shibui* (refined). Materials come in both Western and narrow kimono widths, and there is a large selection of upholstery and curtain fabrics.

Kyoto Silk has a branch in the International Arcade, Ginza; 501–4757. Yuzen prints, scarves, and everything else. Open 10:00 A.M.–6:00 P.M. daily throughout the year.

If you like bargain hunting and have the time to spare, the Asakusa wholesale textile district is fun. Best to have a guide, as the district is confusing. *Fujikake* is one of the biggest and best of the Asakusa shops. Fujikake is at 1–21 Kotobuki Taito-ku; 843–0021, 0026, 841–0217. On the street just off Kikuyabashi on Asakusa-dori Ave.

KIMONO AND OTHER JAPANESE WEAR

You'll find for-tourist-only kimono for sale in the arcade shops, particularly at *Nikko Shokai* (Palace Hotel) and in *Ichi-Fuji* on Ginza, opposite Theater Tokyo.

The best place to do real kimono-viewing is the department stores. Silk kimono prices start at about ¥100,000 and, unlike the tourist-only kimono, are made to order. Elaborate hand-dyed and embroidered kimono begin about ¥180,000 and go way up. Prices for first-rate *obi* are even more expensive.

If you want something fairly spectacular but aren't prepared to pay too much for it, the best thing is to buy a secondhand kimono. Takashimaya's second basement has a good selection of secondhand kimono and obi. Ingenious foreign women, incidentally, long ago discovered that obi, which are made of heavy silk or brocade, can be turned into handsome evening jackets, sheath dresses, or even used to upholster chairs.

Another popular place for secondhand kimono and obi shopping is the International Arcade, behind the Imperial Hotel. Several shops in the arcade sell both new and secondhand kimono, etc. The best is *K. Hayashi* (open 9:30 A.M.–7:00 P.M. daily throughout the year. 501–4014), which also has a branch shop in the Capitol Tokyu (open 9:00 A.M.–7:00 P.M. on weekdays but 9:30

A.M.–6:00 P.M. on Sundays and national holidays. 581–5015). Hayashi has a good collection of secondhand obi, and also of men's black silk formal kimono (discreet *mon*—family crests—on the shoulder and sleeves add to the elegance), which make handsome dressing gowns for men of distinction.

Happi coats are standard tourist items, but it's not always so easy to get the genuine article. The International Arcade has them, and it also has heavy dark blue workmen's aprons.

Blue and White, at Juban in the Azabu district, makes the most attractive goodies out of *yukata* material.

To top your new kimono in proper style, maybe you'd like to buy a geisha wig, made up into a traditional Japanese hairdo. If so, the place to go is *Komachi,* at 2–6 Ginza, Chuo-ku; 561–1586. There you can splurge on a genuine geisha wig or be content with paper models. Either kind is grand for costume parties. Samurai wigs are available for gentlemen. Fans and traditional Japanese hair ornaments also sold here. Some of the combs and pins adapt beautifully to a Western chignon. Komachi is open from 9:30 A.M.–7:00 P.M.; closed Sundays.

To hold over yourself in the rain you need a *bangasa,* a Japanese umbrella made of oiled paper and bamboo. Two Asakusa shops specialize in bangasa, *mingeigasa* (traditional paper umbrellas), and umbrellas for Japanese dancing: *Inami Shoten* (open 8:00 A.M.–6:00 P.M., closed ono Sundays and national holidays. 10–14 Hanakawado, Taito-ku; 841–9524), and *Sekiguchi* (open 9:00 A.M.–5:30 P.M. Closed on Sundays and national holidays. Two minutes from Asakusa Station on Ginza subway line near Matsuya Department Store in Asakusa. 1–10–13 Hanakawado, Taito-ku; 843–4647). Prices from ¥2,500.

KNITWEAR AND OTHER APPAREL FOR LADIES

The Japanese are making excellent knitwear these days, and it's becoming easier to find large foreign sizes in the shops. The *Mitsukoshi* and *Takashimaya* department stores (both in Nihonbashi) have a wide variety. *Isetan* at Shinjuku excels in summer fashions.

Ladies' fashion floors of big department stores in Tokyo are good places to have a dress or suit made to order. Each department store is affiliated to an haute couturier of Paris. The price is lower than you would pay in Europe or America. Two or three fittings, minimum of three weeks required. The affiliated haute couturiers are *Isetan* (Balmain); *Daimaru* (Givenchy); *Takashimaya* (Pierre Cardin); *Mitsukoshi* (Guy Laroche); *Matsuzakaya* (Nina Ricci).

Kiyomizu in Shibuya sells Western-style dresses made up from Kyoto kimono fabrics. Most of the dresses are of much the same style. English is not spoken in this store but everything is clearly labeled and priced. Near Miyamasuzaka-shita intersection and a few yards short of the big Shibuya Post Office; 409–1886. Open 10:30 A.M.–7:00 P.M. on weekdays but closed earlier at 6:00 P.M. on Sundays.

Recently, many cozy boutiques have sprung up in Tokyo as in other big cities around the world. They are scattered along small streets in Nishi-Ginza running parallel with Chuo-dori. You will find some good boutiques in the Roppongi and Aoyama areas, also. For imaginative clothes and accessories for the young and fashion conscious, try *Harajuku.*

Mme. Hanae Mori, probably the most noted Japanese designer in America, has her own building in Harajuku. She has other fashion rooms in the Hotel Okura's South Wing, in the Imperial Hotel's arcade, and in many department stores. *Hanae Mori,* 3–1–6 Kita-Aoyama, Minato-ku; 400–3301. Open 11:00 A.M. to 7:00 P.M. daily throughout the year.

Jun Ashida, for many years designer to Crown Princess Michiko, has several boutiques: Akasaka-Mitsuke, 588–5030/5084; Ginza, 574–8811; Akasaka, 588–5030; and Omote Sando, 479–4733. Open 11:00 A.M.–7 P.M.

Issey Miyake, a designer of international fame, has boutiques on the first floor of From 1st building at 5 Minami-Aoyama, 499–6476; 6th fl. Parco Part 2, Shibuya, 496–0438; and Bi,Tessenkai Bldg., Minami Aoyama, 423–1428. Open 12 noon–8:00 P.M. Closed on Sundays.

Kansai Yamamoto, still another Japanese designer of world renown, has his boutique, *Kansai International Harajuku* in Harajuku fashion town; 3–28–7 Jingumae, Shibuya-ku; 478–1958. Open 11:00 A.M.–8:00 P.M. throughout the year.

SHIRTS

Many Tokyo shops make handmade shirts in a wide range of materials. On the whole, tailored shirts are a fair bargain, but it's best not to go shirt-buying unless you have ample time for at least one fitting and a bit more time for final adjustments. Collar styles are sometimes a bit difficult and it is best to have a model to copy from. Also insist that any material used be preshrunk before cutting. *Moh Long* in the Imperial Hotel Arcade, *Kanebo* at Gallery Center Bldg., Miyuki-dori, and *Tani Shirt Company* in the arcades of Hotel Okura and Imperial Hotel, are all good shops. *Ricky Sarani,* 3–3–12 Roppongi, Minato-ku, phone 587–0648, rents Western-size dress clothes and tailors shirts and suits.

HANDBAGS

Beaded bags are a wonderful bargain in Japan, but you should also have a look at the handsome hand-stenciled cottons, brocades, and fancifully designed leather handbags. *M. Yamamoto* in Sukiyabashi Shopping Center, Ginza, has many lovely items. Handbag sections in Wako and Mitsukoshi Nihonbashi are also good. Shops in the hotel arcades specialize in beaded and brocade bags. For something more Oriental, try any of the dozens of small kimono accessory shops around the Ginza. One of the best is *Izumiya* (sign in English), a tiny shop with an old-fashioned traditional air and a chic clientele of Tokyo's upper-class ladies and higher-class geisha. Two blocks west of Chuo-dori, in the first block south of Harumi-dori.

FURS

An expert on the subject says that Japan's furs now equal those of an American "top second-class furrier." While the quality of the furs themselves is equal, Japanese styling and workmanship aren't up to the high standards of leading foreign furriers. Ranch mink is bred in Japan from stock imported from Canada, Norway, and the United States, and is cured by processes adapted from those used elsewhere. The difference comes in the workmanship—cutting, matching skins, sewing, etc. Ranch mink is available in several grades, a wide variety of mutation colors, and in a fairly good range of styling—nothing spectacular as fur fashion is relatively new to Japan, but good basic styles.

Japan also produces so-called mink items that really come from the lowly weasel. This fur is exported to the United States for trimmings on children's and cheaper garments, but in Japan it turns up in full-length "mink" coats, at, naturally, bargain prices. You're not likely to mistake it for the real thing, but it is simpler to make it clear from the beginning that it's "ranch" mink you're after.

Nutria, marten, fox, and sable are also available in Japan. Among the top Tokyo furriers is *Futaba,* 1–10 Ginza, Chuo-ku; 571–0518. Main store is on the street beside the Imperial Hotel towards Ginza. Open 10:00 A.M.–7:00 P.M. daily throughout the year. Futaba has a branch in the Imperial Hotel. *Nakamura,* 4–3–15 Ginza, Chuo-ku; 563–3451. At Ginza 4-chome on Namiki-dori St. is also this well-known furrier.

POTTERY AND CHINA

The china section in any of the department stores is fun, but *Takashimaya* and *Mitsukoshi* (at Nihonbashi) have the best selections of both Japanese and Western-style ware.

Koyanagi, 1–7–5 Ginza, Chuo-ku; 561–3601. 100 years old, this shop carries first-class Kiyomizu, Kutani, Imari ware. One of the most attractive little shops on the Ginza across the Chuo-dori street from Melsa department store. Open 10:00 A.M.–7:00 P.M. on weekdays, 12:00 noon–6:00 P.M. on Sundays and national holidays. Closed on third Sunday of every month.

Noritake is sold all over town, but the easiest place to inspect the products of this most famous Japanese manufacturer of Western-style dinnerware is the *Noritake,* 1–1–28 Toranomon, Minato-ku; 591–3241. Also on sale here is Okura china, a higher quality porcelain manufactured by Noritake. On the first floor of TOTO Bldg. at Toranomon intersection. Open 10:00 A.M.–6:00 P.M. Closed on Sundays and national holidays.

Takumi (see Paper and Paper Products), one of Tokyo's best-known shops, specializes in Japanese folkcraft. Here you will find pottery from the many small country kilns still operated by farmer-craftsmen. Thanks to the crusading work done by leaders of Japan's folkcraft revival movement, many of the kilns are now turning out pottery in shapes and sizes adapted to the Western table.

Tachikichi, 5–6–13 Ginza, Chuo-ku; 571–2924. The Tokyo outlet of an old (over 200 years) and renowned Kyoto porcelain manufacturer. A small shop, unfortunately with no signboard in English, located two blocks west of Chuo-dori, near Komatsu Store. On Nishi-Gobangai-dori street about 70 meters from Harumi-dori towards Shimbashi. Open 11:00 A.M.–7:00 P.M. Closed on Sundays. On the other side of the street it has Adam & Eve chinaware, and specializes in Western-style dinner sets and glassware.

Kuroda Toen, near Ginza 4-chome intersection (571–3223), sells both crockery for everyday use as well as "works of art" and tea ceremony utensils. It has an unbelievably profuse array of ceramics of all kinds, from inexpensive teacups to a tea bowl of beautiful perfection from Aichi Prefecture, priced at a whopping ¥9,000,000. Kuroda Touen is in the middle of the block past Matsuzakaya Department Store towards Shimbashi, but on the opposite side of Matsuzakaya. Open 10:00 A.M.–7:00 P.M. every day.

Nippon Kogei, Sanshin Building Arcade near Hibiya intersection. A minute shop but worth a visit. Designers of their own "Mikado China," Western-style dinner sets with tasteful Japanese patterns. You can have a set made with your own name painted on in Japanese *kana* or Chinese *kanji* characters. Also small pottery collection. Open 10:00 A.M.–7:00 P.M. throughout the year.

Odawara Shoten, old Kutani and Imari ware. In Imperial Hotel Arcade; 591–0052. Open 9:00 A.M.–7:15 P.M. on weekdays and 9:00 A.M.–6:15 P.M. on Sundays and national holidays.

Though a bit garish for some tastes, the heavily decorated gold Satsuma ware has been a popular tourist item for years, and Satsuma manufacturers long ago learned to turn out coffee cups, tea sets, and the like for the Western table. You can find Satsuma at *Bon Tokyo* in the Nikkatsu Arcade, *Toyo* and *Okubo* in the

Imperial Hotel Arcade, and *Koshida Satsumaya* on the second floor of the
Sukiyabashi Shopping Center. (See Hotel Arcades and One-Stop Shopping for
addresses.)

FOLKCRAFT

Several Tokyo shops specialize in folkcraft, or *mingei* products. They are
good places to go for original and inexpensive gifts.

Takumi Craft Shop, 8-4-2 Ginza, Chuo-ku; 571-2017. Still the acknowl-
edged leader in the field. Specializes in Mashiko ware, the most famous folk
pottery. On Sotobori-dori corner opposite the Hotel Nikko. Open 11:00 A.M.–
7:00 P.M. on weekdays and 11:00 A.M.–5:30 P.M. on national holidays. Closed on
Sundays.

Wafudo, 1st floor of the Marubiru Arcade, in the Marubiru Building in front
of Tokyo Station (201-3639), is a tiny shop packed to the rafters with folkcraft
goodies. Open 9:00 A.M.–6:00 P.M. on weekdays and 9:00 A.M.–3:00 P.M. on Saturdays. Closed on Sundays and national holidays.

Kacho-do, 2nd floor of the Marubiru Arcade, (201-3809), has an interesting,
but less extensive mingei collection. Open 10:00 A.M.–6:00 P.M. on weekdays.
Closed on Saturdays, Sundays and national holidays.

Izumi, 5-26 Ogibuko, Suginami-ku; 391-3645. This shop is a far trek from
the center of town, and only recommended for those who will be in Tokyo for
some time. Outside JR Ogikubo Station in Suginami-ku. It has a big collection
of Mashiko pottery, Nanbu cast iron kettles, pans and ashtrays, bamboo ware,
straw mats and many other folkcraft items. The shop has Izumi written in
English alphabet. Open 10:00 A.M.–7:00 P.M. Closed on Wednesdays.

Tsukamoto, 4-1-19 Mikawadaimachi, Minato-ku; 403-3747. Another shop
specializing in Mashiko ware, few blocks north from Roppongi intersection, on
the left going towards Tameike. Prices here are a little lower than Takumi's.
Open 10:00 A.M.–7:00 P.M. daily throughout the year. in Tomigaya, 4th stop on
Shibuya-Hatagaya bus, sells mashiko ware.

Bingoya at Wakamatsucho in Shinjuku-ku near Tokyo Joshi Idai (Tokyo
Women's Medical University) and in front of Kawadacho bus stop, resembles
a traditional storehouse and has six floors brimming with folk toys, baskets,
pottery, hand-dyed fabrics, lacquerware and country furniture. All are simple,
strong, and practical things. Open 10:00 A.M.–7:00 P.M. Closed on Mondays.

PRINTS

Old prints by the great masters are hard to come by, but good reproductions
abound, and late 19th-century prints are plentiful. The postwar years have
brought a renaissance in the print-making art, and a whole crop of new artists
is creating exciting prints in a variety of styles and techniques.

Watanabe, 8-6-19 Ginza, Chuo-ku; 571-4684. Sells originals and reproductions. In the early years of the 20th century, the head of this old Tokyo firm
became famous for his crusade to revive the then-disappearing art of print
making. The shop has continued its fine tradition of craftsmanship. A block east
of Sotobori-dori Ave., behind the Hotel Nikko. Open 9:30 A.M.–8:00 P.M. on
weekdays, 9:30 A.M.–4:30 P.M. on national holidays. Closed on Sundays.

The Tolman Collection, 2-2-18 Shiba Daimon, Minato-Ku; 434-1300. Modern Japanese prints by leading artists, many in exclusive, small editions, effec-
tively displayed in an old geisha house. Hours, 11 A.M.–6 P.M. Closed Tuesdays.

Kato Gallery, 5-5-2 Hiroo, Shibuya-ku; 446-1530. Old and contemporary
prints, and gift items. Well known for distinctive framing. Hours, 10:30 A.M.–
6:30 P.M. Closed Sundays.

Yoseido, 5–5–15 Ginza, Chuo-ku; 571–1312/2471. One of the first galleries in Tokyo to take up the cause of the new school of modern print artists. Abe Yuji, the owner, speaks English and will be happy to answer your questions on what's going on in the Tokyo art world. The upstairs gallery has shows of modern artists in all media. Framing and *kakemono* (hanging scroll) mounting. On Namiki-dori, behind the Sony Bldg. and two stores from Mikasa Kaikan restaurant complex. Open 10:00 A.M.–6:30 P.M. Closed on Sundays and national holidays.

Honjo Gallery, Palace Aoyama Bldg., 6–1–6 Minami Aoyama, Minato-ku; 400–0277. Traditional and modern prints along with an assortment of antiques. Hours, 10:30 A.M.–6 ·P.M. Closed Sundays.

Amaury St. Gilles, 3–2–9 Ohi, Shinagawa-ku; 775–2040. Imaginative displays of contemporary prints and ceramics. By appointment.

Also three old shops—*Nakazawa, Sakai,* and *Takamizawa*—on the street across from the Imperial Hotel and running towards Ginza. The *Franell Gallery* in the Hotel Okura specializes in the moderns. Franell Gallery opens 10:00 A.M.–6:30 P.M. all the year-round.

ANTIQUES, CURIOS, FINE ARTS

Antique stores are scattered throughout the city, and exploring them in search of treasures is one of the pleasures of collecting. The first two listings are suggested because of the variety of popular goods that they show, thus providing a good introduction to what is available. The others are only a few of the many reputable shops. Of these, the first three are well-known to all serious collectors. Generally only a few pieces are on display.

Hanae Mori Building, 3–6–1 Kita-Aoyama, Minato-ku, Tokyo; 406–1105. In the heart of Omotesando. The downstairs arcade is filled with many shops featuring antiques and good-design products of every description including some foreign goods. There are even shops specializing in clothing (adaptations of Japanese classic designs made from traditional fabrics) and wooden kitchen-wares.

Tokyo Antique Hall, 2–9 Kanda-Surugadai, Chiyoda-ku. Near Maison Franco Japonaise, next to the JR tracks. From Ochanomizu JR station on the Chuo or the Sobu lines, walk towards the next station, Suidobashi. This complex houses a number of small antique and curio shops. They sell a huge variety of curios and antiques, including *netsuke, ukiyo-e* woodblock prints, old clocks and watches, medicine boxes, ancient Korean *tansu* (wardrobe) and old ceramics. Here you can find something to fit your budget, whether it is just ¥1,000 or a million yen—from three-for-¥100 old coins to a *tsubo* pot costing several million yen. The emphasis, however, is on the inexpensive curios and trinkets, so the whole building is like a giant flea market. Open 10 A.M.–7:00 P.M. daily throughout the year.

Otsuka Kogeisha in Nihonbashi next door to Takashimaya Department Store is an old, established store dealing in *kakemono* scrolls, *gaku* framed pictures, and excellent reproductions of Japanese art, mostly *sumie* India ink-brush paintings. The store is on the 3rd floor of Shin-Nihonbashi Bldg. next to Taka-shimaya on its Kyobashi side (to the right as you face the department store). The ground floor is a bank. The store is open from 9:00 A.M. to 5:00 P.M. daily on weekends, but from 9:00 A.M. to 2:00 P.M. on Saturdays except the first and third Saturdays of the month, when it is closed. Closed on Sundays and national holidays. 271–3587.

Mayuyama, 2–5–9 Kyobashi, Chuo-ku; 561–5146. The most famous name among Tokyo's fine art dealers, and a must stop for every visiting museum curator. It specializes in Japanese and Chinese ceramics. A handsome modern building, on the corner one block west of Showa-dori and north of Takara-cho. Open 9:30 A.M.–6:00 P.M. Closed on Sundays and national holidays. Mayuyama has branches in the Imperial and Nikkatsu arcades, but these deal only in jewelry, handbags, ivory, etc.

Kochuko Art Gallery is another shop that handles only the best. Noted for its excellent collection of Oriental ceramics. Opposite Takashimaya department store, south side entrance. In this same block are several other small, discreet shops patronized by connoisseurs.

Heisando, 1–2–4 Shiba Koen, Minato-ku; 434–0588/9. An old Tokyo firm that deals in collector's items but also handles more popularly priced things. Good for screens, lacquer, and *kakemono* (hanging scroll pictures). Near Shiba Park Hotel in Shiba Park. Open 10:00 A.M.–5:00 P.M. Closed on Sundays and national holidays.

Odawara Shoten, Imperial Hotel Arcade; 591–0052. A collection of distinguished antiques and decorative pieces of all kinds. Open from 9 A.M.–7 P.M.; Sundays, 9 A.M. to 6 P.M.

Honma Antiques, 3–4–8 Azabudai, Minato-ku; 583–2950, with a wide selection on display including some small bronzes. A favorite with foreign collectors.

Yokoyama, Inc., the famed Kyoto store, has a branch on the 2nd floor of the Sukiyabashi Shopping Center (572–5066), where modern arts and crafts can be had in addition to a sampling of the Kyoto treasury of antiques. Open 10:00 A.M.–6:00 P.M. Its branch in Hotel Okura Arcade (582–0979) is open 9:00 A.M.–7:00 P.M. on weekdays, 10:00 A.M.–5:00 P.M. on Sundays.

Fuso, 7–6–47 Akasaka, Akasaka New Plaza, 1st fl., Minato-ku; 583–5945. Long established, it has curios in a new shop near Nogi Shrine, about 7 minutes' walk from Nogizaka Station on Chiyoda subway line. Open 10:00 A.M.–6:00 P.M. Closed on Sundays.

Art Plaza Magatani, 5–10–13 Toranomon, Minato-ku; 433–6321. Near Japan Taxfree Center, this is actually two shops, one dealing in antiques and the other selling new Japanese ceramics and folkcraft items. Open 9:30 A.M.–6:30 P.M. daily except Sundays and national holidays.

Ohno, 2–31–23 Yushima, Bunkyo-ku; 811–4365. A popular shop noted for its screen collection. Also good ceramics, bronzes. Be sure to go up to the 2nd floor. Near Yushima Tenjin Shrine and on Kasuga-dori Ave., at Yushima. About three minutes walk from Yushima Station on Chiyoda subway line. Open 10:00 A.M.–6:30 P.M. Closed on Sundays and national holidays. There are several other curio shops nearby, and a shop called *Suzuka,* the only pewter manufacturing company in Tokyo. Beautifully made sake sets, tea pots, and canisters.

Seigado Shimizu Honten (842–3777) is located in the Asakusa amusement area, just behind the famed Kannon Temple. Easily reached by subway from the Ginza. The temple is a tourist attraction, so you can easily combine temple and antique viewing. Open 9:00 A.M.–9:00 P.M. Closed second and fourth Wednesdays of each month.

Japan Art Center, Tokyo Green Heights, 1–22–10 Takadanobaba, Shinjuku-ku; 200–5387. Though small, it is crammed with furniture of an earlier Japanese era. You'll find items such as *tansu, hibachi, andon* (graceful lamps from the days before electricity), teapots and lacquered picnic boxes. About 5 minutes walk from Takadanobaba Station on JR Yamanote loop line. Open 10:30 A.M.–4:30 P.M. every day except Monday, including Sundays and national holidays.

There are several shops owned by foreign residents which are recommended for the visitor. Language is never a problem and questions about age, use and quality are readily and reliably answered. In addition, these dealers are well aware of foreign preferences. Your purchases can be packed and shipped back home for you.

The Gallery, 1–11–6 Akasaka, Minato-ku; 585–4816, across from the Okura Hotel and behind the U.S. Embassy residence. Here you will find the finest of Chinese and Japanese antiquities: fine carpets and furnishings, china, lacquerware, screens, and imaginative one-of-a-kind jewelry. Open 10 A.M.–6 P.M. Closed Sundays.

Harumi Antiques, 9–6–14 Akasaka, Minato-ku; 403–1043. A wide selection of blue and white china, tansu (Japanese chests of drawers) and hibachi. Hours, 10 A.M.–6 P.M. daily.

Antiques Tsurukame, Paseo Sankozaka 2F, 2–1–1 Shirogane, Minato-ku; 447–3990. The owners specialize in tansu and other home furnishings including ceramics and baskets. Open 11 A.M.–6:30 P.M. Closed Mondays and Tuesdays.

Kura, 2–2–18 Shiba Daimon, Minato-ku; 434–1300. Attractive selection of quality antiques in an old geisha house which also features modern Japanese prints. Open 11 A.M.–6 P.M. Closed Tuesdays.

Kurofune, 7–7–4 Roppongi, Minato-ku; 479–1552. Japanese style furnishings and accessories selected for western decorating. Open 11 A.M.–6 P.M. Closed Sundays.

Oriental Antiques: A small gallery in a home setting near Roppongi with both folkcrafts and fine antiques. Phone first for an appointment; 408-1532.

MUSICAL INSTRUMENTS

There are many musical instrument stores near JR Ochanomizu Station. They sell a great variety of instruments for light and classical music—electric guitars, electronic keyboards, drums, strings, woodwinds, and percussions. *Ishibashi* is open from 10:00 A.M. to 7:00 P.M. every day throughout the year, but until 6:00 P.M. on Sundays and national holidays. 291–0541. *Crosawa* is open from 10:00 A.M. to 7:30 P.M. daily throughout the year. 291–9791.

SWORDS

Japan Sword, 3–8–1 Toranomon, Minato-ku; 434–4321/3. If you are a complete novice, this is the place to start. Near Hotel Okura, they handle all the paraphernalia and speak English. Japan Sword also deals in less archaic items of cutlery for daily use. About 4–5 minutes walk either from Toranomon Station on Ginza subway line or from Kamiyacho Station on Hibiya subway line. Open 9:30 A.M.–6:00 P.M. Closed on Sundays and national holidays.

FLOWER-ARRANGING EQUIPMENT

For information and guidance on all flower-arranging topics, including current exhibits in Tokyo, *Ikebana International,* an organization devoted to worldwide promotion of Japanese flower arrangement, has its office at Shufunotomo Bldg., 8th Fl., 1–6 Surugadai, Chiyoda-ku; 293–8188.

Shops selling vases and other ikebana equipment are found in most neighborhoods. The department stores also have large sections devoted to vases and ikebana supplies. The Japanese don't go in much these days for the small tray garden figurines, but you can find a large selection of these in the *Hibiya Kadan* flower shop in the Imperial Hotel Arcade; 503–8781.

You can also buy flower arranging equipment at any of the flower-arrangement schools, such as the *Sogetsu School* on Aoyama-dori near the Canadian Embassy (7–2 Akasaka, Minato-ku; 408–1126), *Ikenobo College* near JR

Ochanomizu Station, and *Ohara Center* at Minami-Aoyama near the Aoyama-dori intersection. (5–7 Minami-Aoyama, Minato-ku; 499–1200.)

FISHING EQUIPMENT

The shop patronized by Japanese experts are *Tosaku* in Ginza 2-chome on Sotobori-dori, three blocks north of Harumi Dori. Tosaku carries a good line of Western-style equipment, but the emphasis is on the local brand. Tosaku is open from 10:00 A.M. to 7:30 P.M. daily except Sundays and national holidays. Address is 2–2–17 Ginza, Chuo-ku; 567–6950. A very good shop with a complete line of Western equipment is *Tsuruya* in Kyobashi on the east side of Chuo-dori. It is open from 10:00 A.M. to 7:00 P.M. daily, but from 11:00 A.M. to 5:00 P.M. on Sundays and national holidays. It is closed on the third Monday of every month. Address is 2–6–20 Kyobashi, Chuo-ku; 563–4071.

PROVINCIAL SPECIALTIES

In the Kokusai Kanko Building, close to the northern entrance, or Yaesu side, of Tokyo Station (that's the side with the Daimaru Department Store above the exits), there are showrooms on the 2nd, 3rd, and 4th floors, where the products of 27 Japanese prefectures are displayed. The display rooms of an additional 12 prefectures are located on the 9th floor of Daimaru. If you do not have time to visit the provinces, you might go here to see what kind of handicrafts you are missing. Some items can be purchased in Tokyo and the officials on duty can tell you where. If your itinerary includes trips to the provinces, it is all the more reason you should visit this center to gain advance knowledge of the specialties available in the places you will visit.

SUPERMARKET

Tokyo's international "supers" are excellent. Shop for food, for picnics, or "box lunch" ideas, at *Kinokuniya's* international store on Aoyama-dori (400–0022), a showplace for fine foods; at *National Azabu* in Hiroo (442–3181) *Olympia* in Harajuku; and at *Meidi-Ya* with popular stores in Roppongi and Hiroo. For more of the taste of Japan, stop at one of the many branches of *Peacock,* or at any of the neighborhood convenience stores. All open every day.

ART GALLERIES

If you want to view traditional prints showing you the Japan you wish you were seeing, almost any hotel arcade will have a gallery just right for your needs. But don't flinch when you see the price tags. The galleries listed below tend to deal in more contemporary artworks. Typically a show will last only six days, opening on a Monday and closing at about 4:00 P.M. on Saturday.

In addition, almost every major department store has a craft or ceramic salon, where weekly shows are staged. Some are very prestige-oriented and the prices of the works displayed reflect that. Others give new craftspeople the exposure they need to begin moving up the ladder of success.

Tokyo is a goldmine of galleries, but those listed below have proven their staying power.

Akasaka Green Gallery, at 4–8–8 Akasaka, 03–401–5255, has a varied schedule of events, leaning heavily toward ceramics. Kiyotsugu Sawa has shown his Shigaraki wares here in the past.

Galeria Grafica Tokio operates out of the Kato Building at 7–8–9 Ginza; 03–573–7731. Specializes in prints, rotating between antique Western (18th- and

19th-century works) and those of contemporary Japanese. Owner, Ms. Reiko Kurita speaks flawless English and has a respected knowledge of the contemporary art scene.

Gallery Inoui is on the 4th floor of the Narihiro Building at 3–9–3 Akasaka; 03–582–9660. Their varied collections are usually ceramics. Prices tend to be moderate on the Japanese scale and many new talents have been introduced here.

Galerie Laranne is in the basement of the Nishi Building at 2–8–2 Ginza; 03–567–5596. Owner Setsuko Sumi's small space is generally hung with printed artworks that herald the outer edge of print making in Japan. Shows include the lithography of Mineo Gotoh and the extremely limited edition woodblock artistry of Toshiharu Maekawa.

Galerie Mukai can be found on the 6th floor of the Tsukamoto Fudosan Building at 5–5–11 Ginza; 03–571–3292. Fine prints include those of Mayumi Oda and a number of rising stars from the United States. Madame Mukai has championed a number of fine artists, including Marion Korn, the late Kenzo Okada, and Morkazu Kumagai. Both the latter two were respected masters before their deaths.

Gallery Seiho is located on the 3rd floor of the Daiichi Iwatsuki Building at 6–7–16 Ginza; 03–573–5678. A sculpture-oriented gallery whose shows include the works of Shiro Hayami from Shikoku.

Gallery Te is found on the 4th floor of the Tojo Building at 8–10–7 Ginza; 03–574–6730. Artists shown here include minimalist Insik Quac and painter/printmaker Shingo Honda.

Gallery Yamaguchi is two blocks behind Matsuya Department Store at 3–8–12 Ginza, on the 3rd floor of the brick-faced Yamato Building; 03–564–0633. The wide range of shows here includes sculpture, prints, and paintings.

Ginzado Gallery is located on the 2nd floor of the Kyohana Building at 3–2–12 Ginza; 03–567–0648. The graphics and drawings of both Ryoji Ikeda and Masuo Ikeda art shown here.

Kakiden Gallery is found just outside the east exit of Shinjuku's JR Station, on the 7th floor of the Oyasu Building at 3–36–6 Shinjuku; 03–352–5118. Tea ceremony items are the type of ceramic ware most often shown here.

Maki Gallery is at 4–9 Nihombashi Honcho, Chuo-ku; 03–241–1310. The list of new talents emanating out of Nobuo Yamagishi's galleries reads like a who's who of Japanese contemporary art. Open daily.

Minami Aoyama Green Gallery is adjacent to the Aoyama Gakushuin University campus off Aoyama-dori, at 5–10–12 Minami Aoyama; 03–407–0050. Shows are almost exclusively ceramics, with such luminaries as Hideto Satonaka and Rikichi Miyanaga regularly displaying their latest kiln efforts.

Miyuki Gallery, located directly above Mune Craft (one of Tokyo's better craft and ceramic galleries) in the Ginza Chushajo Building at 6–4–4; 03–571–1771. Displays an ever-changing array of painting, print, and sculpture collections.

Nichido Garo (Gallery), is on Sotobori-dori Ave., near the Sony Bldg., at 5 Ginza, Chuo-ku; 571–2553. The most influential gallery of the Japanese academic school. There is an annex on the same street.

Q is located on the 4th floor of the Tojo Building at 8–10–7 Ginza (as is Gallery Te, mentioned above); 03–573–1696. Q tends toward experimental, oversize canvas works and arranged constructions of steel beams and rough quarried rock.

Tokyo Gallery is on the street three blocks west of Ginza and three blocks south of Harumi-dori, toward the Shimbashi entertainment district.

PACKING AND SHIPPING

Department stores will pack and ship your purchases overseas. Major hotels have a counter of a shipping agent. Best known worldwide for excellent work is *Odawara Shoten* in the Imperial Hotel Arcade (591–0052). Equally reliable, and more experienced for larger shipments, is *Nippon Express (Nittsu* in Japanese), which guarantees safe arrival of any shipment, including objets d'art and other precious items. If you ask, the shop where you purchase something can telephone Nippon Express, and the latter will pick up the item directly from the shop for shipment to your destination.

 DINING OUT. If you stir outside your hotel restaurants, eating in Tokyo becomes an adventure.

Finding a given restaurant among the thousands in the sprawling metropolis is in itself a task of some magnitude, as Japan does not aid the visitor by having a recognizable address system. Having arrived at your restaurant you will frequently find (if in a Western-style one) that familiar dishes somehow taste quite unlike what you expected or (if it is a Japanese-style one) that there are gastronomic touches of such delicacy and beauty that a whole new world of cuisine opens up before you.

If you are at all in the mood for adventure, you will probably be pleasantly surprised to find that delicacies such as octopus, raw prawns, sea urchin eggs, or eel liver are quite palatable.

Apart from the modestly priced chair-and-table lunch places, which are similar to their counterparts all over the world, Japanese restaurants may be divided into two broad categories: the *o-zashiki* (private room) restaurant, where the meal is served in your own Japanese-style room, and the counter restaurant, where you sit up at a long counter of scrubbed white wood. Generally (although not invariably) the former is more expensive than the latter.

Indeed, the best Japanese restaurants (known as *ryoriya*) charge prices comparable to those leading Parisian restaurants. In general Japanese restaurants specialize in one or two dishes, which are served on a *table d'hôte* basis. Thus you must go to a special *sukiyaki* restaurant, or a special eel restaurant, or a special snap turtle restaurant if your fancy takes you in the direction of those dishes.

At most Japanese-style restaurants the only choice of drinks you will have will be beer, *sake,* or whisky (*Suntory,* the best Japanese brand of whisky, is a good, smooth whisky with a Scotch-like character). Expensive *ryoriya,* however, may have imported liquors.

Japanese tend to eat early and, with only a few exceptions, you must be prepared to arrive at any Japanese-style restaurant before 8:00 P.M.

You should have your hotel front desk phone ahead to any high-class restaurant to make sure that a room is available. Reservations are becoming necessary at higher-priced Western-style restaurants.

Bills and tipping are tricky in Japan.

Japanese who can afford to go to the best *ryoriya* (mostly on expense accounts) generally have charge accounts and the bill is sent to their offices. For those who wish to pay cash, a small slip of paper with the total charge is discreetly handed to them at the end of the meal. There is no itemized bill. This is supposed to include a service charge, but since the patrons of such restaurants are expected to have great *face,* they are expected to add a generous tip as well. This should not be less than 1,000 yen, no matter what your bill is. If the bill is over 10,000 yen, you should make the tip at least 2,000 yen.

These subtleties, however, are best left to those lucky (and wealthy) enough to be regular patrons of such places. For most ordinary mortals, including most Japanese, the situation is much simpler—and blessedly easy on the wallet. Routine tipping of the Western variety is a custom alien to the Japanese. Nine times out of ten there is not the slightest need to pay more than the sum at the bottom of your bill. There will be no churlish looks when you pocket your change, and if you leave money on the table, more often than not the waitress will assume you did so by mistake and will hurry after you to return it.

A word about locating the restaurants listed below. The only sure way of finding them on your own, given Tokyo's idiosyncratic address system, is to have a detailed map leading from the nearest landmark, usually a railway station, to the restaurant's door. Obviously this was impossible to provide, given the concise nature of this book, but there are two practical alternatives: (1) Have the front desk at your hotel phone ahead and draw you a map according to the instructions he/she receives; or (2) give the restaurant's phone number to your taxi driver and have him phone ahead for directions—assuming he doesn't know the place to begin with, which, in Tokyo, is more than likely. Only those bent on proving something would try to find a Tokyo restaurant unaided. Old hands who have been here for many years, not to mention the Japanese themselves, would not dream of doing such a thing.

Note: The rate of mortality among new restaurants in Tokyo is extremely high. There are restaurants which have stood on the same site for 200 years—but many more last less than one year, and some have gone into bankruptcy even before they opened their doors! This means that it would take a weekly publication to keep an up-to-date list of operating restaurants—and there are estimated to be about 500,000 of them in metropolitan Tokyo! It would therefore be advisable to consult with your hotel desk or read local English-language publications before setting out for any of the restaurants listed below.

Our price categories for the listings below are per person as follows: *Super Deluxe,* ¥20,000 and up; *Deluxe,* ¥10,000–20,000; *Expensive,* ¥5,000–10,-000; *Moderate,* ¥2,000–5,000; and *Inexpensive,* up to ¥2,000. "All major credit cards" means that establishment takes American Express (AE), Billion, Diamond, Diner's Club (DC), Japan Carte Blanche (JCB), MasterCard (MC), UC, and Visa (V).

JAPANESE STYLE

When American and European diners pay astronomical prices for dining out they are in part paying to become celebrities for the evening, "the observed of all observers"; the pleasure is almost as much social as gastronomical. Japanese diners, on the other hand, pay the highest prices for the privilege of withdrawing from society altogether, into a private, cocoonlike room where they are treated like emperors or sultans. The entrance of the restaurant is almost certain to be small, dark, and hidden down a narrow back street. As everything about restaurants of this type is unfamiliar to the visitor from abroad, much the best way to experience them is to be taken by a sympathetic and bilingual Japanese companion. Indeed, without one it will be difficult even to make a reservation—it may even be impossible.

This is particularly true of Tokyo's *kaisekiryori* (tray cuisine) restaurants, but any of those little hole-in-the-wall joints that look at first glance as if they'd be likely to serve you instant coffee in a cracked cup need to be approached warily. Smallness denotes intimacy; the Japanese language does not distinguish between "customer" and "guest" so walking in off the street is like gate crashing someone's kitchen. Grit your teeth and brazen it out and you'll probably get served, but the experience may be a bizarrely chilly one.

In all such places a Japanese companion, or competence in speaking Japanese, is the prerequisite of an enjoyable evening. But the many larger, cheaper, or more internationally minded Japanese restaurants pose no such problems. The word "accessible" below denotes restaurants that are not likely to prove difficult for the casual foreign customer.

Super Deluxe

Hamadaya. 13–5, Nihonbashi, Ningyo-cho 3-chome, Chuo-ku; 661–2648. Hamadaya is one of a number of central Tokyo *kaisekiryori* restaurants that must rank among the most expensive places to eat in the world. Your meal here will be a full-blown introduction to Japanese aesthetics; every aspect of the decor, the service, the tableware, and the foot itself will reflect the Japanese preoccupation with delicacy, harmony, and attention to detail. The food will be served on trays in a private tatami-matted room. No credit cards.

Ichinao. 8–6, Asakusa 3-chome, Taito-ku; 874–3032. Another super-pricey kaiseki restaurant, this one located in Asakusa, the legendary old entertainment quarter on the east side of town. No credit cards.

Deluxe

Goeimon. 2–39–14 Hakusan, Bunkyo-ku; 812–0111. Where it has gained entry at all, tofu remains a second-class citizen in the Western kitchen, but in this exquisite, Kyoto-like restaurant it attains its apotheosis. Goeimon is a gourmet Japanese restaurant of the highest caliber, which just happens to use tofu as a basic ingredient in many of the dishes. A pretty garden and running water enhance the experience. Open 5:00 to 10:00 P.M. Tuesdays through Saturdays; 3:00 P.M. to 8:00 P.M. Sundays and holidays. Closed Mondays. No credit cards.

Holytan. 2–30–10 Kabuki-cho, Shinjuku-ku; 208–8000.. Located behind Koma Stadium in the heart of Kabuki-cho, Tokyo's naughtiest square mile, Holytan is an impressive teppanyaki steak restaurant with a variety of other dishes on the menu, including seafood. Open 5:00 P.M. to 2:00 A.M. weekdays and 4:00 to 10:00 P.M. on Sundays. A branch in Hibiya (501–2454) closes earlier (and on Sundays) but opens for weekday lunches, and offers *kaiseki ryori.* Accessible. All major credit cards.

Houmasa. 2–21, Moto—Azabu 3—chome, Minato-ku, Tokyo; 479–2880. One of Tokyo's *kaiseki* restaurants most esteemed by those who know—the sort of restaurant where a truly knowledgeable companion is indispensable. The menu offers dishes in a variety of catagories such as *namamono,* "raw things"; *nimono,* "simmered things;" *agemono,* "fried things"; and so on. This is a tiny restaurant where everything is perfect. A taxi ride away from Roppongi. Open from 6:00 P.M. to about 10:30 P.M., closed Sundays and holidays. No credit cards.

Inagiku. 9–8 Nihonbashi, Kayaba-cho 2-chome, Chuo-ku; 669–5501. A venerable (80-year-old) *tempura* shop that cooks some of the lightest, freshest tempura in town at its old headquarters near Nihonbashi, heart of the EdoPeriod merchant's quarter. A small branch on the 7th floor of Shinjuku's Keio Plaza Hotel maintains comparable standards but with lower prices (344–0111). All major credit cards.

Jisaku. 14–19 Akashi-cho, Chuo-ku; 541–2391. A large old restaurant on the bank of the Sumida River, behind St. Luke's Hospital. The specialty is *mizutaki,* country-style sukiyaki using fish or poultry in place of beef. Other dishes are served too. Reservations preferred. Open noon to 10:00 P.M. All major credit cards.

Kissho. 8–7, Akasaka 4-chome, Minato-ku; 403–2621. Located near Aoyama Dori. Kissho has three different restaurants, one on each floor, with the most expensive at the top. Specialties of the house are sukiyaki, shabu-shabu, and tempura, and the atmosphere is quiet and elegant. Open 11:30 A.M. to 11:00 P.M. Accessible. All major credit cards.

Shiruyoshi. 6–2–12 Akasaka, Minato-Ku; 583–7244. Located in front of Shin Kokusai Bldg.; West Annex. An authentic and classy Japanese restaurant where the tempura is prepared before your eyes. The full course dinner is between ¥35,000 and ¥40,000; the lunch menu is the same, with a "modestly" priced item being the tempura at ¥15,000. Open for lunch, and for dinner to 11:00 P.M.

Expensive

Ashibe. Tsukiji; 543–3540. One of the many fine fish restaurants strategically located near Tsukiji fish market, Ashibe's specialty is *fugu,* the blowfish whose liver and ovaries contain tetrodotoxin, .024 of an ounce of which can kill a grown man in hours. Ashibe, like all fugu shops, is government-licensed, and they've never lost a customer! Most fugu eaten in Japan is frozen, but Ashibe's is fresh and therefore only available between October and March. The rest of the year console yourself with the shop's delicious *suppon* (snapping turtle) dishes. Open 11:30 A.M. to 1 P.M., and 5:00 P.M. to 10:00 P.M. No credit cards.

Chinzanso. 10–8, Sekiguchi 2-chome, Bunkyo-ku; 943–1111. A gigantic restaurant set in a magnificent garden. A specialty is teppanyaki barbecue, a splendid feast. The enjoyment is increased by the entertainment—Hawaiian bands, *Son et Lumière* presentations. Fireflies are released in the garden during the summer months. Open daily until 9:00 P.M. Accessible. All major credit cards.

Edo Gin. 5–1, Tsukiji 4-chome, Chuo-ku; 543–4405. Reputed to be one of the best sushi shops in Japan, Edo Gin is not only on the doorstep of Tsukiji fish market, but the restaurant's interior is dominated by a huge tank in which the evening's ingredients swim blithely about. Raw fish doesn't come any fresher. Edo Gin is big, too, which helps to make it more accessible than other places in the vicinity. Open daily till 9:30 P.M., closed Sunday. All major credit cards.

Five Farmers. Square Building, 10–3 Roppongi 3-chome, Minato-ku; 470–1675. Traditional food served in a rustic, snow-country ambience. Reservations are preferred. All major credit cards.

Fuku Sushi. 7–8, Roppongi 5–chome, Minato-ku; 402–4116. Another famous sushi shop, this one is in the fashionable and international Roppongi section. Reservations are preferred. Open till 11:00 P.M., closed Sundays. All major credit cards.

Furusato. 4–1 Aobadai 3-chome, Meguro-ku; 463–2310. At the top of Dogenzaka Street in Shibuya, near Osaka-ue bus stop. A 300-year-old farmhouse dismantled, brought to Tokyo and re-erected, Furusato (Old country home) offers a wide range of local Japanese dishes, such as *shabu-shabu* and *nabemono.* Definitely accessible and full of charm—though perhaps a bit of a tourist trap; there is a "foreign tourist course" priced ¥6000 to ¥10,000. Lunch 11:30 A.M. to 2:00 P.M., dinner 5:30 P.M. to 10:00 P.M. Closed Mondays. All major credit cards.

Happo-en. 1–1, Shiroganedai 1-chome, Minato-ku; 443–3111. Two restaurants in one the tatami-matted *Nihonkan,* serving *kaiseki* dishes, and the Western-style restaurant, with a menu including sukiyaki. Open 11:30 A.M. to 9:00 P.M. reservations preferred. AE, DC.

Kiraku. 12–1, Tsukiji 4-chome, Chuo-ku; 541–0908. Another highly recommended Tsukiji sushi shop. Open daily until the supply of fresh fish runs out, usually about 8:30 P.M. Visa.

Kushi Hachi-ten. 10–9 Roppongi 3–chome, Minato-ku; 403–3060. When Jimmy Carter paid a return visit to Kushihachi, his favorite Tokyo yakitoria, in 1983, the news magazine *Focus* captioned the photo "only the yakitori hasn't changed." Most yakitoria are bright and garish, but this classy specimen is decorated with antiques and has a cozy atmosphere. The prices are less than presidential. AE, DC, JCB.

Kyubei. 5–23 Ginza 8-chome, Chuo-ku; 571–6523. The famous Ginza sushi shop, with branches in the Hotel Okura, Hotel New Otani, and Keio Plaza Hotel. Open 11:30 A.M. to 2:00 P.M., 5:00 P.M. to 10:00 P.M. All major credit cards.

Okahan. Ginza Kanetanaka Bldg, 6–16 Ginza 7-chome, Chuo-ku; 571–1417. Okahan's specialty is *sukiyaki,* served in classically Japanese surroundings. There's another branch at the New Otani. Open noon to 10:00 P.M. except Sundays. Reservations preferred. Accessible. All major credit cards.

Sasanoyuki. 15–10, Negishi 2-chome, Taito-ku; 873–1145. A pioneer of *tofu* cuisine, Sasanoyuki is a large restaurant that has managed to keep a friendly, solicitous atmosphere typical of the proletarian eastern quarter in which it is located. *Every* dish has tofu in it—which may seem too much of a good thing, though the variety of preparations amazes. Accessible: there's an English menu. Open 11:00 A.M. to 9:00 P.M., closed Mondays. Diamond.

Seryna. 12–2, Roppongi 3-chome, Minato-ku; 403–6211. A famous restaurant with French and Chinese as well as Japanese menus. Seryna is renowned for its shabu-shabu and sukiyaki as well as its *Kani Seryna,* made with fresh crab daily. Accessible. All major credit cards. Open 12:00 noon to 10:30 P.M.

Shabu Zen. 17–16, Roppongi 5-chome, Minato-ku; 585–5388. A highly accessible Roppongi restaurant specializing in *shabu-shabu* and *sukiyaki.* Private rooms available, and the kimono-clad waitresses speak English. Open 5:00 P.M. to midnight, to 11:00 P.M. on Sundays.

Ten-Ichi. 6–5, Ginza 6-chome, Chuo-ku; 571–1949. Ten-Ichi's well-intentioned local advertising, which shows a row of aproned *gaijin* (foreigners) tucking in to the tempura, might be counterproductive if it leaves the impression that the place is a tourist trap. True, it welcomes foreign guests, but there is no need to fear you are being taken for a ride—Ten-Ichi's reputation is solid. All major credit cards accepted. Open 11:30 A.M. to 9:30 P.M. Branches at the Imperial Hotel's Imperial Tower, Akasaka Plaza of Akasaka Tokyu Hotel, and 1st basement of West Shinjuku's highrise Mitsui Building. All major credit cards.

Zakuro. TBS Kaikan, 3–3, Akasaka 5-chome, Minato-ku; 582–6841. A famous chain of shabu-shabu restaurants with branches in central Akasaka, Kyobashi, Marunouchi, and Nihonbashi besides the main restaurant in Akasaka. Open daily 11:00 A.M. to 10:00 P.M. Reservations preferred. All major credit cards

Moderate

Aoi Marushin. 4–4, Asakusa 1–chome, Taito-ku; 841–0110, 841–5439. In the old east side entertainment quarter, Aoi Marushin's varied menu includes yakitori, tempura, and sukiyaki. Open daily 11:00 A.M. to 10:00 P.M. All major credit cards

Chikuyotei. 14–7, Ginza 8-chome, Chuo-ku; 542–0787. Very conveniently located next to the Lion Beer Hall at the main Ginza intersection with Harumidori Avenue, Chikuyotei specializes in *unagi* (broiled eel) dishes. Open 11:30 A.M. to 8:00 P.M. There are three other branches in the city center.

5-Chome Tsubo-Han. 3–9, Ginza 5-chome, Chuo-ku; 571–3467. An island of elegant antiquity in racy, high-rising Ginza, with interior walls of dark wood, dimly lighted from behind *shoji* paper and dotted with folkcraft tableware, Tsubo-Han is the place to come for an authentic and undiluted image of Japan which is so strong that afterwards it is almost impossible to shake from the memory. The cuisine is far removed from the sukiyaki and tempura standards: *zosui,* a rice stew with fish, chicken, or vegetables, and *o-chazuke,* rice with green tea, *nori* seaweed and, in the case of *sake chazuke,* salmon. It's the sort of food the Japanese eat every day, but in marvelous surroundings. Open 4:30 P.M. to 11:00 P.M. Closed Sundays and holidays.

Hassan. Blf, Denki Building, Roppongi, Minato-ku; 403–9112. Hassan's interior is designed in the style of a *sukiya-zukuri* tea house—rustic-looking, a little gloomy, but full of subtle refinement. Reasonable prices, tremendous portions: all the shabu-shabu you can eat for ¥4,300, for example. Also sukiyaki, tempura, sashimi (raw fish), tea ceremony cuisine. Accessible. Open daily 11:30 A.M. to 11:00 P.M.

Ichioku. 4–4–5 Roppongi, Minato-ku; 405–9891. Small restaurant in backstreet Roppongi that transcends categories. Menu includes mussels, spring rolls, tofu steak, dumplings, garlic toast . . . gasp at the eclectic imagination of the chef. Located behind the Self-Defence Agency. Open 5:00 P.M. to 12:30 P.M.

Inagiku. Roppongi Branch: Hotel Ibis, 14–4, Roppongi 7-chome, Minato-ku; 403–5507; Shinjuku Branch: Keio Plaza Hotel, 2–1, Nishi-Shinjuku 2-chome, Shinjuku-ku; 344–0592. Shibuya Branch: 15–1, Udagawa-cho, Shibuya-ku; 464 –6887; Tokyo Stn. Branch: Tokyo Station Building, 9–1, Marunouchi 1–chome, Chiyoda-ku; 212–7777. Inagiku is the fine tempura specialist whose Nihonbashi headquarters appeared in the *Deluxe* section. The word is that the branches are almost as good—and a lot cheaper.

Inakaya. Akasaka Social Building, 12–7, Akasaka 3-chome, Minato-ku; 586– 3054. In a robatayaki restaurant a wide variety of ingredients—various kinds of fish, vegetables, tofu, meat—are grilled by the chef, put on the end of a long paddle, and passed to the customers sitting at the semicircular counter. Ordering-by-pointing is effective, the atmosphere is friendly and informal, and the food is generally cheap. *Inaka* means "the country," *inakaya* "country house" and that's the best description of the ambience. Definitely accessible.

Noboritei. 1–12–6 Shimbashi, Minato-ku; 571–0482. You shouldn't leave Japan with investigating what the Japanese do to eel—*unagi,* as it's called. It's art. They bone, steam, and broil it until it is rich and succulent, a deep amber in color, then serve it, often on a bed or rice, in lacquered boxes. Noboritei is a fine place to sample this dish at its best. Open 11:00 A.M. to 8:00 P.M.

Minokichi. Roi Roppongi, 5–1, Roppongi 5-chome, Minato-ku; 404–0767. Kaiseki ryori and shabu shabu served in an ambience of old Kyoto. Open 11:30 A.M. to 11:00 P.M. All major credit cards.

Tenmi. 10–6, Jinnan 1-chome, Shibuya-ku; 496–9703. The leading natural food restaurant in tokyo, Tenmi serves a good variety of excellently cooked vebetarian Japanese dishes, notably *o-fukuro no aji,* "flavors of mother," a plate of up to a dozen different exquisite tastes in small portions, served with steamed brown rice, miso shiru (soup), and pickles. Downstairs is a natural food supermarket that sells organically grown vegetables and much else besides. Open 11:30 A.M. to 2:30 P.M., 5:00 P.M. to 8:30 P.M., Sundays and holidays 11:30 A.M. to 6:00 P.M. Closed 3rd Wednesday of the month. Highly accessible.

Inexpensive

There is a great deal of inexpensive food available in Tokyo, much of it approximately Japanese. A lot of it, however, is not terribly wholesome. Sometimes it seems that the Japanese have learned their Western lessons a good deal too thoroughly, for the cheap restaurant food is laden with preservatives, artificial coloring, and monosodium glutamate. It's probably much healthier to eat cheap in a relatively poor country like neighboring Korea, where the chefs are less sophisticated and the ingredients relatively pure.

If you can ignore that aspect of it, however, you will find that every miniscule shopping street has its array of restaurants. Among the tastiest Japanese-style dishes offered almost everywhere are *soba* (buckwheat noodles), *oden* (see below), *donburi* style (scrambled egg with meat or chicken on a bed of rice) and *udon* (thick, white, wheat-based noodles in broth). There are also many cheap *sushi* shops, including some where the sushi travels around on a little conveyor belt and the diners pick the dishes they fancy, but we strongly recommend that you save up your pennies for the more expensive version. There's a world of difference.

The handful of restaurants listed below combine superb food with really cheap prices. It's not surprising that they are few and far between. In their own way they are as distinguished, and as Japanese, as the ¥ 20,000 plus kaiseki ryori places.

Musashino Sobadokoro. 55–11, Nakano 5-chome, Nakano-ku; 389–4751. *Soba,* buckwheat noodles usually served in broth, is a Japanese favorite that foreign visitors are apt to overlook because it is so cheap and humble-seeming. When it is made by hand and only the purest ingredients are used, however, it can be a real treat. Tucked away among the nightclubs of Nakano, west of Shinjuku on the Chuo line, this little shop serves some of the best soba in town. Open 6:00 P.M. to 2:00 A.M., closed Sundays.

Otako Honten. 4–4 Ginza 3-chome, Chuo-ku; 561–8246/8298. *Oden* is a mystifying and little-known Japanese dish consisting of bits of *kamoboko* (fish sausage), vegetables, fried and stuffed tofu, and many other puzzling bits and pieces kept bubbling in a great vat of stock and eaten with hot mustard. It is most enjoyable on a cold winter's night, washed down with tumblers of hot, cheap sake in one of those tent-like bars that litter the fringes of Tokyo's railway stations. Otako in the Ginza is one of the two classiest oden places in town. The other is Yasuko, described below. Otako is Kanto, i.e., Tokyo-style, which means the stock is fish- (not chicken-) based, and the flavor is saltier. Open noon to 2:00 P.M. and 5:00 P.M. Closed Sundays and holidays.

Tong Fu. 28–9, Minami-Aoyama 2-chome, Minato-ku; 403–3527. Unique restaurant with an essentially Chinese menu that also includes Japanese and Vietnamese dishes. Good value lunch at ¥ 1,000 might include kidney beans with mince, soup, rice, pickles, and salad, followed by a sherbet dessert and coffee. Near Bell Commons store. Open 11:30 A.M. to 4:30 A.M.

Yabu Soba. 10, Kanda Awaji-cho 2-chome, Chiyoda-ku; 251–0287. A really high quality *soba* shop located in Kanda, conveniently close to the center of town. Open 11:30 A.M. to 7:00 P.M.

Yasuko. 4–6 Ginza 5-chome, Chuo-ku; 571–0621. Not far from Otako (above) in Ginza 5-chome, *Yasuko* means "cheap" and "happy"; the quality of the food and the size of the bill should explain why. This is Ginza's other *oden* shop; the stock is chicken-based and the flavor (and decor) are seomwhat lighter than Otako's. Open 4:00 P.M. to 11:00 P.M. daily.

AMERICAN

Deluxe

Fisherman's Wharf. Dobashi Bldg., B1, 17–8, Akasaka 3-chome, Minato-ku; 583–0659. Tokyo branch of San Francisco's famous seafood restaurant. Reservations preferred. Open 11:00 A.M. to 2:30 P.M., 5:00 P.M. to 11:00 P.M., closed 3rd Sunday of every month. All major credit cards.

Expensive

Hard Rock Café. 4–20, Roppongi 5-chome, Minato-ku; 408–7018. Hamburgers, steaks, other American classics in an ambience redolent of the '50s and '60s. Open 4:00 P.M. to 2:00 A.M. daily.

Spago. 7–8, Roppongi 5-chome, Minato-ku; 423–4025. First Japanese branch of Austrian-born chef Wolfgang Puck's creation, Spago is the place for California cuisine. "Spago" is actually Italian slang for pasta, but there's a lot more to the menu than that. Open 5:30 P.M. to 11:00 P.M. daily. Spago may be the only restaurant in Tokyo that encourages tipping! AE, DC, JCB, Visa.

BRAZILIAN

Moderate

Saci Perere. PL Yotsuya Bldg., 9 Honshio-cho, Shinjuku-ku; 353–7521. Authentic Brazilian food with samba and bossa nova performances. Open 6:00 P.M. to 2:00 A.M.; closed Sundays and holidays.

BRITISH

Moderate

The Rising Sun. 2d floor, Shinsei Building, 9–3, Yotsuya 1-chome, Shinjuku-ku; 353–8842. Lovable, authentic British pub with mad Irish landlord Jerry Hegarty. Noted for its masterpieces of British cuisine: shepherd's pie, bangers and mash, fish and chips. Open 6:00 P.M. to midnight, closed Sundays and holidays.

CAMBODIAN

Inexpensive

Angkor Wat. 44–12, Yoyogi 1-chome, Shibuya-ku; 370-3019. Near Yoyogi Station. The first Cambodian restaurant in town, opened by Cambodian refugees. Very simple and inexpensive, with a menu of traditional rice-based dishes. Open 11:00 A.M. to 2:00 P.M. and 5:00 P.M. to 11:00 P.M.

CHINESE

There are plenty of moderately priced Chinese restaurants in Tokyo, and innumerable extremely cheap ones. Most of them use too much monosodium glutamate (*aji-no-moto,* as it's known in Japan, the country in which it was invented), which is the problem with cheap Chinese food all over the world. In the cheap places, the food has also undergone substantial adaptations to suit it to the Japanese palate, so true aficionados may get a shock. Undoubtedly the most popular Chinese dish locally—perhaps the single most popular food—is *ramen,* Chinese-style noodles swimming in broth. About ¥500 will buy you a basic bowl of ramen, hot, nourishing, and tasty (if you can forget about the additives).

Below we have listed some of the more expensive Chinese restaurants, where you are more likely to be served authentic Chinese food.

Expensive

Bodaiju. 2nd fl., Bukyo Dendo Center Bldg., 3–14, Shiba 4-chome, Minato-ku; 456–3257. "Unique" is an overworked word, but it applies to Bodaiju, which is the first and only restaurant in Japan to specialize in Chinese vegetarian dishes. Many visitors to Hong Kong will have seen the incredibly crafty imitations of meat dishes produced by vegetarian restaurants in the Colony, and now they're available here too. The owner, Mr. Numata, is the man responsible for putting Buddhist bibles alongside the Christian ones in many of Japan's hotels. Open 11:30 A.M. to 2:30 P.M., 5:30 to 9:00 P.M.; closed Sundays. Closest subway stations are Mita (on the Tori No. 6 Mita line) and Tamachi on the Yamanote line. AE, Diamond, DC.

China Doll. 27–19, Minami-Aoyama 2-chome, Minato-ku; 479–0201. Next to Orange House in Aoyama. A famous restaurant with a wide range of dishes. Open 11:30 A.M. to 11:30 P.M. All major credit cards.

Fu-Ling. 8–4, Roppongi 4-chome, Minato-ku; 401–9769. A Cantonese-style restaurant that is open from morning to late at night—as late as 4:00 A.M. All major credit cards.

Heichinrou. 28th fl. Fukoku Seimei Bldg., 2–2, Uchisaiwaicho 2-chome, Chiyoda-ku; 508–0555. A branch of the oldest restaurant in Yokohama's China-town, Heichinrou has an elaborately Chinese interior and a great view of the Imperial Palace moat. The Cantonese cuisine is prepared by a chef sent from one of Hong Kong's leading hotels. Open 11:00 A.M. to 9:30 P.M.; closed on Sundays and national holidays. All major credit cards.

Heichinrou. Shibuya Branch, 2nd fl., Shibuya Hillside, 19–3, Jinnan 1-chome, Shibuya-ku; 464–7888. The Shibuya branch of the famous restaurant, near Parco II Department Store, specializes in Cantonese-style fresh seafood. Open daily 11:00 A.M. to 9:30 P.M. All major credit cards.

Hoa Hoa. Roppongi, Minato-ku; 402–8787. Five minutes walk from Rop-pongi intersection towards Shibuya. Another example of the East-West mar-riages that have been cropping up in *haute cuisine* lately, Hoa Hoa's chefs provide Cantonese cuisine cooked in a French manner. Open 11:30 A.M. to 11:00 P.M. (last orders, 10:30 P.M.). Open noon to 10:00 P.M. on Sundays and holidays. All major credit cards.

Hokkai-En. 12, 1, Nishi-Azabu 2-chome, Minato-ku; 407–8507. Located close to the Almond coffee shop at Roppongi intersection. A large restaurant that is widely believed to be one of the best Peking-style places in town. It's also expensive. Open 11:30 A.M. to 10:00 P.M. All major credit cards.

New Asia Restaurant. 3–2, Shiba Daimon 2-chome, Minato-ku; 434–0005. Shanghai cuisine, with a menu that changes daily. Open from lunchtime to 10:00 P.M. Reservations are preferred. Hamamatsu-cho is the nearest Yamanote line station.

South China. 35, Jingumae 6-chome, Shibuya-ku; 400–0031. Also at 14–10, Sakuragaoka-cho, Shibuya-ku; 461–7592. Two Cantonese restaurants with high reputations. Open 11:30 A.M. to 11:00 P.M. All major credit cards.

Tokyo Daihanten. JC Bldg., 17–3, Shinjuku 5-chome, Shinjuku-ku; 202–0121. With over 200 dishes on the menu and reportedly over 60 chefs to prepare them, this is a very special Szechuan-style restaurant. Open daily from 11:00 A.M. to 10:00 P.M. AE, Diamond, DC, UC, Visa.

CZECHOSLOVAKIAN

Moderate

Castle Praha. Tonichi Bldg., 2–31, Roppongi 6-chome, Minato-ku; 405–2831. Czechoslovakian cuisine with Bohemian music. Open lunchtime from 5:30 P.M. to 10:30 P.M. Reservations preferred.

FRENCH

Deluxe

Crescent. 8–20, Shiba-Koen 1-chome, Minato-ku; 436–3211. Rebuilt in late-Victorian style; live musical entertainment accompanies the food. Open daily

11:30 A.M. to 10:00 P.M. Closed on Sundays in the summer. All major credit cards.

L'ecrin Ginza. Ginza Mikimoto Pearl Bldg., 5–5, Ginza 4-chome, Chuo-ku; 561–9706. The chef de cuisine is a member of France's prestigious Academie Culinaire. Open lunch, tea, and dinner; closed on Sundays. Reservations preferred. Open 11:30 A.M. to 10:00 P.M.All major credit cards.

Ile de France. Com Roppongi Bldg, 11–5 Roppongi 3-chome, Minato-ku; 404–0384. Unpretentious, low-key restaurant famous for the extraordinary quality of its classic French cuisine. Duck dishes particularly good. Open 11:30 A.M. to 2:00 P.M., 5:30 P.M. to 10:30 P.M. All major credit cards.

John Kanaya Azabu Restaurant. Kanaya Hotel Mansion, 1–25, Nishi-Azabu 3-chome, Minato-ku; 402–4744. A sleek spot, fashionable with diplomats and fast-lane locals. Open 5:30 P.M. to 11:00 P.M. All major credit cards.

Maxim's de Paris. Sony Bldg., 3–1, Ginza 5-chome, Chuo-ku; 572–3621. A clone of the famous Parisian original with French chef and manager direct from Paris, Maxim's is in the basement of the Sony Bldg. in the heart of the Ginza. Lunchtime set menu a hefty ¥6,600; dinner set menu ¥20,000. Open 11:30 A.M. to 2:30 P.M.; 5:30 P.M. to 11:00 P.M.; bar open 11:30 A.M. to 11:00 P.M.; closed on Sundays. AE, DC, V.

Prunier. Imperial Hotel, 1–1, Uchsaiwai 1-chome, Chiyoda-ku; 504–1111. Tokyo's branch of the famous Parisian establishment, in the capital's oldest five-star hotel. All major credit cards. Open 12:00 A.M. to 9:30 P.M.

Rengaya. Daikanyama branch: 29–18, Sarugaku-cho, Shibuya-ku; 463–8377. The cuisine of Lyon in the famous "brick house." Daikanyama shop (1st stop on Toyoko Line from Shibuya) open 10 A.M. to 9 P.M. All major credit cards.

Virgo. Hotel New Otani, 4 Kioi-cho, Chiyoda-ku; 238–0020. La nouvelle cuisine prepared by a Parisian chef. Terrific views of Tokyo from the top floor of the New Otani Tower. All major credit cards. Open noon to 10:00 P.M.

Expensive

Bistro Lotus. JBP Bldg., 8–17, Roppongi 6-chome, Minato-ku; 403–7666. Changing menu, respectable cellar of French wines. Reservations preferred. All major credit cards. Open noon to 10:30 P.M.

Chez Figaro. 4–1, Nishi-Azabu 4-chome, Minato-ku; 400–8718. Tokyo's best bistro, wildly popular with French residents. The ¥2,000 lunch served Tuesday through Saturday is an especially outstanding bargain. Private parties (4 to 30 persons) catered. Reservations preferred. Open for lunch and from 6:00 P.M. to 10:00 P.M. All major credit cards.

Isolde. Hokushin Bldg., 2–1, Nishi-Azabu 3-chome, Minato-ku; 478–1055. Impressively authentic French cuisine in an elegant Parisian ambience. Live music, reservations preferred. Open every day 11:30 A.M. to 10:30 P.M. All major credit cards.

Pantagruel. TBS Kaikan Bldg., 3–3, Akasaka 5-chome, Minato-ku; 582–5891. Reservations preferred. All major credit cards. Open 11:00 A.M. to 3:00 P.M., 5:00 P.M. to 10:00 P.M.

Le Poisson Rouge. 3–10, Minami-Aoyama 5-chome, Minato-ku; 499–3391. Reservations preferred. All major credit cards.

La Promenade. Sanshin Bldg., 4–1, Yuraku-cho 1-chome, Chiyoda-ku; 504–3668. Very popular restaurant, menu changes daily. Reservations preferred. All major credit cards. Open noon to 10:00 P.M.

Regence. 32nd fl., Toho Seimei Bldg., 15–1, Shibuya 2-chome, Shibuya-ku; 406–5291. Authentic French cuisine at the top of Shibuya's tallest building. Open daily 11:30 A.M. to 2:00 P.M., 5:30 P.M. to 9:30 P.M., 8:30 P.M. on Sundays and holidays. All major credit cards.

GERMAN

Expensive

Alte Liebe. 29–8 Minami Aoyama 2-chome, Minato-ku; 405–8312. Ginza branch: 8, Ginza 7-chome, Chuo-ku; 573–4025. Live music at the Ginza shop. Reservations preferred. Open 11:00 A.M. to 10:00 P.M.

Bei Rudi. 11–45, Akasaka 1-chome, Minato-ku (Dai-san Kowa Building B1); 586–4572. Said to serve the best German food in town, Bei Rudi has a cheerful, beer hall atmosphere, with live music. Open 5:00 P.M. to midnight; closed Sundays. Nearest stations Toranomon and Akasaka.

Lohmeyer's. Igami Bldg., 3–14, Ginza 5-chome, Chuo-ku; 571–1142. A well-established restaurant in Ginza, near the Sony Bldg. Open daily 11:30 A.M. to 10:00 P.M.

GREEK

Moderate

Double Ax. Koshi Bldg., 10–4, Roppongi 3-chome, Minato-ku; 401–7384. Tokyo's only Greek chef prepares a wide variety of dishes, in a carefree Greek atmosphere. Dinner course: ￥8,000 for two. Open 5:30 P.M. to 11:00 P.M. daily.

INDIAN

Moderate

Ajanta. 3–11, Niban-cho, Chiyoda-ku; 264–4255. One of Tokyo's classy Indian restaurants, open 24 hours daily. Saris for sale. Open 11:30 A.M. to 9:00 P.M.

Ashoka. Pearl Bldg., 9–18, Ginza 7-chome, Chuo-ku; 572–2377. Sitar music, incense. Many delicious specialties, bland or hot. Open from 11:30 A.M. to 9:30 P.M., noon to 7:30 P.M. on Sundays.

Maharaja. Takanao Bldg., 26–11, Shinjuku 3-chome, Shinjuku-ku; 354–0222. Located in the "World Snack," a floor of international restaurants in the Takano Fruits Parlour Bldg., which stands on what is alleged to be the most expensive land in the world, near Shinjuku Station. Fortunately this is not reflected in Maharaja's prices. Nan and tandoori cooked before your eyes by Indian chefs. Other branches near Ginza's Mitsukoshi Bldg. and in basement of Sogo Department Store in Yokohama Station Bldg.

Maharao. Hibiya Mitsui Bldg., 1–2, Yurakucho 1-chome, Chiyoda-ku; 580–6423. Very popular, always crowded. A sister shop to Maharaja, above.

Moti. Roppongi branch: Roppongi Hama Bldg. 3rd fl., 2–35 Roppongi 6-chome, Minato-ku; 479–1939, 479–1955. Akasaka branch: Akasaka Floral Plaza 2nd fl., 8–8, Akasaka 3-chome, Minato-ku; 582–3620. Also at Akasaka 2-chome: 584–6640. The best Indian food in Japan, many say. Piping hot, balloon-like *nan,* delicious *sagh.* Open 11:30 A.M. to 10:00 P.M.

Nair's. 10–7, Ginza 4-chome, Chuo-ku; 541–8246. A little piece of India, friendly, informal and sometimes delicious. Open noon to 9:30 P.M.

The Taj. Pagoda Bldg., 2–7 Akasaka 3-chome, Minato-ku; 586–6606. Next to Moti's in Akasaka. A stylish, international interior, sophisticated service, unusual and delicious dishes. Open noon to 10:30 P.M.

INDONESIAN

Moderate

Bengawan Solo. 18–13, Roppongi 7-chome, Minato-ku; 408–5698. National dishes, strongly spiced. Open 3:00 P.M., 5:00 P.M. to 11:00 P.M.

Indonesia Raya. 4–3, Shinbashi 4-chome, Minato-ku; 433–7005. Exotic decor with Indonesian folk art objects; waitresses in traditional attire. Open 11:30 A.M. to 10:30 P.M.; closed Sundays and holidays.

Sederhana. 5–4, Kami-Osaki 3-chome, Shinagawa-ku; 473–0354/5. Meguro is the nearest station; the restaurant is upstairs in the Tanaka Bldg. on the corner of No. 2 Expressway. A rarity in Japan, a totally un-phony neighborhood-style ethnic restaurant, run by an Indonesian family, with the wife taking the orders and her husband doing the cooking. The food is entirely authentic and there's an English language menu. Open noon to 2:00 P.M., 6:00 P.M. to 10:00 P.M. daily.

ITALIAN

Expensive

La Cometa. 1–7 Azabu Juban, Minato-ku; 470–5105. A cozy and authentic little restaurant serving Italian fish and meat dishes. Dinner menu hovers around ¥ 7,000; lunch menu is more in the moderate category. Open 11:45 A.M. to 2:00 P.M. and 6:00 P.M. to 10:30 P.M.

Moderate

Antonio's. 3–6, Minami-Aoyama 7-chome, Minato-ku; 797–0388. Daikanyama Branch: Hillside Terrace D, 29–9, Sarugacho, Shibuya-ku; 464–6041. Famous for ravioli, antipasto platter, Barbera wine. Long established, with a high reputation. Open noon to 2:30 P.M., 5:00 P.M. to 10:30 P.M.

Borsalino. S. K. Heim Bldg., 8–2, Roppongi 6-chome, Minato-ku; 401–7751. Authentic dishes in a relaxing black-and-white interior. Open noon to 2:00 A.M., Sun. 6:00 P.M. to 11:00 P.M., Closed on Mondays.

Nicola's. Roppongi Plaza, 12–6, Roppongi 3-chome, Minato-ku; 401–6936. Owned by Nicola V. Zapetti, this restaurant is famous for its 50 varieties of pizza. Also spare ribs and New York-cut steaks. Open daily noon to 3:00 A.M.

Roma Sabatini. Center Bldg., 29–8, Dogenzaka 2-chome, Shibuya-ku; 461–0495. Italian chef; the menu is a copy of the original in Rome. The restaurant is Japan's only recipient of the Diploma di Benemerenza, awarded by Turismo di Roma. Open 11:30 A.M. to 2:00 P.M., 5:30 P.M. to 11:00 P.M.

Sabatini di Firenze. 7th fl., Sony Bldg., 3–1, Ginza 5-chome, Chuo-ku; 573–0013. The first overseas branch of this famous restaurant, superbly appointed. Open noon to 2:30 P.M. and 5:30 P.M. to 11:30 P.M.

KOREAN

Moderate

JuJu. 1F Kotsu Anzen Kyoiku Bldg., 3–24–20 Nishi Azabu, Minato-ku; 405–9911. *Yakiniku* in cool surroundings in Roppongi. Open 5:00 P.M. to 1:30 A.M.

Sankoen. Asami Bldg., 11–16 Azabu Juban 1-chome, Minato-ku; 585–6306. Open 11:30 A.M. to 2:00 A.M.; Sundays 11:30 A.M. to 1:00 A.M.; closed Wednesdays.

Seikoen. 6–6, Ginza 1-chome, Chuo-ku; 561–5883. Open 11:30 A.M. to 11:00 P.M.; Sundays and holidays 3:00 P.M. to 10:00 P.M.

LATIN AMERICAN

Moderate

Restaurante Gaucho. Nomura Bldg., 4–8, Yonban-cho, Chiyoda-ku; 262–8621. Live Latin music, a relaxed, carefree, and cheerful atmosphere. A popular item on the menu is Churrasco Libre, barbecued chicken, pork, and beef. Open 11:30 A.M. to 2:00 P.M., 5:00 P.M. to 11:00 P.M.; closed Sundays and holidays.

MIDDLE EASTERN

Moderate

Laila. Roppingi Forum, 2nd fl., 16–52, Roppongi 5-chome, Minato-ku; 582–8491. Probably the first Middle-Eastern restaurant in Japan. Belly dancing and a real Afghan-cum-Middle-Eastern atmosphere. Open daily from 5:30 P.M. to 2:00 A.M.

PAKISTANI

Moderate

Gandhara. Ginza Five Star Bldg., 8–13, Ginza 5-chome, Chuo-ku; 574–9289. Tokyo's only authentic Pakistani restaurant. Open 11:30 A.M. to 2:00 P.M.; 5:00 P.M. to 9:30 P.M.; closed Sundays.

RUSSIAN

Moderate

Volga. 3–5–14 Shibakoen, Minato-ku; 433–1766. Onion domes outside, pre-Revolutionary gloom within. Open 11:00 A.M. to 10:30 P.M.

SPANISH

Expensive

Patio Flamenco. 10–12, Dogenzaka 2-chome, Shibuya-ku; 464–8476. Open 5:00 P.M. to 11:00 P.M. daily. Live flamenco. Paella, seafood dishes.

Los Platos. Terrace Akasaka Bldg., 13–11, Akasaka 6-chome, Minato-ku; 583–4262. Flamenco guitarist. Open 11:30 A.M. to 10:30 P.M.; closed Sundays.

SWEDISH

Expensive

Stockholm. Sweden Center, 11–9, Roppongi 6-chome, Minato-ku; 403–9046. Swedish smorgasbord and other Scandinavian delicacies in a large restaurant with live music. Open throughout the year, 11:00 A.M. to 10:30 P.M.

SWISS

Moderate

Movenpick. Shinjuku Center Bldg., Annex, 25–1, Nishi Shinjuku 1-chome, Shinjuku-ku; 344–5361. A handsome, low-rising, polygonal building among the skyscrapers of West Shinjuku houses the very best place in town for quiche Lorraine and other pie dishes, as well as a number of hard-to-come-by European delicacies. Open daily, from breakfast to dinner. Ginza branch: Ginza Sanwa Bldg. B2, 6–1, Ginza 4-chome, Chuo-ku; 561–0351.

Tokyo Swiss Inn. Tokyo Bed Bldg., 1–16, Roppongi 4-chome, Minato-ku; 584–0911. Swiss-managed, this intimate restaurant features good veal dishes. Open 5:00 P.M. to 11:00 P.M.

THAI

Moderate

Chiang Mai. Kaitei Building 6–10, Yuraku-cho 1-chome, Chiyoda-ku; 580–0456. Friendly, intimate, Thai-managed restaurant with fiendishly hot items on the menu. Open 11:30 A.M. to 11:00 P.M.; closed Saturdays.

VIETNAMESE

Moderate

Aodai. Akasaka Trade Bldg., 4–14, Akasaka 5-chome, Minato-ku; 583–0234. Open 5:00 P.M. to 11:00 P.M.; closed Sundays.

Hi Lac Nam. 9–16, Kita Shinjuku 3-chome, Shinjuku-ku; 369–5431. Open 10:00 A.M. to 10:00 P.M.; closed first and third Mondays.

NATURAL FOOD RESTAURANTS

Inexpensive to Moderate

Ashun. Shimo-Kitazawa Credit Bldg., 2nd fl., 26–2, Kitazawa 3-chome, Setagaya-ku; 465–7653. Believe it or not, curry rice is one of the most popular of all dishes, Japanese or foreign, in Japan. This is a brown rice-based vegetarian curry house with a number of highly original dishes—like fried *natto* (fermented soybeans). Open 4:00 P.M. to 11:30 P.M., 2:00 P.M. to 11:30 P.M. on weekends; closed on Mondays. Shimokitazawa Station on the Odakyu Line is five minutes away on foot.

Manna. 16–5, Shinjuku 1-chome, Shinjuku-ku; 344–6606, 342–2659. Long-established, somewhat severe, vegetarian restaurant run by Seventh Day Adventists. Open 11:00 A.M. to 8:30 P.M.; 11:30 A.M. to 3:00 P.M. on Fridays; closed Saturdays, holidays, and some Sundays.

Mominoki House. LCP Bldg, 18–5, Jingumae 2-chome, Shibuya-ku; 405–9144. Located in Harajuku. Noted for its dancers and fashion models. Relaxed mood, extensive menu. Open 11:00 A.M. to 11:00 P.M.

Nippon Kenko Shizenshoku Centre, 26–3, Shinbashi 3-chome, Minato-ku; 573–4181. Old-established health food restaurant and shop. Open 9:30 A.M. to 6:00 P.M., dining room open 11:30 A.M. to 2:00 P.M.; closed Sundays and holidays.

Tenmi. This famous Shibuya natural food center is listed in the Japanese section.

Tofuya. 1st fl., Sanyo Akasaka Bldg., 5–2, Akasaka 3-chome, Minato-ku; 582–1028. Classic Japanese tofu dishes plus rice dishes. Open 11:30 A.M. to 1:30 P.M.; 5:00 P.M. to 10:30 P.M.; closed Saturdays, Sundays, and holidays.

Tojinbo. B1, New Shinbashi Bldg., 16–2, Shinbashi 2-chome, Minato-ku; 580–7307. Very near Shinbashi Station. Wild vegetables, delicious Japan Sea fish specialities, no MSG. Open 5:00 P.M. to 11:00 P.M., closed on first and third Saturday and Sunday of the month and holidays.

STEAK AND PRIME RIBS

Due to the artificially high price of beef in Japan, eating steak is an expensive business. This doesn't deter the serious steak man, and a number of fine Tokyo restaurants serve this dish.

Deluxe

Aragawa. Hankyu Kotsusha Bldg., 3–9, Shinbashi 3-chome, Minato-ku; 591
–8765. Open from noon to 11:00 P.M. Painstakingly reared beef, lovingly prepared for the table. All major credit cards.

Hama. No. 5 Polestar Bldg., 7th fl., 6–12. Ginza 7-chome, Chuo-ku; 573–
0915. Roppongi shop: 2–10 Roppongi 7-chome, Minato-ku; 403–1717. Teppanyaki and seafood as well as steak are specialities of Hama, noted for its
elegance. Open 11:00 A.M. to 2:00 P.M.; 5:00 P.M. to 2:00 A.M.; closed on Sundays.
All major credit cards.

Expensive

Benihana of New York. 3–7, Ginza 6-chome, Chuo-ku; 571–9060. Hibachi
and Teppanyaki steak are specialties of the house, though the New York-cut
steak is said to be more popular. There are 50 Benihana restaurants in the
United States now. Open 11:00 A.M. to 10:00 P.M. All major credit cards.

Colza. Clover Bldg., 15–10, Roppongi 7-chome, Minato-ku; 405–5631. Next
to Meiji-ya in Roppongi. Colza specializes in teppanyaki, steak, and seafood.
Open noon to 2:00 P.M.; 5:00 P.M. to 9:00 P.M.; Sundays and holidays 5:00 P.M. to
9:00 P.M. All major credit cards.

Moderate

Chaco Atago Ten. MY Bldg., 4–1, Nishi Shinbashi 3-chome, Minato-ku;
432–4850.

Suehiro. Ginza branch: Kintetsu Bldg., 4–10, Ginza 4-chome, Chuo-ku;
562–0591. Others at Ginza 6-chome: 571–9271; Harajuku: 401–4101; Ikebukuro: 985–6232; and Shinjuku: 356–4656. A chain famous for the quality of its
Kobe steak.

OTHERS

American fast food is very well established in Tokyo, and nobody nostalgic
for the taste of a Big Mac need remain nostalgic for long. **McDonald's**—
"Makudonurarudo" it comes out in Japanese—far and away leads the field, but
**Kentucky Fried Chicken, Wendy's Hamburgers, Barby's Beef Sandwiches,
Mister Donut,** and **Baskin-Robbins** are all hanging in there. Local imitations
have sprung up, among them **Morinaga** and **First Kitchen.**

Japanese chain restaurants that sell reasonable and inexpensive food include
Fujiya, Morinaga, and **Coq d'Or.** Most big buildings in central Tokyo have
concentrations of cheaper restaurants in their basements. The Yuraku Food
Center, under the elevated expressway at Sukiyabashi, between Ginza and
Hibiya, also has numerous small restaurants of various kinds. Other good bets
are the city's numerous German-style beer halls, including **New Tokyo** at
Sukiyabashi, between Ginza and Hibiya subway stations. **Kirin Beer Hall** near
Sukiyabashi; **Munchin Beer Hall,** and **Lion Beer Hall,** Shinbashi both accessible from Ginza and Shinbashi subway stations,; the **World Service Snack Bar**
in the Sanshi Bldg., Ginza; and the dining rooms of department stores.

British-style pubs with fish and chips or tidbits and darts include **Eri's Cabin,
Uncle Michael,** and the **Bull and Bear** (no darts), all at Roppongi station on
the Hibiya line, and the **Rising Sun** at Yotsuya station on the Marunouchi and
Chuo lines.

In locating these bars you will find the area maps printed in *Tokyo Journal*
(monthly ¥300) and *Tour Companion* (weekly, free) an invaluable aid.

The visitor who seriously needs to cut his everyday expenditure will find that
many small coffee shops offer "morning service." During the morning hours

only, these shops include something extra—a boiled egg and toast, perhaps, or a sandwich—for the price of a cup of coffee or tea. "Morning service" is almost the same in Japanese—*moningu sabisu.*

Heading out of the center of town and into the suburbs, visitors may be amazed to see how American-style roadside restaurants have caught on. **Denny's,** for example, has more than 150 family restaurants in the Tokyo region.

HOTEL DINING

Expect hotel dining rooms to be *Deluxe* and *Expensive;* snack bars, tea lounges and coffee shops fall in the *Moderate* and *Inexpensive* ratings.

Akasaka Prince Hotel. 1–2, Kioi-cho, Chiyoda-ku. Near Akasaka-Mitsuke subway station; 234–1111. Tokyo's striking new landmark offers terrific views from the *Blue Gardenia* on 40th floor. Other restaurants in the tower are: *Potomac* Western cuisine, 3rd fl.; *Kioi,* Japanese cuisine; *Tachibana,* sushi; *Kiri,* tempura; and *Riou,* Cantonese—all in the basement. *Ohmi* steak house is in the diminutive annex, while the original building, constructed before the war as the palace of a Korean prince (hence the hotel's name), houses the French restaurant *Torianon.*

Capitol Tokyu, formerly Tokyo Hilton. 2–10–3 Nagato-cho, Chiyoda-ku. A taxi ride from Akasaka-Mitsuke subway station; 581–4511. The Tokyo Hilton became the Capital Tokyu when the lease reverted to the owner (the Tokyu Corporation) in January 1984. On September 1, 1984, the Tokyo Hilton International relocated to West Shinjuku, near the Century Hyatt. The Capital Tokyu retains the old Hilton's reputation for excellent food. The *Keyaki Grill* features gourmet food and a well-stocked cellar of select wines. Noon to 3:00 P.M., 5:30 P.M. to 10:30 P.M. *Genji-no-ma* features Japanese specialties in Japanese atmosphere and has a *Teppan-yaki* counter and a *Sushi* counter. Cocktail and tea lounge serves breakfast buffet, 7:00 A.M. to 10:30 A.M.; luncheon buffet, noon to 2:30 P.M. (except Sundays and holidays). The *Star Hill Chinese Restaurant* has 177 dishes on the menu, on Sundays and National Holidays all-you-can-eat for ¥6,000 (lunchtime) and ¥7,000 (evenings). *Coffee Shop,* informal and versatile, has a view over the Japanese garden.

Century Hyatt. 2–7–2 Nishi-Shinjuku, Shinjuku-ku. A taxi ride from Shinjuku subway and national railway stations; 349–0111. From the simple to the sumptuous, in 10 restaurants and lounges. Japanese food is Kansai-style, Chinese food is Beijing and Shanghai-styles. The Italian restaurant *Caterina* is the only one in Japan operated by a hotel itself. *Chenonceaux* is a French restaurant on the 27th floor—super-elegant.

Ginza Dai Ichi 1–2 Shinbashi, Monato-ku. Near Shinbashi subway and national railway station; 542–5311. *Lumière.* A large room offering quick service and prices that may be termed moderate by the standards of Tokyo's top hotels—¥6,000 and up for dinner. The Japanese restaurant *Kuruma-ya* serves shabu-shabu and other Japanese dishes in a comparable price range.

Ginza Tokyu. 5–15–9 Ginza, (huo-ku. Near Ginza subway station; 541–2411. *Grill:* Good food. The roast beef is particularly worthwhile. Trout in season is also a specialty. *Kujakucho:* Chinese buffet with an elaborate selection of dishes and plenty of room. Lunchtime, and for dinner from 5:30–9:30 P.M. Moderately expensive.

Hilton International. 344–5111. Second floor restaurants in the new Shinjuku Hilton include *Musashino,* for sushi, tempura and teppan-yaki, and *Dynasty* for Chinese dishes.

Hotel Okura. 2–10–4 Toranoman, Minato-ku. A taxi ride from Toranomon and Kasumigaseki subway stations. Right behind the U.S. Embassy; 582–0111.

As befits Tokyo's most luxurious hotel, the Okura is swarming with restaurants. *Continental Room,* open for lunch and dinner, serves European food and overlooks downtown Tokyo. *Orchid Room* (French Restaurant), open for breakfast, lunch and dinner, has band music at night. *Yamazato:* An attractive Japanese restaurant serving yakitori, suki-yaki, and the like. *Toh-ka-lin:* An excellent Cantonese restaurant. *Starlight Lounge:* piano and combo music, 6:00 P.M. to 11:00 P.M. *Terrace Restaurant,* informal and pretty, is open from 7:00 A.M. to 9:00 P.M., and serves Chinese food. *La Belle Epoque* in the South Wing, 19th-century in style, serves European cuisine and has room for dancing.

Imperial. 1-1-1 Uchisaiwai-cho, Chiyoda-ku. Near Hibiya subway station; 504-1111. The top-floor *Fontainebleau* French restaurant, open for lunch and dinner, is outstanding any time, often memorable. The last Friday of each month is the *Diner Gastronomique,* for which you will want to schedule long in advance. *Rainbow Room,* 17th fl., open 6:00 P.M. to 11:00 P.M. except Sun. & holidays, gives a superb night view of Tokyo. Organ music in *Rainbow Lounge,* 17th fl., 6:30 P.M. to 11:00 P.M. *Prunier* is now part of the Main Dining Room. Excellent fish dishes. The new coffee shop, *Cycles,* facing street specializes in pancakes. The Imperial's mighty new Imperial Tower has a number of new restaurants in the basement: *La Brasserie,* French; *Peking, Sushi Gen, Ten-Ichi* (tempura) and *Kiccho,* Japanese. The 1st floor has a *Salon de Thè.*

Keio Plaza Hotel. 2-2-1 Nishi-Shinjuku, Shinjuku-ku. Near Shinjuku subway and national railway station; 344-0111. Full complement of restaurants from basement to 45th floor. *Aurora Lounge* at the highest level is open from 10:00 A.M. to midnight. On clear days, Mt. Fuji can be seen in the distance.

Marunouchi. 1-6-3 Marunouchi, Chiyoda-ku. Near Tokyo Station; 215-2151. *Bamboo Room:* an attractive grill that serves fine food.

Miyako Hotel. 1-1-50 Shirogane-dai, Minato-ku. By taxi from Meguro or Shinagawa national railway stations; 447-3111. *La Cle d'Or* dining room specializes in beef. Periodically, the menu of a state dinner party from the original Miyako, in Kyoto, is re-planned. Szechuan-style food served in Chinese restaurant. *Silver Hill* coffee shop has a buffet breakfast; chef's special at lunchtime—bouillabaisse.

The New Otani. 4 Kioi-cho, Chiyoda-ku. Near Akasaka-Mitsuke subway station; 265-1111. *Virgo:* French nouvelle cuisine. *Top of the Tower,* buffet restaurant, breakfast, lunch, and dinner. *Trader Vic's,* the first in the Orient. Chinese snack-style buffet, lunch and dinner, in the revolving *Blue Sky Lounge.* *Taikan-En:* Chinese food, atmosphere. *Kioi:* Japanese restaurant. *La Tour d'Argent:* a French restaurant on the 16th floor, branch of a Paris restaurant famous for duck. *Rib Room* in the basement offers good steak and is well worth a visit. *Barbecue* in ten-acre Japanese garden. Open year-round.

Pacific Meridien. 3-13 Takanawa, Minato-ku. Near Shinagawa national and private railway station; 445-6711. *Garden Restaurant Ukidono,* and music 5:00 P.M. to 11:00 P.M. *Sky Lounge Blue Pacific,* 5:00 P.M. to 11:00 P.M., for drinking and dancing. Cellar bar *El Vencedor,* 5:00 P.M. to 11:00 P.M. Koto music in the *Tea and Cocktail Lounge,* 5:00 P.M. to 7:00 P.M.

Palace Hotel. 1-1-1, Marunouchi, Chiyoda-ku. Near Otemachi subway station; 211-5211. The 10th-floor *Crown Room* overlooks the Imperial Palace moat and grounds. Elegant dining, menu, and wine-list supervised by Paris-trained head-chef. Food is also good in the moat-side *Swan Room,* the hotel's main dining room. The basement houses the *Grill and Prunier* and a pub-restaurant *Ivy House.* Also in the basement is the café-restaurant *Humming,* open from 6:00 A.M. to 1:00 A.M., which serves everything from coffee to steak.

Takanawa Prince. 3–13–1 Takanawa, Minato-ku. Near Shinagawa national and private railway station; 447–1111. A chef imported from France prepares his own specialities for royalty in *Le Trianon,* open from 7:00 A.M. to 11:00 P.M.

Tokyo Prince. 3–3–1 Shiba Koen, Minato-ku. Near Shiba Keon subway station; 432–1111. *Beaux Sejours* is a French restaurant on the 3d floor, especially noted for its fish dishes. On the 1st floor is the *Porto* "American-style" coffee shop, open from 6:30 A.M. to 2:00 A.M. *Gotoku* for sushi and *Fukusa* room for tempura. The garden-view *Prince Villa* is a simple, cheerful (somewhat Japanized) European restaurant open till 10:00 P.M. with chicken, seafood, steak, good pilaffs, and a young clientèle. Prices unbelievably low for Tokyo, prompt, efficient service.

 NIGHTLIFE. Japanese cultural tradition is conducive to a flourishing nightlife, much of which is geared to the male Japanese. In a country where a sort of marital division of labor exists and the home is conceded to be the wife's castle, husbands do their entertaining on the outside. To accommodate them, countless bars, cabarets, and other kinds of nightspots have sprung up, making the entertainment areas of Japan among the most active in the world.

As night starts to fall in Tokyo, varicolored neons begin to blaze along the major streets. Behind the brilliantly lighted main drags, in dark little alleys and byways that twist and crisscross in mazelike patterns, are a multitude of nightspots, where women, as gorgeous as beauty parlors can make them, sit primly in kimono and Western dress and wait for business. Starting as early as 6:00 P.M., for the sidewalks are rolled up early in Japan, business comes—in the form of men who buy them drinks, complain about their wives and bosses, and air their troubles in general to sympathetic ears, while avid eyes watch the bill run up. This keeps up until about midnight, when a silence suddenly overtakes most areas (except where after-hours joints abound) as closing time arrives.

Nightlife in some variation on this theme has had a long history in Japan's traditionally male-dominated society. Ladies of the night reached their peak in the mid-18th century when the *oiran* reigned as queen of the Yoshiwara entertainment district, during the Tokugawa Shogunate. *Geishas* then were entertainers who sang and danced as a preliminary to an evening with an oiran, who was specially trained for her part. If some of the glowing reports of her accomplishments are correct, she surpassed even the fabulous *hetaerae* of ancient Greece in the knowledge and practice of the art of love.

The Yoshiwara, called Tokyo's Gay Quarters in the days before "gay" took on its current meaning, began to decline at the end of the 18th century and finally lost all claim to its so-called gaiety in 1958, when the Diet, under pressure from female members, outlawed prostitution. In so doing, it also removed the area from Tokyo's tourist attractions. It is now a far cry from what it was, even from what it had been in the postwar years before its legal demise. It is dotted with cheap bars and "massage" parlors where one can get a sort of massage if he insists.

As the oiran declined, the geisha rose in importance and, in the 19th century, took over as the main source of after-dark entertainment. But the geisha was a different sort of entertainer. Her forte was and still is singing, dancing, and playing the *samisen.* Geisha are very much in evidence today, and a geisha party is still the place where important business and political deals are sealed. Few foreigners, though, will have an opportunity to attend one, except as a guest. Proper standing in Japanese society along with a proper introduction is necessary.

Nightlife for foreigners centers around bars, cabarets, those restaurants that provide stage shows, discos, and nightspots of questionable character. In general, few places close their doors to foreigners. Those that do are not xenophobic. They are, instead, fearful of the language barrier. They are also worried about the foreigner's reaction to the bill, which may strike him as a figure taken from Japan's GNP. From past experience they know that the non-Japanese, especially the Caucasian, does not hesitate to make his views known. Since loud voices and threatening gestures are foreign to the Japanese way of life, a bar can lose regular customers when such an altercation arises.

The main nightlife areas of Tokyo include the **Ginza,** the heart of the city, with plenty of places for both foreigners and Japanese; **Shibuya,** about half an hour west of the Ginza, with a number of bars and clubs operating on a nonsegregated basis (its nightlife continues rather later than that of the Ginza area); **Shinjuku,** also about half an hour west of the Ginza, a large entertainment quarter that once included one of Japan's biggest red light districts, and now contains numerous theaters, bars, and nightclubs; and **Roppongi,** which has burgeoned recently as a competitor to the Ginza. In addition to its bars and clubs, many of which cater to foreigners, Roppongi is the center of the popular discos. Whereas the other districts tend to shut down at about 11:30 P.M., the night prowler in Roppongi can always find something going on.

Akasaka, ten minutes west of the Ginza, has geisha and a number of nightclubs catering to foreigners and to Japanese on the expense-account circuit. **Asakusa,** a center of nightlife for the ordinary working-class Japanese, lies to the north about half an hour from the Ginza. It is a fascinating place to visit at night but its small bars and clubs should not be visited unless you are with a Japanese who knows his way around.

Foreign women are accepted where Japanese women don't go, for example, at geisha parties, bars, and nightclubs. However, this is still not commonplace. Women accompanying their husbands, male friends, or associates to such places tend to be regarded (especially by the hostesses) with the curiosity reserved for visitors from Mars. And, in general, although the streets of Tokyo are safe at any time, a woman alone at night is looked at askance. Women can expect to feel comfortable at discos, kabuki theater, the movies, and restaurants with stage shows, but even in these cases, it is still the practice to go with a friend or with a male companion.

One other Japanese phenomenon should be mentioned here, and that is escort clubs for women only. Theses are places where women go and have young men dance and talk with them for a fee, just as hostesses entertain the men at the male-oriented clubs. Many of the customers are neglected Japanese wives. Three such establishments are: *Aoi Tori* (Blue Bird), at 7–17–12 Roppongi (486–4059), reservations from 4:00 P.M. to 3:00 A.M.; *Club Taboo* in Shibuya (464–4438), two hours for ¥10,000; and *Mr. Blue* in Roppongi (582–6887), two hours for ¥25,000.

The pleasure-seeking foreign male will find himself welcome in most places in Tokyo's entertainment areas. Throughout the narrow byways he will find a wide variety of nightspots. There are the bars without hostesses, often called "stand-up bars" because they formerly had no seats. In such places a knowledge of Japanese will help. As one goes up the scale to those spots where hostesses are provided, the price rises. Not only are the drinks subject to payment, but so are the women, in terms of hostess charge and tip, the latter being negotiable. Then there are the nightclubs, which provide some type of stage show along with hostesses, drinks, food, and dancing. Prices sometimes vary with the show, where higher cover charges are exacted relative to the fame of the entertainer. Prices at nightclubs cost from ¥20,000 on up per person. Finally, there are the high-class bars, which are the most expensive of all despite the fact that they provide no floor show. In such bars one might run across a prominent politician, a giant of industry, or a star entertainer on any given night. At the high-class bars the tab can run as high as ¥100,000 each.

In the tempestuous struggle for existence in the entertainment areas, where Darwin's rule of the survival of the fittest prevails, some interesting types of bars have sprung up. One is reported to dress up its hostesses as nuns to appeal to some people's subconscious quirk. Another provides a wall with a photograph holder in which customers are invited to place a picture of their boss or wife or someone else who has caused them frustration and throw glasses and bottles at it. Relieved of their frustrations, they do not complain about the bill for the glassware. Another, to appeal to the shortness of elderly Japanese, hires women under five feet as hostesses and calls itself a "transistor" bar.

Tokyo is also filled with hundreds of *karaoke* bars, the majority of which are in the Shinjuku area. Karaoke equipment consists of tape machine and micro-phone for the frustrated singers among the guests. Though foreigners are wel-come at such bars, they should remember that the songs are generally popular Japanese songs with which they may not be familiar.

Discos have brought something new to Tokyo nightlife, another type of female companion, the foreign model, who is given free entrance and a free meal, because "she brings in the customers," just by being there. In this way, she is very much like her Japanese colleagues, whose function is exactly the same.

Tokyo discos can be, and often are, selective as to whom they allow in. Proper attire, though flexible in definition, is required. Discos have taken over with the younger generation and with those who would like to be or believe they are members of that age group. Foreign celebrities are found in many of them, as the discos undoubtedly remind them of home.

There is nothing wrong with Tokyo's nightlife that a well-filled wallet cannot cure. Without that wallet, though, it is not necessarily dull. Tokyo's nightspots have developed over the years in such a way as to suit almost every budget, and no person need feel left out because of lack of cash.

Here are charges that will be tacked on to a bill in addition to what one eats and drinks:

Service charge. Rate is dependent upon the type of service. Where only drinks and food are involved, it is about 10 to 15 percent. Where a hostess serves the client and sits at the table with him, acting as an absorbent for the story of his life, its trials and tribulations, it could be as much as 85 percent of the bill. In addition to this, there is a **hostess charge,** which is itemized separately from the service charge.

Tax. In pubs and restaurants where there are no hostesses, bills up to ¥2,500 are not charged a tax. Where a hostess is involved, as little as a ¥1,000 charge is taxable.

In the following list of nightclubs and bars, *Expensive* is anything over ¥20,000 a person; *Moderate* are those where one can expect a bill of from ¥10,000 to ¥20,000; *Inexpensive* are nightspots where a normal bill will be under ¥10,000.

Note. Nightspots of any sort are high-risk businesses in Tokyo as in any place else. By the time this book is published, some may have gone out of business, changed their name, or changed ownership. The list below is current at press time. For additional information on many of the places mentioned, or for more listings of places used to catering to foreign visitors, you might also consult the English-language *Tour Companion.*

Each entry below gives the name of the establishment, the district it's in, and the phone number. The simplest and most practical thing for visitors to do is to have someone, perhaps the hotel doorman, phone for directions and give them to the cab driver.

We have listed nightclubs and high-class bars together. To the Japanese mind, the difference is vague, except for the extremes like Copacabana on the one hand and Hime on the other. As one progresses toward the center, though, the differences disappear, and the names can stand for one or the other.

NIGHTCLUBS AND BARS

Expensive

Club Casanova. Roppongi; 584–4558. Open 8:00 P.M. to 3:00 A.M., with hostesses available until midnight. Drinks, food, hostesses. Bill will run from ¥25,000 a person, all inclusive. AE, DC.

Copacabana. Akasaka; 585–5811. Open from 6:00 P.M. to 2:00 A.M., except Sundays. Two shows nightly at 9:45 P.M. and 11:30 P.M. Cover charge ¥6,000 and hostess charge ¥3,000 an hour. Club service charge of 20 percent added to the bill as is a tax of 10 percent. Food is available, but the *Little Copa* above the nightclub has some of the best roast beef in Japan, as well as other food. At the Little Copa a 15 percent service charge and 10 percent tax is tacked on to the bill. At the nightclub a cost of ¥30,000 to ¥40,000 a person is considered reasonable. AE, DC.

Gres. Ginza; 573–0777. Open 7:00 P.M. to midnight. Live piano music, with drinks, food, hostesses. Bill will run to ¥40,000 per person, all inclusive. AE, DC.

Hime. Ginza; 572–2423. Open from 7:30 P.M. to midnight. Live music for entertainment, with drinks, food, hostesses. Bill will run from ¥50,000 to ¥100,000, including hostess, service charge, and tax. Price also depends on whether one is on the company expense account or is paying it out of one's own pocket and whether the customer is a regular or a first-time visitor. AE, DC.

El Morocco. Tameike; 585–5141. Open from 7:00 P.M. to 1:30 A.M. Live band with drinks, food, and hostesses. Bill will run to ¥22,000 per person, all inclusive. AE, DC.

The New Latin Quarter. Akasaka; 581–1326. Open 7:00 P.M. to 1:30 A.M., except Sundays. Floor shows at 8:30 P.M. and 10:30 P.M. Hostess charge is ¥4,000 an hour; cover charge is ¥6,000; drinks from ¥1,700. Special steak dinner at ¥12,000 if reserved a day in advance. Price includes food, cover charge, drinks, service charge, and tax. Chinese cuisine also available. Otherwise service charge is 20 percent and tax is 10 percent. With a hostess, the bill will come to ¥30,000 or more. AE, DC.

Le Rat Mort. Ginza; 571–9296. Open 7:00 P.M. to midnight. Live piano music, with drinks, food, hostesses. Bill will run from ¥35,000 to ¥60,000 a person depending on number of guests. Alone, the bill can come to almost ¥60,000, all inclusive. With two or more it could come to ¥35,000 a person. AE, DC.

Moderate

Club Fontana. Roppongi; 584–6758. Open 7:00 P.M. to 1:00 A.M., except Sundays. Cover charge of ¥3,000, hostess charge of ¥3,000 an hour, drinks at ¥1,000 each. No shows but piano and vocalist. AE, DC.

Club Maiko. Ginza; 574–7745. Open from 6:00 P.M. to midnight, except Sundays and holidays. Four shows nightly at 7:40 P.M., 8:40 P.M., 9:40 P.M. and 10:40 P.M., featuring geisha and maiko (apprentice geishas) dances. Performers wait on customers before and after shows. Table d'hôte menu at ¥8,000 a person with two drinks. Additional drinks at ¥1,000 each, plus tax and service charge. Japanese food available on request at ￥15,000 to ￥20,000 a person. Japanese credit cards accepted; otherwise, cash only.

Club Morena. Roppongi; 402–9337. Open from 7:30 P.M. to 1:00 A.M. Cover charge of ￥1,500 per person. Hostess charge ￥4,000 an hour and a compulsory plate of peanuts and other tidbits called "charm" at ￥800 a person. Drinks from ￥1,000 each. English-speaking hostesses. AE, DC.

Club Penthouse. Akasaka; 582–1803, 586–5929. Open 8:00 P.M. to 2:00 A.M. except Sundays. No shows but live band. Hostess charge at ￥7,000 a person for two hours. Cover charge at ￥4,000. Also, a 30 percent charge and 10 percent tax is added. About ￥25,000 a person will be sufficient. AE, DC.

Cordon Bleu. Akasaka; 582–7800. Open from 7:00 P.M. to 3:00 A.M., except Sundays. Nightly topless shows at 8:00 P.M. and 10:00 P.M. French cuisine with table d'hote menu at ￥15,000 plus 10 percent tax, or hors d'oeuvres only at ￥12,000 plus 10 percent tax. Hostess charge at ￥8,000 for two hours. Count on ￥20,000 a person as reasonable to budget for an evening. AE, DC.

May Flower. Ginza; 563–2426. Open from 6:00 P.M. to 11:30 P.M. except Sundays and holidays. Live band but no shows. Hostesses available. About ￥20,000 a person will take care of an evening, inclusive of service charge and tax. AE.

Mikado. Akasaka; 583–1101. Open from 6:00 P.M. to 11:30 P.M., except Sundays. Nightly shows featuring Japanese and Western dances at 8:10 P.M. and 10:10 P.M. Count on ￥20,000 a person which includes cover charge of ￥3,500, hostess charge of ￥3,000 per hour, and ￥1,000 a drink. No cover charge for foreigners. Mikado claims to be the largest cabaret with hostesses in the world, boasting of 600 women and a capacity for 1,300 customers. It has its own dancing team and four regular bands. Food such as spareribs and sandwiches served. AE, DC.

Monte Carlo. Ginza; 571–5671. Open from 6:30 P.M. to 11:45 P.M., except Sundays and holidays. Japanese and foreign show nightly at 9:00 P.M. and 10:30 P.M. Special price of ￥10,000 to foreigners, which includes five drinks, a hostess to serve, cover charge, and tax. Additional drinks at ￥1,000 each. English-speaking hostesses available. AE, DC.

Playboy Club. Roppongi; 478–4100. Open from 6:00 P.M. to 2:00 A.M. except Sundays and holidays. Nightly shows at 7:30 P.M., 9:00 P.M., and 10:30 P.M. Drinks at ￥750 for scotch, ￥550 for beer. Playboy Club cardholders only. AE, DC.

Inexpensive

Bag Pipe. Shibuya, 499–1097; and Roppongi, 401–0580. Open from 5:00 P.M. to 5:00 A.M. daily. English-style pub. About ￥5,000 per person will cover two kinds of snacks, drinks, service charge, and tax. Drinks from ￥500. Japanese credit cards. DC.

Club Charon. Akasaka; 586–4480. Open from 7:30 P.M. to 12:00 A.M., except Saturdays, Sundays, and holidays. Piano and singer. Scotch at ￥900 or more, depending on brand. Small bottle of beer at ￥800. Hostess charge at ￥4,000 an hour. Table charge at ￥1,000 a person. Service charge and tax at 10 percent each. AE, DC.

Club Lee. Shinjuku; 208–6385/8566. Open from 6:00 P.M. to midnight. Two shows nightly at 8:30 P.M. and 10:30 P.M., featuring Japanese singers. Between 6:00 P.M. and 8:00 P.M., about ￥12,000 will cover drink, service, hostess charge, and tax. After 8:00 P.M. budget ￥15,000 for the evening. AE, DC.

Cross Tokyo. Roppongi; 402–8553. Open from 6:00 P.M. to 4:00 A.M., except Sundays and holidays. Table charge at ￥1,300 including one drink. Live band. Food available from ￥800 and drink from ￥800. AE, DC.

Crystal Room. Akasaka; 265–8000. Open from 6:00 P.M. to 11:30 P.M. Two top-class Parisian shows nightly at 7:30 P.M. and 10:00 P.M. Table d'hote menus at ¥16,500 and ¥22,000. Hors d'oeuvres only at ¥11,000. A la carte menu also available. No hostesses. AE, DC.

El Cupid. Roppongi; 405–6339. Open from 7:30 P.M. to 2:30 A.M., except Sundays and holidays. Filipino trio from 7:30 P.M. Drinks from ¥1,000. Cover charge ¥1,500. English-speaking hostesses at ¥3,000 an hour. Cover charge at bar only ¥500. Sandwiches at ¥1,000 and steak at ¥5,000 available. AE, DC.

The Glasshopper (sic). Akasaka; 586–3579. Open from 11:30 A.M. to 2:30 A.M. Drinks from ¥400, beer at ¥600, mixed drinks from ¥600, food from ¥450 but steak is ¥1,800. Popular with young Japanese. AE, DC.

High Grade Pub My Place. Roppongi; 401–3111. Open from 6:00 P.M. to 4:00 A.M., except Sundays and holidays. Table charge at ¥4,000 including two drinks. Food and drink from ¥1,000. AE, DC.

Hot Co-Rocket. 5–8, Roppongi 2-chome, Minato-ku; 583–9409. Live reggae music by West Indian bands. Open from 7:00 P.M. to 3:00 A.M. Very reasonably priced.

Lamp Light. Aoyama; 499–1573. Open from 5:30 P.M. to 2:00 A.M., except Sundays and holidays. Piano music. No hostesses. Will run about ¥8,000 to ¥10,000 a person. AE, DC.

My Scotch. Roppongi; 402–6649. Open daily from 6:00 P.M. to 2:00 A.M. Live music from 8:00 P.M., except Sundays and holidays. Drinks from ¥700, food from ¥700. Cover charge of ¥500 per person, which includes "charm." Service charge and tax at 10 percent each.

Nawanoren. Uchisaiwaicho, behind the Imperial Hotel; 508–9660. Open from 4:00 P.M. to 4:00 A.M. Japanese sake from ¥350, beer at ¥400, whiskey at ¥400, food from ¥500. Cash.

Peter and the Rabbits. Akasaka; 263–0400. Run by a television personality. Open from 7:00 P.M. to 4:00 A.M. This is a bottle club where the customer must buy his own bottle from ¥6,000 to ¥12,000. Table charge at ¥1,000 and "charm" at ¥500. Service charge and tax at 10 percent each. Chinese food available. Ice and water at ¥500. DC.

Potato Club. Akasaka; 584–1348. Open from 6:30 P.M. to 3:00 A.M., except Sundays. Live band music. No hostesses. About ¥10,000 will be enough. AE, DC.

Pub Central. Shinjuku; 356–0073. Open from 5:00 P.M. to 11:30 P.M. Drinks from ¥400. Table charge of ¥300. About ¥5,000 a person should be sufficient and would include some snack. DC.

Pub Grazie. Shinjuku; 209–8989. Open from 6:00 P.M. to 1:30 A.M., except Sundays. About ¥5,000 a person should be enough. Drinks from ¥500 and table charge at ¥1,000. DC, V.

Pub Happy Box. Shibuya; 476–2734. Open from 2:00 P.M. to midnight, except Sundays and holidays. Drinks from ¥450. Table charge at ¥500. About ¥4,000 per person should be enough. Cash only.

Pub House Royal Kan. Akasaka; 584–9426. Open 5:00 P.M. to 5:00 A.M. Drinks from ¥500, food from ¥600, table charge at ¥700. Before 7:00 P.M. all food is half the menu price. About ¥5,000 a person should be enough. Japanese credit cards.

Pub Passport. Ginza; 574–7576. Open from 6:00 P.M. to 11:30 P.M., except Sundays and holidays. About ¥5,000 per person will cover reasonable number of drinks, service charge, and tax. Snacks available. Drink starts at ¥500. Japanese credit cards or cash.

Pub Yagurachaya. Ginza; 571–3494. Open from 5:00 P.M. to midnight. Old Japanese country-style bar. Beer at ¥380, sake at ¥240, whiskey from ¥440, food from ¥180 to ¥880. Menu in English with colored pictures for better understanding. Guests must remove shoes on entering but chairs and stools available. Can accommodate 260 customers. Cash.

La Siesta. Ginza; 573–1021. Open from 5:00 P.M. Table charge of ¥500, whiskey from ¥450, draft beer at ¥350, food from ¥450. Tax, 10 percent. No service charge. Cash.

Suntory the Cellar. Akasaka; 470–1071. Quaintly named pub run by a whiskey manufacturer. Open from 5:00 P.M. to 11:00 P.M., daily. Suntory whiskey from ¥400. Graciously offers scotch at ¥500. Suntory beer from ¥500. Food available. Service charge and tax at 10 percent each. For bills over ¥2,500 there is a consumption tax. AE.

RESTAURANTS WITH STAGE SHOWS

The restaurants listed here require prior reservations.

Furusato. Shibuya; 463–2310. Open from 5:30 P.M. to 10:00 P.M. Open daily. Two shows a night at 7:00 P.M. and 8:30 P.M., featuring traditional Japanese dances. Set menu, including only Japanese food, available to foreigners at ¥6,000 to ¥10,000 inclusive of service charge and tax. AE, DC.

Matsubaya. Yoshiwara; 874–9401. Open from 6:00 P.M. to 10:00 P.M. Two shows nightly at 7:00 P.M. and 9:20 P.M. Table d'hôte menu from ¥6,000 plus 15 percent service charge and 10 percent tax. Private room available at ¥60,000, excluding food. Show features 18th-century courtesan, the *oiran*, dressed in kimono of that period and other authentic items of clothing. Food is Japanese *kaiseki-ryori*. DC, but cash preferred.

Miyarabi. Kudan; 261–3453. Open from 5:00 P.M. to 11:00 P.M., except Sundays and holidays. Okinawan restaurant with nightly show featuring Okinawan traditional dances at 8:00 P.M. Table d'hote menu of Okinawan food from ¥7,000 to ¥12,000 plus 20 percent service charge and 10 percent tax. Cash only.

DO-IT-YOURSELF BARS

The two bars listed below are high class yet not so expensive. There are other piano bars, but the ones listed here are representative, refined, and usually patronized by customers who speak English.

Little Manuela. Akasaka; 582–0469. Open from 7:00 P.M. to 1:00 A.M., except Sundays and holidays. Jet setters and top Japanese entertainers meet here. Its unique attraction is a jazz combo of piano, bass, and drum plus a saxophone, steel guitar, trumpet, and clarinet that are available for the clients to try their hand at with the combo accompanying them. Standard jazz is the fare. Table charge including "charm" is ¥2,500 for women; ¥3,000 for men. AE, DC.

Reverie. Akasaka; 582–8017. Open 7:00 P.M. to 1:00 A.M., except Sundays. Tokyo Jet Setters frequent this one and the one below. Hiroyuki Nishtoka, the very able pianist, is the drawing card. Vocalist sings from 9:00 P.M. Table charge of ¥800. Drinks from ¥900. No service charge but 10 percent tax. About ¥5,000 will produce a pleasant evening, where one can even check out his voice quality on songs he is familiar with, as pianist Nishioka knows almost all of them. What he does not know, he will pick up from a few hummed bars. AE, DC.

KARAOKE BARS

The Best Ten. Roppongi; 405–9934. Open from 6:30 A.M. to 3:30 A.M. Table charge is ¥1,000 with "charm" (tidbits) compulsory at ¥500. Drinks start from ¥600. A bottle of Suntory Black Label is ¥4,800. Ice and mineral water available at ¥500. Service charge and tax are 10 percent each. One bottle with two guests would come to ¥5,000 per person for the three. AE.

Karatto. Shibuya; 464–7073. Open from 6:30 P.M. to 2:00 A.M., except Sundays and holidays. Cover charge ¥1,000. Music charge to ¥1,000. Drinks from ¥800. Table d'hôte menu, including cover and music charge, "charm," and drinks at ¥4,400. Otherwise about ¥7,000 will insure a good evening. Japanese credit cards or cash.

Sharps and Flats Nodojiman Dojo. Roppongi; 405–7929. Open from 6:00 P.M. to 4:00 A.M., except Sundays and holidays. ¥3,500 will cover all drinks, tax and service charge. Cash.

DISCOS

Chakras Mandala. Roppongi; 479–5600. Open from 5:00 P.M. to 11:30 P.M. It is a favorite with the gilded youth, many of whom promenade on Sundays along the notorious or noted Harajuku Pedestrian's Paradise. Entrance fee of ¥3,500 for men and ¥2,500 for women includes all drinks and food. Three shows nightly, at 8:30 P.M., 10:00 P.M. and 11:00 P.M. AE, DC.

The Giza. Roppongi; 403–6538. Loud music, Egyptian decor and topless dancers make it a favorite among those whose eyes force the eardrums to take it. Entrance fee after 8:00 P.M., ¥3,000 for men and ¥2,500 for women, includes drinks and sushi. AE, DC, Visa.

The Lexington Queen. Roppongi; 401–1661. Reputedly the best disco in Tokyo, attracting local and visiting fashion personalities, musicians, film stars, and other celebrities. Entrance fee of ¥3,000 covers the cost of most drinks and also includes ¥1,000 worth of sushi at the club's sushi bar. Most of the staff speak some English. The club also employs American and European waiters. Among foreign celebrities visiting the club have been Sylvester Stallone, Stevie Wonder, Rod Stewart. AE, DC, Visa.

Make Up. Roppongi; 479–1511. Open from 5:00 P.M. to midnight. Admission charge ¥3,000 for men and ¥2,000 for women, ¥500 less for those who come before 8:00 P.M. Price includes all drinks and all the salad and noodles desired.

Mugen. Akasaka; 584–4481. Claims to be the very first disco in Tokyo. Open from 6:30 P.M. to 1:00 A.M. Table d'hôte menu of ¥3,000 for men and ¥2,000 for women, including one drink. Additional drinks are ¥300 for soft drinks, ¥400 for beer and ¥500 or more for whiskey. Food from ¥500. Cash only.

Nepenta. Roppongi; 470–0751. Open from 5:00 P.M. to midnight. Weekday admission charges are ¥2,500 for men and ¥2,000 for women. On Saturdays and Sundays the charge is ¥2,500 for men, but remains the same for women. After 8:00 P.M. it is ¥3,000 for men and ¥2,000 for women. Price includes all drinks and all the noodles one may want. AE, DC.

The Pacha. Roppongi; 479–0522. Another favorite oasis for the fashion crowd. Entrance fee of ¥4,000 includes two drinks. AE, DC, Visa.

Samba Club. Roppongi; 470–6391. Dark-is-elegant is apparently the theme of this lively nightspot. Its decor combines black velvet with mirrored walls and it is popular with the older disco crowd. Open from 6:00 P.M. to midnight. Entrance charge is ¥4,000, which includes three drinks, food, service charge, and tax. Additional drinks are from ¥800. French cuisine, as the club describes it, is available. AE, DC.

Tsubaki Ball. Roppongi; 478–0087. Attracts a younger crowd, lots of punk fashion and new-wave music. Chic lounge area upstairs. Dynamic dance area downstairs. Entrance fee is ¥3,000 for women and ¥3,500 for men and includes drinks and the club's buffet. AE, DC, Visa.

HOTEL DANCING

Hotel Century Hyatt. Shinjuku; 349–0111. A lively disco, the *Samba Club Regency,* provides loud music for guests. All international credit cards accepted.

Hotel Keio Plaza. Shinjuku; 344–0111. Visitors can dine, drink and dance until 11:30 P.M. in the 2nd floor *Consort Room.* Shows at 8:00 P.M. and 10:00 P.M. All international credit cards accepted.

Hotel New Otani. Akasaka; 234–2321 or 265–1111. *Tap Chips,* a restaurant on the 1st floor of the new wing, provides dancing until 2:00 A.M. in addition to food and drinks. All international credit cards accepted.

Hotel Pacific. Shinagawa; 445–6711. Dancing at the romantically named *Blue Pacific* Restaurant on the 30th floor to live music, from 7:00 P.M. to midnight. All international credit cards accepted.

Imperial Hotel. Hibiya; 504–1111. Dancing at the *Rainbow Room* Restaurant on the 17th floor, overlooking the bustling Ginza on one side and the Imperial Palace grounds on the other. A pleasant evening for those who still enjoy the old-fashioned way of dancing. All international cards accepted.

Takanawa Prince Hotel. Shinagawa; 447–1111. Dancing to live music at the 1st floor *Night Spot* until midnight. All international credit cards accepted.

TOKYO

FIVE-MINUTE JAPANESE

No one can hope to get very far with any language in five minutes. The purpose of the following vocabulary is not so much to make you into a linguist as to help you have a little fun. Whenever you are in a fix, someone whose English is better than your Japanese is sure to come forward to save you. Remember in Japanese that every syllable has equal stress. Pronounce the vowels as: *a* as in father; *e* as in pen; *i* is somewhere between ink and machine; *o* as in rope; and *u* as in put. Good luck!

English	Japanese	English	Japanese
Good morning	o-ha-yo	go back (turn around)	modote
Good afternoon	kon-nichi-wa		
Good evening	kon-ban-wa	hurry	hayaku
Goodnight (on retiring)	o-yasumi-nasai	go slowly	yukkuri
		stop	tomatte
Goodbye	sayonara	left	hidari
Thank you	domo arigato	right	migi
I'm sorry, please excuse me	sumi-masen	next	tsugi
		corner	kado
Yes	hai	toilet	toi-re
No	i-ie	information desk	an-nai-sho
Maybe	tabun	hotel	ho-teru
Wait a minute	chotto-matte	room	heya
I don't understand	wakarimasen	key	ka-gi
I	watakushi (for a lady)	eat	tabe-masu
		drink	nomi-masu
	boku (for a man)	meat	niku
You	anata	fruit	kudamono
he	ka-re	water	mizu
she	ka-no-jo	hot water	oyu
today	kyo	coffee	co-hi
tomorrow	ashita	tea	o-cha
yesterday	kino	money	kane
how much?	ikura deska?	One	Ichi
expensive	takai	Two	Ni
Anything cheaper?	Motto yasui no wa?	Three	San
		Four	Shi
I'll buy this	Itadakimasu or Kaimasu	Five	Go
		Six	Roku
telephone	denwa	Seven	Shichi
Please telephone and ask	Denwa de Kiite kudasai	Eight	Hachi
		Nine	Ku
taxi	tak-shi	Ten	Ju
bus	bus-u	Eleven	Ju-ichi (10 + 1, etc.)
train	densha		
subway	chika-tetsu	Twenty	Ni-ju (2 × 10, etc.)
station	eki		
ticket	kippu	Thirty, etc.	San-ju (3 × 10, etc.)
airport	hi-ko-jo		
street	michi	Hundred	Hyaku
Where is . . . ?	. . . doko deska?	Thousand	Sen
shop	mi-se	Ten thousand	Man or Ichi-man
stamp	kit-te		(thus, 25,000 is
police box	koban		ni man go sen)

INDEX

FODOR'S TRAVEL GUIDES

Here is a complete list of Fodor's Travel Guides, available in current editions; most are also available in a British edition published by Hodder & Stoughton.

U.S. GUIDES

Alaska
American Cities (Great Travel Values)
Arizona including the Grand Canyon
Atlantic City & the New Jersey Shore
Boston
California
Cape Cod & the Islands of Martha's Vineyard & Nantucket
Carolinas & the Georgia Coast
Chesapeake
Chicago
Colorado
Dallas/Fort Worth
Disney World & the Orlando Area (Fun in)
Far West
Florida
Fort Worth (see Dallas)
Galveston (see Houston)
Georgia (see Carolinas)
Grand Canyon (see Arizona)
Greater Miami & the Gold Coast
Hawaii
Hawaii (Great Travel Values)
Houston & Galveston
I-10: California to Florida
I-55: Chicago to New Orleans
I-75: Michigan to Florida
I-80: San Francisco to New York
I-95: Maine to Miami
Jamestown (see Williamsburg)
Las Vegas including Reno & Lake Tahoe (Fun in)
Los Angeles & Nearby Attractions
Martha's Vineyard (see Cape Cod)
Maui (Fun in)
Nantucket (see Cape Cod)
New England
New Jersey (see Atlantic City)
New Mexico
New Orleans
New Orleans (Fun in)
New York City
New York City (Fun in)
New York State
Orlando (see Disney World)
Pacific North Coast
Philadelphia
Reno (see Las Vegas)
Rockies
San Diego & Nearby Attractions
San Francisco (Fun in)
San Francisco plus Marin County & the Wine Country
The South
Texas
U.S.A.
Virgin Islands (U.S. & British)

Virginia
Waikiki (Fun in)
Washington, D.C.
Williamsburg, Jamestown & Yorktown

FOREIGN GUIDES

Acapulco (see Mexico City)
Acapulco (Fun in)
Amsterdam
Australia, New Zealand & the South Pacific
Austria
The Bahamas
The Bahamas (Fun in)
Barbados (Fun in)
Beijing, Guangzhou & Shanghai
Belgium & Luxembourg
Bermuda
Brazil
Britain (Great Travel Values)
Canada
Canada (Great Travel Values)
Canada's Maritime Provinces plus Newfoundland & Labrador
Cancún, Cozumel, Mérida & the Yucatán
Caribbean
Caribbean (Great Travel Values)
Central America
Copenhagen (see Stockholm)
Cozumel (see Cancún)
Eastern Europe
Egypt
Europe
Europe (Budget)
France
France (Great Travel Values)
Germany: East & West
Germany (Great Travel Values)
Great Britain
Greece
Guangzhou (see Beijing)
Helsinki (see Stockholm)
Holland
Hong Kong & Macau
Hungary
India, Nepal & Sri Lanka
Ireland
Israel
Italy
Italy (Great Travel Values)
Jamaica (Fun in)
Japan
Japan (Great Travel Values)
Jordan & the Holy Land
Kenya
Korea
Labrador (see Canada's Maritime Provinces)
Lisbon
Loire Valley
London

London (Fun in)
London (Great Travel Values)
Luxembourg (see Belgium)
Macau (see Hong Kong)
Madrid
Mazatlan (see Mexico's Baja)
Mexico
Mexico (Great Travel Values)
Mexico City & Acapulco
Mexico's Baja & Puerto Vallarta, Mazatlan, Manzanillo, Copper Canyon
Montreal (Fun in)
Munich
Nepal (see India)
New Zealand
Newfoundland (see Canada's Maritime Provinces)
1936 . . . on the Continent
North Africa
Oslo (see Stockholm)
Paris
Paris (Fun in)
People's Republic of China
Portugal
Province of Quebec
Puerto Vallarta (see Mexico's Baja)
Reykjavik (see Stockholm)
Rio (Fun in)
The Riviera (Fun on)
Rome
St. Martin/St. Maarten (Fun in)
Scandinavia
Scotland
Shanghai (see Beijing)
Singapore
South America
South Pacific
Southeast Asia
Soviet Union
Spain
Spain (Great Travel Values)
Sri Lanka (see India)
Stockholm, Copenhagen, Oslo, Helsinki & Reykjavik
Sweden
Switzerland
Sydney
Tokyo
Toronto
Turkey
Vienna
Yucatán (see Cancún)
Yugoslavia

SPECIAL-INTEREST GUIDES

Bed & Breakfast Guide: North America
Royalty Watching
Selected Hotels of Europe
Selected Resorts and Hotels of the U.S.
Ski Resorts of North America
Views to Dine by around the World

AVAILABLE AT YOUR LOCAL BOOKSTORE OR WRITE TO FODOR'S TRAVEL PUBLICATIONS, INC., 201 EAST 50th STREET, NEW YORK, NY 10022.